Religion, Health, and Aging

Recent Titles in
Contributions to the Study of Aging

RELIGION, HEALTH, AND AGING

A Review and Theoretical Integration

Harold George Koenig,
Mona Smiley,
and Jo Ann Ploch Gonzales

Foreword by David O. Moberg

Contributions to the Study of Aging, Number 10

GREENWOOD PRESS
NEW YORK • WESTPORT, CONNECTICUT • LONDON

Library of Congress Cataloging-in-Publication Data

Koenig, Harold George.
  Religion, health, and aging : a review and theoretical integration
/ Harold George Koenig, Mona Smiley, and Jo Ann Ploch Gonzales.
    p.   cm.— (Contributions to the study of aging, ISSN
0732–085X ; no. 10)
  Bibliography: p.
  Includes indexes.
  ISBN 0–313–26208–X (alk. paper)
  1. Aged—Health and hygiene. 2. Aged—Religious life. 3. Health—
Religious aspects. I. Smiley, Mona. II. Gonzales, Jo Ann Ploch.
III. Title. IV. Series.
RA777.6.K63 1988
613'.0438—dc 19   88–17779

British Library Cataloguing in Publication Data is available.

Library of Congress Catalog Card Number: 88–17779
ISBN: 0–313–26208–X
ISSN: 0732–085X

First published in 1988

Greenwood Press, Inc.
88 Post Road West, Westport, Connecticut 06881

Printed in the United States of America

∞

The paper used in this book complies with the
Permanent Paper Standard issued by the National
Information Standards Organization (Z39.48–1984).

10 9 8 7 6 5 4 3 2 1

This book is dedicated to the American Veterans of World War I and World War II both living and dead whose courage and faithfulness to their country enables us today to live in a free country where men and women may engage in the occupation of their choice, speak whatever is on their minds and hearts without fear of governmental retaliation, and worship their God in the manner they choose. It is our hope that those veterans who experience physical or emotional illness in their later years might have their burden eased through the progress of scientific research in medicine and the social sciences, that they might identify and fully utilize the resources available to them, and that we as scientists might listen to these men and women and learn from their experience.

CONTENTS

FOREWORD

David O. Moberg

Three significant contemporary trends meet in this book. One is the expansion of the aging population that provides a large proportion of the patients of most medical specialties and health services. The second is an increasing emphasis on the unity of each person that is reflected in such concepts as "total wellness," "wholistic well-being," and "holistic medicine." The third is the rising interest in spirituality that is evidenced by a wide range of renewal phenomena in traditional Christianity, as well as by numerous new religious movements and countless pseudo-religious cults and practices.

High-technology medicine is accomplishing much, but its limitations are obvious to many. It has emphasized the mechanical, physiological, and biochemical means for restoring health and sustaining physical life, but it has tended to minimize or even ignore the psychological, social, and especially the religious and spiritual dimensions of healing. In contrast there is a growing recognition that all aspects of human nature, including a person's beliefs and activities, influence and are influenced by his or her physical and mental health, illness, and therapy. Along with expanding awareness of the importance of psychosomatic elements in the etiology, symptomatology, and therapy of illness and disability, there is increasing consciousness that a spiritual dimension also underlies and is interwoven with all human concerns and behavior.

Spirituality is linked with religion, although not synonymous with it, for a central goal of most religions is the development and nurturance of the spiritual well-being of their members. This is especially true of the Judeo-Christian orientations and traditions that are dominant in

Europe and the Americas. Most of the research related to this subject has centered around various aspects of religion, even though spirituality extends far beyond its bounds, and many of the concerns of religious institutions and their personnel do not directly relate to spiritual well-being.

There are numerous findings from empirical research on the relationships between various aspects of religion and health among older people, but they are so widely scattered that most people in gerontology, geriatrics, the health and human service fields, the social and behavioral sciences, and even the religious professions are completely unaware of the predominant direction of the results. Here at last is an encyclopedic resource that pulls together the bits and pieces of studies that have included religion as one variable among many, as well as those that centered specifically upon the relationship of religion to various aspects of health and clinical medicine. The fragments and chunks have been pulled together from diverse sources. Some of the findings were serendipitous results on the periphery of studies devoted primarily to topics other than religion. Others—including several previously unpublished studies incorporated into several chapters—are from investigations expressly analyzing selected aspects of religiosity in relationship to the health and therapeutic treatment of aging and the elderly.

This book is not an apologetic treatise that stacks up all the evidence on one side of controversial perspectives on the relationships between religion and health in the later years, ignoring contrary findings. Instead, its emphasis is placed upon the findings of research. It is not a collection of the mere opinions and exhortations that are so abundant, especially in proreligious and antireligious circles. It attempts to summarize all the findings of empirical and clinical research on the subject, whatever the direction of such findings might be. Conclusions are carefully qualified by calling attention to alternative explanations, methodological issues like sampling and measurement limitations that might have influenced the results, and the complications connected with generalizing from the research findings.

Because it is an interdisciplinary volume, this book is all the more valuable. It will significantly help physicians, surgeons, nurses, educators, therapists, and other people in all the medical and paramedical professions; but it also will be very useful to clinical and counseling psychologists, social workers, the clergy, chaplains, other pastoral care specialists, and the leaders, staff members, and volunteers in the wide variety of services and agencies that work with and for the aging and elderly. It will make a significant contribution to geriatrics and gerontological education, helping to increase awareness of and sensitivity to the importance of religious and spiritual variables among older people. It will stimulate researchers to explore countless topics related to the subject, for numerous hypotheses emerging from previous studies and other suggestions for further research are presented throughout its pages, and many more are implicitly recommended. It should help to improve communication across the boundaries of disciplines concerned with research on the reciprocal interactions of religion and health among the aging such as epidemiology, geriatrics, and other branches of medicine, gerontology, nursing, psychology, psychiatry, religious studies, and sociology.

This state-of-the-art masterpiece will prove itself to be very interesting and helpful for informative personal reading, for use as a textbook, for stimulating further research, and for use as a reference volume by which to locate research reports and interpretations on specific subjects related to religion and aging. Its substantial contributions to both the applied and academic aspects of our knowledge of the relationships between religion and health in the later years of human life will help strategically to improve the well-being and life satisfaction of the aging, and thus enhance the present and future physical, mental, and spiritual health of us all.

ACKNOWLEDGMENTS

A special thanks to Charmin Marie Koenig who gave her time and talent, as well as encouragement and support, to the preparation of this text. We are grateful to Dr. Erdman Palmore for his advice and constant encouragement, as well as to David Bowman for his teaching and wisdom. Thanks to Stuart Barr who assisted with manuscript preparation. Dr. Keith Meador is recognized for his firm support as a colleague, counselor, and friend. Dr. David Moberg's critical review of our manuscript prior to publication was deeply appreciated.

Religion, Health, and Aging

INTRODUCTION

Old age can be a time of multiple losses and major life changes that may result in considerable stress and anxiety for the mature adult. Hinkle and Wolff (1958), writing in the *Annals of Internal Medicine*, note that susceptibility to illness varies inversely with ability to cope with stress, and that illness occurs when people perceive their lives as unsatisfying, threatening, overdemanding, and filled with conflict. The relationship between stress and illness has now been well substantiated by a number of retrospective and prospective studies (Selye, 1956; Perlman, Ferguson, and Bergum, 1971; Cohen, Teresi, and Holmes, 1985; Lin et al., 1979; Rabkin and Streuning, 1976). The following illnesses have been linked with psychosocial stress: cardiovascular disease (Rosenman et al, 1975; Haynes et al., 1980); hypertension (Elk and Nash, 1985); cancer (Shekelle et al., 1981; Greer, 1983); asthma (Hall, 1966); tuberculosis (Hawkins, 1957); pneumonia and pulmonary infections (Jacobs, 1970); diabetes (Kisch, 1985; Landis, 1985; Johnson, 1979; Grant, 1974; Hinkle and Wolff, 1952); Crohn's disease (Berbert, 1979); peptic ulcer disease (Cobb and Rose, 1973; Bradley, 1967; Pflanz, 1971; Sturdevant, 1976); and rheumatoid arthritis (Baker, 1982; Cobb, 1971). In old age, a time in life when health is often in a precarious balance with illness, one might expect that stress could have a significant impact.

Of considerable interest for geriatricians and gerontologists alike is the search for personal resources and coping strategies that buffer the ill effects of stressful life changes on the elderly. Studies have repeatedly shown the utility of *personal resources* such as good health, adequate financial resources, and available social support (health, wealth, and love) in helping persons to cope better with stressful life events (George, 1980; Larson, 1978). Little information, however, exists concerning effective *coping strategies* (George, 1980).

Coping strategies have been subdivided into cognitive and behavioral types (Lazarus, 1966; Mechanic, 1974). More specifically, a person may cope with stressful life events by either intrapsychic maneuvers that serve to change the interpretation of the event (i.e. from unpleasant or threatening to something less disturbing), or active behaviors designed to change the situation and make it less stressful. In younger age groups, an active coping strategy is generally felt to be more effective. In older individuals, however, this may not always be the case. Active behaviors focused on correcting the stressful situation may be counterproductive at times and actually stress-inducing, especially for a sick or disabled elderly person with little financial or social resources and little control over his or her environment. This person may have to rely entirely on intrapsychic coping strategies (Folkman and Lazarus, 1980).

The rationale behind the effectiveness of cognitive strategies has been emphasized by Lazarus and his colleagues. They argue that the decisive factor in coping with stress is the individual's appraisal or interpretation of the event, rather than any purely objective feature of the stressful situation itself (Folkman and Lazarus, 1980; Lazarus, 1974). Two thousand years ago the ancient Greek Stoic philosopher Epictetus said, "people are not upset as much by what happens to them as by the views they take of what happens" (Merrill, 1982, p. 33). In fact, the theory behind "cognitive therapy," a widespread psychotherapeutic technique for treating depression, is based on the hypothesis that thought processes concerning events and situations determine one's affective state (Beck, 1976). Hence, cognitive as well as behavioral coping strategies may be vital for older adults when encountering stressful life changes.

In the search for coping strategies and resources to facilitate adaptation to stressful life events Mechanic (1974) has suggested that attention be turned to the influence of adaptive strategies that have their roots in the culture of a society. Religion is a firmly ingrained part of the culture of the current elderly cohort. Recent Gallup polls have shown that among people over age sixty-five, more than 80 percent consider religion to be an important influence in their lives, and nearly 50 percent attend church at least weekly (Princeton Religion Research Center, 1982). The elderly person today is more likely to be involved in church groups than in all other social organizations combined (Payne et al., 1972; Cutler, 1976; Kulka et al., 1979; Youmans, 1963; Mayo, 1951; Webber, 1954). Indeed, Palmore (1980) states that the church is the "single most pervasive" resource available to the elderly. Among all forms of adult education, religious study courses are those most frequently participated in by older Americans (Moberg, 1968; Payne, 1973).

In a study of religious activities and attitudes of older persons attending a geriatric medicine clinic, half (50.0%) of the sample noted the following statement to be definitely true for them: "My faith involves all my life" (Koenig et al., 1988a). Similar responses were given to statements such as: "Nothing is as important to me as serving God the best I know how" (48.4%); "My religious beliefs are what really lie behind my whole approach to life" (49.5%); or "One should seek God's guidance in making every important decision" (65.6%). A study of senior center participants in central Illinois, eastern Iowa, and central Missouri found similar responses (see Table 1). The results of these studies and the Gallup national surveys underscore the major impact that religion has on the lives of older adults in this country.

While Starbuck (1899) and others have vigorously claimed that people become more religious as they age, there is continuing debate on this subject. Several investigators have reported findings suggesting that elderly people do not become more religious with increasing age (Orbach, 1961; Busse and Pfeiffer, 1969; Oakes, 1974). More recent work—both cross-sectional and longitudinal—has shown that although church attendance becomes less regular because of illness and disability after age seventy, religious beliefs become increasingly important with age and are expressed in nonorganizational activities such as prayer, religious reading, and private devotion (Blazer and Palmore, 1976; Mindel and Vaughan, 1978; Guy, 1982; Harris and Associates, 1975; Moberg, 1975).

Does this widespread prevalence of and interest in religion among today's elderly indicate that religion has value as a coping strategy or personal resource? (See Figure 1.) Alternatively, does this concern with religion simply represent a cultural phenomenon that is specific to this current cohort of elderly Americans, and in reality has no relationship to coping or health? The purpose of the present empirical review and synthesis is to provide evidence that might help to answer these questions.

First, what is meant by the term "religion?" Although admitting that definitions vary according to individual perspectives, David Moberg (1970, p. 175) has defined religion as "the personal beliefs, values, and activities pertinent to that which is supernatural, mysterious, and awesome, which transcends immediate situations, and which pertains to questions of final causes and ultimate ends of man and the universe." Moberg goes on to describe two major orientations of religion: one personal and the other institutional. An institutional orientation concerns group-related behaviors such as church attendance and other organi-

Table 1

Religious Attitudes of Geriatric Patients[1] and Senior Center Participants[2]

Location (N)	Definitely True %	Tends to be True %	Unsure %	Tends Not to be True %	Definitely Untrue %
"My faith involves all my life"					
Geriatric Clinic (98)	50.0	24.5	6.1	6.1	13.3
Burlington, IA[3] (86)	46.5	36.0	10.5	3.5	3.5
Springfield,IL[3] 162)	53.1	32.7	8.6	2.5	3.1
Columbia, MO[3] (15)	53.3	26.7	6.7	0	13.3
"Nothing is as important to me as serving God the best I know how"					
Geriatric Clinic (95)	48.4	32.6	7.4	7.4	4.2
Burlington, IA (89)	36.0	44.9	11.2	5.6	2.2
Springfield, IL (159)	51.6	36.5	5.0	4.4	2.5
Columbia, MO (15)	64.3	21.4	7.1	0	7.1
"My religious beliefs are what really lie behind my whole approach to life"					
Geriatric Clinic (95)	49.5	29.5	3.2	5.3	12.6
Burlington, IA (89)	33.7	33.7	20.2	22.3	1.1
Springfield, IL (156)	42.9	40.4	7.7	7.1	1.9
Columbia, MO (15)	57.1	35.7	7.1	0	0
"My religious faith is the most important influence in my life"					
Geriatric Clinic (95)	54.7	27.4	---	7.4	10.5
Burlington, IA (82)	36.6	43.9	---	11.0	8.5
Springfield, IL (156)	44.2	43.6	---	7.1	5.1
Columbia, MO (13)	46.2	46.2	---	7.7	0
1982 Gallup Poll* (265)	42	40	---	4	11
"One should seek God's guidance when making every important decision"					
Geriatric Clinic (96)	65.6	19.8	4.2	6.3	4.2
Burlington, IA (82)	50.0	32.9	7.3	9.8	0
Springfield, IL (158)	59.5	30.4	6.3	1.9	1.9
Columbia, MO (13)	61.5	30.8	7.7	0	0

1 From Koenig et al. (1988a). Religious statements come from Hoge's (1972) intrinsic religiosity scale.
2 Unpublished data (Koenig)
3 Senior Centers. Questionnaires were distributed on site by senior center managers, a single distribution was performed for most centers. 70% response rate was obtained. See Koenig et al. (1988b) for more detail on methodology. Sample characteristics included the following: 73% women, mean age 74.3 yrs, 74% living on <600/mo, 77% Protestant, 22% Catholic.
* Princeton Religion Research Center, 1982, p 112

Figure 1
Simplistic model of the interaction between stress and illness, with factors that might affect this relationship. Religion is incorporated into the model where its influence may be significant.

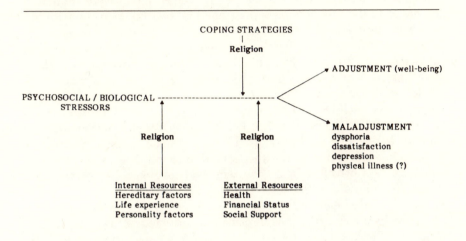

zational types of religious activities. A personal orientation reflects beliefs and attitudes of the individual.

FREUD, JUNG, AND OTHERS

In the early 1900s, the men who gave birth to modern psychiatry disagreed sharply over the probable effects of religion on mental health. Debate often centered on whether religion's influences on the psyche were positive and health inducing or, in contrast, reflective of neurosis and illness producing. Freud strongly defended the latter hypothesis, while Jung and Pfister favored the former.

Fromm, in a commentary on the limitations of Freudian concepts, refers to Freud as the "enemy of religion" who believed religion to be an "illusion" that blocked man from reaching maturity and independence (Fromm, 1979, p. 107). Freud considered religion to be a temporary institution created by man to deal with his powerlessness against nature and felt that it would eventually disappear as the "primacy of the intellect" replaced it. At the age of seventy-one Freud commented in "Future of an Illusion" the following:

Religion would thus be the universal obsessional neurosis of humanity; like the obsessional neurosis of children, it arose out of the Oedipus complex, out of the relation to the father. . . . Historical residues have helped us to view religious teachings, as it were, as neurotic relics, and we may now argue that the time has probably come, as it does in analytic treatment, for replacing the effects of repression by the results of the rational operation of the intellect. (Strachey, 1962, pp. 43–14)

Religious activities and rituals (prayer, for example) were compared by Freud to the repetitive acts performed by neurotic persons with obsessive-compulsive disorder. According to Freud these religious activities served the primary function of defending and protecting against anxieties and dangers in life. The suppression or renunciation of instinctual impulses by these activities, however, was seen as neither completely effective nor final and left the individual sitting on a time-bomb of repressed feelings and emotions that were constantly threatening to be released. In 1907 Freud concluded that "in view of these resemblances and analogies, one might venture to regard the obsessional neurosis as a pathological counterpart to the formation of religion, to describe this neurosis as a private religious system, and religion as a universal obsessional neurosis" (Strachey, 1959, vol. 2, p. 34).

After Freud's death in 1939, however, some personal information was revealed by a colleague. This information consisted of the contents of a letter that Freud wrote to his friend, Oskar Pfister, three years after publishing his article "Obsessive Acts and Religious Practices" from which the above quote was taken. Pfister was a Protestant theologian, a widely published psychoanalyst, a student of Freud, and a close family friend with whom Freud corresponded frequently over the thirty plus years of their acquaintance. After Freud's death, Pfister turned the many letters which he had saved over to Freud's wife. In one of these letters, dated June 1910, Freud admitted the following:

I cannot face with comfort the idea of life without work; work and the free play of the imagination are for me the same thing, I take no pleasure in anything else. . . . What would one do when ideas failed or words refused to come? It is impossible not to shudder at the thought. Hence, in spite of all the acceptance of fate which is appropriate to an honest man, I have one quite *secret prayer*: that I may be spared any wasting away and crippling of my ability to work because of physical deterioration. In the words of King Macbeth, "let us die in harness." (Meng and Freud, 1963, p. 146).

After publishing "Future of an Illusion" in 1927, Freud's major concern during the final twelve years of his life was centered on topics relating to religion and philosophy (*Civilization and its Discontents* 1930; *New Introductory Lectures*, 1933; *Why War?* 1933; *Moses and Monotheism*, 1939; see Strachey, 1962, for these works). God represented in the unconscious the powerful father figure of the Oedipus complex that Freud felt was at the origin of much psychic conflict. He believed that religion was created by man to help him deal with his insecurities and helplessness in the face of the powerful, uncontrollable forces of nature. This view-point, though presented in a negative light, does support a major role for religion as a coping behavior—one that even Freud himself may have secretly entertained.

In contrast, Freud's contemporary Carl Jung approached religion and its influence on the human psyche from an entirely different perspective. In discussing the differences between himself and Freud, Jung expresses the following reservations over his colleagues views:

For my part, I prefer to look at man in the light of what in him is healthy and sound, and to free the sick man from that point of view which colours every page Freud has written. Freud's teaching is definitely one-sided in that it gen-eralizes from facts that are relevant only to neurotic states of mind; its validity is really confined to those states.... Freud's psychology is not a psychology of the healthy mind. (Jung, 1933, p 117)

Referring specifically to Freud's attitudes toward religion, Jung notes:

... man has, everywhere and always, spontaneously developed religious forms of expression, and ... the human psyche from time immemorial has been shot through with religious feelings and ideas. Whoever cannot see this aspect of the human psyche is blind, and whoever chooses to explain it away, or to "enlighten" it away, has no sense of reality.... This father-complex [Oedipus], fanatically defended with such stubborness and over-sensitivity, is a cloak of religiosity misunderstood. (Jung, 1933, p. 122)

Jung reflects his own experience in this area:

During the past thirty years, people from all the civilized countries of the earth have consulted me. I have treated many hundreds of patients, the larger number being Protestants, a smaller number Jews, and not more than five or six believing Catholics. Among all my patients in the second half of life—that is to say, over thirty-five—there has not been one whose problem in the last resort was not that of finding a religious outlook on life. It is safe to say that every one of them fell ill because he had lost that which the living religions of every age have given to their followers, and none of them has been really healed who did not regain his religious outlook. (Jung, 1933, p. 229)

The intense disagreement among mental health professionals on this subject has hardly abated in more recent years. In 1980, Bergin and Ellis engaged in a lively discussion of this topic in a series of articles published in the *Journal of Consulting and Clinical Psychology*. A.E. Bergin, from Brigham Young University, strongly argues for the positive impact of religion on mental health and the need to include it in psychotherapy (Bergin 1980a, 1980b). On the other hand, Albert Ellis, founder of the

Institute for Rational-Emotive Therapy, articulately disagrees with Bergin. Ellis notes the following in response to Bergin's article:

Devout, orthodox, or dogmatic religion (or what might be called religiosity) is significantly correlated with emotional disturbance. People largely disturb themselves by believing strongly in absolutistic shoulds, oughts, and musts, and most people who dogmatically believe in some religion believe in these health-sabotaging absolutes. The emotionally healthy individual is flexible, open, tolerant, and changing, and the devoutly religious person tends to be inflexible, closed, intolerant, and unchanging. Religiosity, therefore, is in many respects equivalent to irrational thinking and emotional disturbance. (Ellis, 1980, p. 637)

While opinions abound, little systematically collected data from carefully designed research that has utilized random sampling methods and attempted to control for investigator bias supports one or the other of the opinions thus far presented. These opinions were based primarily upon personal experience and experience anecdotally gained through contact with individual patients, often those with mental illness. The latter sources of information, however, tell little about the majority of older persons in the community or those with medical illness who do not have serious psychiatric illness, but instead face adjustment difficulties to very real and stressful life changes. In the past thirty to forty years, studies from a variety of sources have provided systematically collected data in this regard. While study design may have been far from ideal in a number of these investigations, such inquiries represent serious attempts by researchers to apply the scientific method to an amazingly complex and fascinating topic.

EARLIER AND RECENT REVIEWS

Maves (1960), Heenan (1972), and Fecher (1982) have previously reviewed the social sciences literature on religion and adjustment in old age.

Jarvis and Northcott (1987) provide a thorough review of research examining the effects of religion on morbidity and mortality, particularly the impact of religious denomination (101 references). Included are studies performed among Muslims, the clergy, Parsis, Hutterites, and other groups. Not much attention, however, is given to the impact of specific religious behaviors and attitudes—regardless of denomination—on health and well-being. Levin and Vanderpool (1987) have reviewed with a critical eye many of the studies examining the impact of church attendance on physical health and have set forth important groundwork for the emergence of an epidemiology of religion. Although these latter two reviews are not focused on the elderly, their contents are relevant to the degree that older persons were included in most of the studies reviewed. Jarvis and Northcott hypothesize that religion may impact both positively and negatively on health by the following mechanisms: (positively) encouraging behavior that prevents illness or death or that assists in treatment of sickness; discouraging behavior that is harmful to life or that would hinder treatment; placing a person in a support group that can, depending on the strength of the group, assist in times of need; cultivating attitudes that may give the individual a helpful perspective with which to face stressful life situations; (negatively) encouraging behavior that is harmful to life or health care; discouraging behavior that may prevent illness or have a positive effect on treatment.

Our review will build upon and update the work of these reviewers, with a more concentrated focus on the impact of religion on the mental and physical health of the elderly. Three dimensions of religiosity will be considered: belief, ritual, and experience. These dimensions were chosen because they represent the most salient of Glock and Stark's original five dimensions of religiosity (Glock and Stark, 1965), and have most consistently been found among the dimensions of religiosity proposed by sociologists of religion (King and Hunt, 1975; Lenski, 1963; Fichter, 1969) and used in studies relating religion and health variables. Studies will be presented here that address the influence of these dimensions of religiosity on mental health (adjustment and coping, personal well-being, and psychiatric illness) and physical health in the elderly.

OVERVIEW

The general outline for this work will proceed as follows. First, important terms or constructs will be defined and issues concerning measurement will be considered in Chapter 2. In Chapters 3 through 7, an empirical review is conducted of studies that have examined the relationship between religion, health, and aging. Where studies are not available for older populations, investigations among younger samples are presented and their generalizability to the elderly commented upon. In Chapter 8, a model of how religion fits into the complex interaction between stress and illness is presented and explained on the basis of research noted in earlier chapters. In Chapter 9, case studies emerging from the clinical and research experience of a geriatric medicine specialist are presented and implications discussed. Chapters 10 through 12 give perspectives of professionals from multiple disciplines on the interaction between religion, health, and aging. Finally, in Chapters 13 and 14, implications for clinicians and avenues for future research are discussed and conclusions are drawn. Appendix I primarily addresses issues of religious questionnaire construction and provides an example of an instrument recently validated in the elderly. Appendix II is list of organizations from which the interested reader may seek additional information. The bibliography is followed by other references and recommended readings.

2

MEASUREMENT OF RELIGION, MENTAL, AND PHYSICAL HEALTH

RELIGIOSITY

There has been little agreement among investigators on the positive, negative, or neutral impact of religion on mental and physical health. This controversy may be at least partly attributable to the great variety of instruments used to measure religiosity, a consequence of the lack of a universally acceptable characterization of the religiosity variable. There is considerable controversy over whether religiosity is a uni-dimensional or multi-dimensional concept (Gorsuch, 1984). Many studies both in the past and present measure religiosity solely in terms of either church attendance or church membership (J. Wilson, 1978). The multi-dimensional concept, however, has become widespread since Glock and Stark's presentation in 1965 of five dimensions of religiosity: belief, ritual, experience, knowledge, and consequences (Glock and Stark, 1965). Other investigators have dropped some of these dimensions and added others through the method of factor analysis (King and Hunt, 1975). Unfortunately, there has been little agreement on which dimensions are most relevant or how these should be measured (Gorsuch, 1984; J. Wilson, 1978).

Also regrettable is the lack of communication and collaboration between social gerontologists and sociologists of religion who have developed more sophisticated religiosity scales (Heenan, 1972). Consequently, recent surveys and research studies have only seldom used the more refined, multi-dimensional instruments (Heenan, 1972); instead, investigators have tended to use instruments of their own genesis, which are often lacking in formal tests of validity or reliability. Validity itself has been difficult to achieve, because of the nebulous concept of religiosity and a lack of consensus on its salient features. There is little wonder, then, at the diverse outcomes from studies, each using different instruments that measure different aspects of a possibly multi-dimensional variable.

In an attempt to address this problem, Koenig et al. (1988 a, b) have constructed an instrument that incorporates the generally agreed upon dimensions of religiosity into a single questionnaire (the Springfield Religiosity Schedule [SRS]), which was then validated by pastors' judgments. (See Appendix I.) A factor analysis of items comprising the questionnaire was performed (based on the results of a community sample of 836 elders—mean age 73.4). Four major clusters of items with high intercorrelations were found (along with three others that were less well defined). These factors were belief, intrinsic religiosity, religious well-being, and organized religious activity. Although this effort is by no means definitive, it represents an attempt to derive a practical instrument that may be used for older populations to capture important aspects of religion.

MENTAL AND PHYSICAL HEALTH

Difficulties are not, however, restricted to the religious variable. Similar problems have been encountered with the definition and measurement of mental and physical health. Mental health includes both the absence of major psychiatric illness and the presence of subjective well-being. Psychiatric illness is well-defined by criteria set forth in the *Diagnostic and Statistical Manual of Mental Disorders* (3rd ed.). Depressive disorders are the most common psychiatric problems encountered in late life. The prevalence of major depression among community-dwelling older adults is quite low—less than 1 percent (Kramer et al., 1985). However, dysthymias and adjustment disorders are considerably more common. More germane for the great majority of the elderly population are the less severe forms of mental ill-health, such as dissatisfaction with life and unhappiness. Subjective well-being is an important indicator of "quality of life," and hence reflects an important aspect of mental health. Numerous instruments exist for the measurement of well-being, often in the form of self-report questionnaires that are more easily utilized in large population surveys.

Denier (1984) reports in a review of the topic that personal well-being consists of multiple dimensions such as life satisfaction, happiness, mood, and morale, a finding confirmed by George (1986). George also notes that of all the dimensions of well-being, life satisfaction is a more direct, stable, and accurate measure of personal well-being. Different from happiness (a transient, rapidly changing experience), life satisfaction reflects an individual's concept of life in a cognitive rather than emotional sense (George, 1980; George, 1986).

Fortunately, several easily administered self-report scales exist to measure life satisfaction and related concepts among geriatric populations (Life Satisfaction Index, Philadelphia Geriatric Center Morale Scale, MUNSH) (Denier, 1984). Unfortunately, these instruments have seldom been utilized in studies relating religiosity variables.

In looking at the relationship between religion and subjective well-being, investigators often use terms such as life satisfaction, happiness, and morale, interchangeably (Kane and Kane, 1981). As noted previously, these terms are not synonymous. Some data, however, does exist to support the presence of a common underlying factor related to subjective well-being that crosses all of its dimensions (Denier, 1984). In fact, tests for convergent validity between measures of life satisfaction, morale, happiness, and positive affect, have demonstrated high values (.65)—especially for the most common multi-item geriatric scales in use today (Lohmann, 1977). The presence of a similar underlying common factor that infuses or cuts across all dimensions of religiosity has likewise been suggested, though data to support this contention has been less solid than that for well-being (Moberg, 1974).

Similar confusion with terminology has plagued the concept of adjustment and coping. Although closely related, adjustment, coping and subjective well-being are also distinct concepts. George (1980) notes that adjustment is characterized by two conditions: first, the individual's ability to meet the demands of the environment and second, the individual's experience of personal well-being in relationship to the environment. Adjustment, then, represents both the process of coping and the results of that process, a sense of well-being. Unlike well-being, however, coping (the active, more objective component of adjustment) has been difficult to measure directly (Cohen and Lazarus, 1983).

Earlier studies on adjustment and religion did not always clarify the concepts that were being measured. The majority of studies in the 1940s and 1950s used the Burgess-Cavan-Havighurst Attitudes Inventory. This instrument measures satisfaction with activities and status, general happiness, and feelings of usefulness (Cavan et al., 1949). Here the distinction between well-being and personal adjustment becomes quite fine, if present at all. Later studies have distinguished adjustment as a distinct and separate variable from subjective well-being. Hence, to provide recognition of the distinction between concepts such as adjustment, coping, and well-being, we have chosen to report separately the studies examining religion's impact on adjustment and coping, from those on subjective well-being; nevertheless, one must bear in mind the synonymous use of these concepts in some studies.

For the measurement of physical health, investigators have asked patients to check physical symptoms or medical illnesses out of standardized inventories of the like, to report a global self-assessment of their health (poor, fair, good, excellent) or to undergo physical examination by health professionals. The latter method becomes impractical in terms of cost and time for studies involving large numbers of participants. Some investigators, however, have questioned the validity of instruments relying on the older person's subjective self-assessment of his or her health, which may differ significantly from physician ratings (Tessler and Mechanic, 1978). Researchers utilizing self-report measures defend their position by pointing to studies that show an individual's perception of his or her health is quite valid, and may be a more important determinant of health care seeking behavior than physician assessments (Maddox and Douglas, 1973). Our problem exists in comparing studies that have used different methods for assessing health, with no assurance that these instruments are measuring the same aspects of health or are equally valid.

Thus, the wide variety of instruments and constructs measured causes problems even when measuring relatively objective variables such as health. As we have seen, this poses a particularly serious problem when measuring highly subjective and ambiguous variables such as religiosity and personal well-being. Self-administered questionnaires have been particularly popular because of the relatively low cost of such methods and the ability to survey large numbers of people. This strategy, however, has its own inherent problems of selection bias and poor response rates, especially among elderly populations.

In summary, due to methodological diversity, ambiguity in definitions, and use of closely related variables, numerous reasons exist for the disparity in results between studies. Keeping these problems in mind, we proceed with a review of the medical, social, and psychological literature, with the objective of clarifying the issue of religion's impact on the mental and physical health of older adults.

3

RELIGIOUS BELIEFS AND MENTAL HEALTH

In this section we will examine studies focusing on the impact of religious beliefs and attitudes on various dimensions of mental health, such as coping ability, subjective well-being, and psychiatric illness.

ADJUSTMENT AND COPING

Ability to cope with and adjust to stressful life changes with aging (physical illness, bereavement, fears concerning death) is an important determinant of well-being and mental health (Cohen and Lazarus, 1979). In a review of seven common behaviors used to cope with physical illness, Moos and Tsu (1977) include religious belief as relevant in this regard:

When life's happenings seem capricious and uncontrollable, as with the sudden onset of serious illness, it is often easier to manage if one can find a general purpose or pattern of meaning in the course of events . . . Belief in a divine purpose or in the general beneficence of a divine spirit may serve as consolation or as encouragement to do one's best to deal with the difficulties one encounters. (p. 14)

If this is indeed the case, where is the evidence?

The evidence supporting a positive influence of religious beliefs and attitudes on coping in later life comes from several sources. First are results from a number of national surveys, conducted over the past fifteen years, that asked older people directly whether or not religion helped them during times of stress. An example of this type of question is the following: "Are your religious beliefs a help to you during times of stress and unhappiness?" Second are surveys asking similar questions, but in a "negative" fashion. For instance, people are asked to respond with varying degrees of agreement or disagreement to the following statements: "While dealing with difficult times in my life, I *don't* get much personal strength and support from God" or "I rely *very little* on religious beliefs when dealing with tension in my life." Rather than simple assent, the latter questions require considerable deliberation as respondents are forced to express disagreement or objection if they feel that religious beliefs really are a source of help. Third are studies in which checklists of general coping strategies (including religious attitudes and behaviors) are administered to samples of older people, with frequencies of response noted. The later design still allows for bias in terms of social desirability, since it may be "fashionable" among the present cohort of older persons to mark religious items as coping behaviors. There also are other issues of reactivity, such as possible subtle suggestion from the setting of the interview, the way the appointments are made, the presence of the interviewer, and cues that were intentionally or unintentionally provided.

Fourth are data arising from unstructured or semistructured interviews that include open-ended questions designed to elicit *spontaneous* responses from older adults on how they got through or coped with difficult time periods in their lives. These spontaneous responses would appear to be less influenced by social appropriateness and therefore would more accurately reflect behaviors that really helped the person. Even with this study design, however, difficulties with memory and influences of current coping behaviors and attitudes probably interfere to some degree with the accuracy of these spontaneous reports. Finally, there is data acquired from population studies examining the relationship between successful adjustment in later life, and religious beliefs and attitudes. We will now review studies in each of the above five design categories.

DIRECT POSITIVELY WORDED COPING QUESTIONS

The Americana Healthcare Corporation (1980–81) conducted a survey of the community-dwelling adults age sixty and over in the United States using a random digit sampling technique. Their final sample consisted of 505 participants. Among the items was a "positively" worded question inquiring about religion as a help in times of stress and unhappiness: 89 percent of the sample answered affirmatively. The Gallup organization likewise surveyed a random sample of Americans age sixty-five and over, seeking responses, agreement, or disagreement to the following

statement: "I receive a great deal of comfort and support from my religious beliefs" (Princeton Religion Research Center, 1982); 58 percent
of the sample reported completely true and 29 percent mostly true. This
contrasts with responses of people under thirty years of age who noted
completely true only 23 percent of the time.

DIRECT NEGATIVELY WORDED COPING QUESTIONS

Koenig et al. (1988a) recently asked a series of "negatively" worded
questions about religion and coping to a consecutive series of 106 patients
(mean age 74) attending a geriatric medicine outpatient clinic in Springfield, Illinois. These questions were interspersed with eighty-eight other
questions on religious behaviors and attitudes. Agreement or disagreement was sought to the statement: "I rely very little on religious beliefs
when dealing with stress and difficulties"; 73 percent disagreed or
strongly disagreed. Another statement was the following: "God is not
a source of support during difficult times"; to this item, 74 percent
expressed strong or moderate disagreement.

MULTIPLE-CHOICE CHECKLISTS

Several studies have included religious items in checklists of coping
behaviors. Older adults were then asked to note which behaviors helped
them to cope or get through a difficult situation that they recalled from
the past. Conway (1985) distributed a checklist of coping behaviors and
resources to a random sample of sixty-five elderly women residing in
the Kansas City area. Two categories of coping behaviors were examined:
action-oriented (12 items) and cognitive-oriented (8 items). These behaviors were elicited with regard to medical problems that they had
recently experienced. The five most frequently reported action-oriented
behaviors were the following: (1) pray (91%); (2) go to the doctor or
other professional (89%); (3) seek more information (72%); (4) stay home
more (71%); and (5) rest (71%). Among the top five cognitive-oriented
strategies were the following: (1) think of religion (86%); (2) realize that
I am better off than most people (86%); (3) think that I am able to manage
(72%); (4) realize I'm not as bad as first thought (63%); and (5) think
that I have to get through (60%). In a similar study, Manfredi and Pickett
(1987) surveyed a sample of fifty-one older community-dwelling adults
in Rhode Island with the Ways of Coping Checklist (Folkman and Lazarus, 1985). Among the sixty-six items in the checklist, the following
were the top five responses: (1) prayer; (2) remind myself things could
be worse; (3) maintain pride; (4) look for a silver lining; and (5) turn to
work/activity. Although these studies dealt with small samples and only

one was randomly selected (Conway, 1985), a consistent finding is that religion tops these lists as the predominant coping behavior.

SPONTANEOUSLY MENTIONED COPING BEHAVIORS

Nevertheless, the situation may still be that participants are responding in socially acceptable ways. For this reason, a series of studies have been conducted that examine *spontaneously* offered coping responses of older adults to stressful life events. Rosen (1982) examined the spontaneously mentioned coping behaviors of a sample of 148 low-income elderly (age > 65) residing in the Athens, Georgia, area. The sample was predominantly women (78%), the less educated (74% < 8 years of schooling), and equally divided between blacks (52%) and whites. The following question was asked: "Judging from the things that you have told me today, you seem to be active and able to keep going even though you've had a hard life. What would you say keeps you going?" Religious coping behaviors were the most common response, occuring in 51 percent of blacks and 28 percent of whites. Considering the nature of the sample, these findings are not surprising. Women, the less-educated, and people of lower social class have been consistently associated with greater religious activity (Princeton Religion Research Center, 1982). Likewise, Swanson and Harter (1971), studying coping behaviors of blacks in New Orleans, have emphasized the heavy reliance of blacks on religious beliefs and attitudes for coping.

Koenig et al. (1988c) have recently examined the spontaneous coping behaviors of a sample of 100 adults, age fifty-five to eighty, participating in the Second Duke Longitudinal Study in Durham, North Carolina. Participants were selected using a stratified-random sampling technique to achieve a balance in terms of sex and social class. The resulting sample was equally divided between men and women, all white, and most had at least some college. Social class was moderate to high, given a substantial number of retired professionals in the group. Participants were interviewed for two to four hours using a semistructured format. They were asked about three stressful periods or events in their life: the worst event in their whole life, the worst event in the past ten years, and the worst event or situation in the present. The coping question was asked in several different ways to enhance understanding and maximize the information obtained. Typical questions for the three worst events or periods included the following: "How did you get through it?" "How did you manage to keep going?" "What kept you going?" "How did you keep yourself on an even keel?"

A total of 556 coping strategies were mentioned in response to 289 stressful events or periods. Religious coping behaviors were most frequently mentioned. Almost half the sample (45%) mentioned that a religious coping strategy had helped them to get through at least one of the three difficult periods or experiences. Over a quarter of the sample (26%) reported religious coping behaviors for two or all three of the stressful situations. A closer examination of the types of religious strategies employed in coping revealed that personal or private religious behaviors (faith and trust in God, prayer) were present in 91 percent of cases in which religion was employed. Religious group or social activity (church attendance, involvement in church activities, church friends) alone or in combination with private religious behaviors was present only 33 percent of the time. As in other studies (Manfredi and Pickett, 1987; Conway, 1985) among older populations, religious attitudes and private activities appear to predominate over the "social function" of religion in coping. The above study also demonstrated that religious coping behaviors are not restricted to the poor, uneducated, and minority group populations.

Recently, two studies conducted among hospitalized and outpatient elderly veterans (Durham, North Carolina), have examined spontaneously mentioned coping behaviors used to deal with physical illness and disability. In the first, coping behaviors were examined in a consecutive series of 109 men age seventy or over, hospitalized with acute or subacute medical or neurological illness. This was part of a larger study that examined the prevalence of depression among hospitalized veterans (see Koenig et al., 1988d for population characteristics). During a forty-five to sixty minute interview at the bedside, numerous questions were asked about mental and physical problems. The following coping questions were asked: "How do you keep yourself from getting depressed despite your physical illness and disability?"; "What keeps your spirits up?"; "What keeps you going?"

The predominant response, once again, was religious in nature, with 36% (39/108) of the group noting such behaviors. Among patients with major depression, religious coping behaviors were mentioned less frequently (3/12 or 25%) than among the nondepressed (35/96 or 36%), but this difference was not significant ($x^2 = .10$, p > .50).

In a second related study, a group of community-dwelling elderly veterans (mean age 69) attending a hospital-sponsored exercise class were surveyed with regard to the same question. Again, religious coping behaviors predominated, with 35 percent (12/34) of the group noting them. Depressive symptoms were slightly less prevalent among those older veterans using religious coping behaviors than among those not (6.25 vs. 6.50 on Geriatric Depression Scale), though the difference was not significant (T = .14, p > .50) (Koenig et al., 1988g). In an earlier study, Jeffers and Nichols (1961) tested 251 elderly volunteers in the First Duke Longitudinal Study of Aging using the Activity Inventory of Cavin, Burgess, and Havighurst in order to investigate the relationship between attitudes and health in older persons. They found an inverse relationship between physical functioning and religion. For the older, disabled subjects in particular, religion meant more to them as the end of life became near. They concluded that religion was serving to help these older individuals to cope with their increasingly limited life situation. If (1) older and more disabled individuals are more likely to turn to religion to help them cope, and (2) depressive symptoms are more common among the disabled and those in poor health, then the finding that depressive symptoms are no more frequent among religious copers than nonreligious copers suggests that religion may buffer some of the deleterious effects of illness and disability on well-being. The latter idea, however, represents a hypothesis with only marginal support at present. Idler (1987) has found that at a given level of chronic illness, religious older men perceived their functional health status at higher levels than did the nonreligious.

In one of the few longitudinal studies on this subject, O'Brien (1982) examined the role of religion in the adjustment of patients on hemodialysis. Her sample was composed of 126 chronic hemodialysis patients age twenty-one to seventy-five purposively selected from three large hospitals in Washington D.C. The time period between the first (T1) and final (T2) interviews was three years. Patients interviewed at both T1 and T2 were predominantly black (75%), Protestant (69%), and equally divided by gender. It was possible to locate only half of the sample (N = 63) for the final interview. Both qualitative and quantitative data were acquired during the interviews.

In the initial interview, 74 percent of patients noted that religious or ethical beliefs were to some degree associated with adjustment to their disease and its treatment regimen; 28 percent stated that their religious faith was always associated with adjustment to their illness condition. Those who reported the most positive attitudes regarding religious belief and adjustment 28% also reported the highest degree of interactional behavior with others, the highest compliance with their treatment regimen, and the least amount of alienation (Dean Alienation Scale) (Dean, 1961).

Three years later, 27 percent of the patients located for followup noted (qualitatively) that their dependence on their religious faith had significantly increased; over half of these changed their view of religion from having no influence to having a strongly positive one. Only one patient changed his perception of religion as a source of comfort and strength from a positive one to a negative one. The mean age of patients reporting a positive increase in their faith was forty-five years. The mean time on dialysis for these patients was approximately five years. Several patients noted that having church members and/or their minister coming to visit and praying for them helped greatly in their ability to face their condition. Scale item responses (quantatively) indicated that 40 percent of the sample became more positive in their perceived importance of religious faith in adjusting to their illness, whereas 16 percent perceived a decreased importance of religion in their lives. Despite their advancing illness, 33 percent of the sample reported attending church services more frequently; 29 percent decreased church attendance, half of these being attributed to increasing disability. In summary, O'Brien notes that religion was found to be a notable influence for long-term adjustment to end-stage renal disease and chronic hemodialysis.

Although overall a good study and excellent sample size, it could have benefited from inclusion of a statistical analysis of the data and a better description of the demographic characteristics of the original sample. Nevertheless, these findings do confirm those of others who have found religion to be important for adjustment among chronically ill hemodialysis patients (Baldree et al., 1982). This study is also one of the few that has documented an increase in use of religious faith over time in medical patients adjusting to chronic illness.

A valid criticism of the above studies is that most took place in the southeastern U.S., an area frequently referred to as the Bible Belt, where religion holds a particularly strong cultural influence. Nevertheless, studies performed in Rhode Island, Washington D.C., and central Illinois, places well-removed from the Bible Belt, have yielded similar results (Manfredi and Pickett, 1987; O'Brien, 1982; Koenig et al., 1988b). Studies outside this country have also found religion to be an important source of comfort for many older persons. Reid et al. (1978) studied the religious beliefs and attitudes of a random sample of 501 older people in West Scotland. Over half (54%) reported that they received much comfort from their religion. A similar percentage (55%) claimed much comfort from religion when losing someone close to them through death. The investigators concluded that religious beliefs were important in the lives of the majority of the elderly population of Scotland at that time, and that religion was a major source of strength and comfort to these people. The European psychiatrist Viktor Frankl (1959) also underscored the importance of religious faith in maintaining mental and physical health in the destructive environment of a Nazi concentration camp.

It appears that Judeo-Christian religious beliefs and attitudes are ubiquitously claimed by older adults to be of comfort and support to them, and to help them cope with stressful life experiences. This is true regardless of the geographic location of the study, be it central Illinois, eastern Kansas, Rhode Island, Georgia, North Carolina, or western Scotland.

ASSOCIATIONS BETWEEN RELIGIOUS BELIEFS AND SUCCESSFUL ADJUSTMENT

If indeed religious beliefs and attitudes are effective and useful coping behaviors, one would expect to see some relationship between successful adjustment or coping and these intrapsychic religious variables. In fact, several investigators have shown a positive association between religious beliefs and overall personal adjustment in elderly individuals. In two early studies, Moberg found that strong religious belief was significantly correlated with good adjustment in old age. In a study done in 1953, he examined 219 elderly "believers" and "non-believers" in terms of personal adjustment. The former group was found to be better adjusted (Moberg, 1953). In the same study, Moberg (1958) interviewed a sample of sixty-eight elderly persons, and looked at personal adjustment scores of the "fundamentalist" and "non-fundamentalist" members in terms of religious beliefs. He concluded that the holding of orthodox or conservative Christian beliefs is related to positive adjustment.

More recently, Hunsberger in a Canadian study of eighty-five elderly volunteers, found a significant correlation between subjects reporting religious beliefs to be very important and those claiming high levels of personal adjustment (r = .24). "Importance of religious beliefs" was further related to "happiness" and "health" (r = .30 and .25 respectively). "Agreement with beliefs taught while growing up" was similarly associated with personal adjustment (r = .31 and happiness r = .45). All of the above variables, however, were addressed using single-item measures (Hunsberger, 1985). Gass (1987), in a study of coping behaviors among a sample of one hundred widows age sixty-five to eighty-five, (using Folkman and Lazarus' Ways of Coping Checklist; Folkman and Lazarus, 1985), also found that religious beliefs and rituals were positively correlated with measures of mental health.

Acklin et al. (1983) explored the role of religious values in coping with cancer in a study taking place in Atlanta, Georgia. They examined a small sample of twenty-six cancer patients age twenty to seventy-six (mean age 48 and eighteen medical controls with chronic or acute medical conditions other than cancer. Mean intrinsic religiosity (IR) scores (Allport and Ross, 1967) and church attendance were slightly lower for cancer than noncancer patients, though these differences were not significant. Intrinsic religiosity was significantly related to scores obtained on the Life Meaning Scale (72 item scale) in the cancer (r = .41, p < .05) and in noncancer (r = .72, p < .001) groups. Both IR and frequency of church attendance were inversely related to measures of anger-hostility (− .34 and − .39, respectively) and each of the five other subscales of the Grief Experience Inventory; results were similar for cancer and noncancer patients. The small number of patients in the sample, however, precludes adequate comparison of cancer with noncancer patients. Nevertheless, for both cancer and noncancer patients, religious orientation was related to meaning in life and the experience of psychological well-being during serious medical illness.

Koenig and Blake (1986) examined the relationship between the likelihood of using religious beliefs and prayer during stress and two variables reflecting healthy coping: (1) the self-reported ability to handle stress and (2) the likelihood of talking to a person when having a problem with them. The sample consisted of 304 community-dwelling elderly persons (mean age 75) participating in a seniors' lunch program. It was found that among the younger elderly (age 60 to 74) who were highly likely to use religious beliefs and prayer to cope, 40 percent reported they handled stress well, compared with 23 percent among those with a low likelihood of using religious behaviors (p < .10). Religious copers were also more likely to talk with a person in order to resolve the problem (40% vs. 14%, p < .01). Similar trends were found among the old elderly (> 74), but associations were not as marked. The major critique of this study is the low response rate (43%) and the use of relatively crude measures of successful coping and religious coping. Furthermore, other potential covariates, such as sex, health, financial status, and social support were not controlled.

In a similar, but larger study, Koenig et al. (1988b) examined the relationship between religiosity and well-being in a sample of 836 community-dwelling elderly (mean age 73). As a measure of subjective coping, the following statement was presented: "I handle tension in my life very well." Participants were asked to rate on a scale of one to four their agreement with the statement. Responses were correlated with religious activity and intrinsic religiosity (a measure of religious attitudes and commitment). After controlling for health, social support, objective and subjective financial status, sex, and age, intrinsic religiosity was significantly correlated with this coping measure (r = .13, p < .001). Subjective well-being, measured using the Philadelphia Geriatric Center Morale Scale (Lawton, 1975), was highly correlated with the subjective coping item (r = .42).

In one of the few longitudinal studies addressing religion and aging, Blazer and Palmore (1976) examined data collected as part of the Duke University's first longitudinal study of aging extending from 1955 to 1975. Their sample consisted of 272 volunteer community residents whose mean age was 71. Using the Chicago Inventory of Activities and Attitudes (Burgess, Cavan, and Havighurst, 1948) and the Cavan Adjustment Scale (Cavan et al., 1949), they found several significant correlations between religion (both activities and attitudes) and happiness, feelings of usefulness, and adjustment. Religious attitudes were measured by two items: (1) religion as a source of comfort and (2) importance of religion in life. Attitudes alone were not significantly related to happiness, but were related to feelings of usefulness (r = .16) especially among those elderly from manual occupations (r = .24). Religious attitudes had a small correlation with adjustment (r = .13), which became significant among those from nonmanual occupations (r = .24). Because of the higher correlations found with religious activity, they concluded that overt religious behaviors were more important than attitude in influencing adjustment. However, longitudinal analysis over eighteen years showed that despite a general decline in religious activities, religious attitude remained stable and the correlations with personal adjustment increased as people aged. The increasing correlation found between adjustment and religious behaviors/attitudes as people age suggests that as other personal resources such as health, wealth, and social support decline, religion remains as an effective and durable coping behavior.

NEGATIVE REPORTS

Not all studies, however, have shown positive associations between religious belief and adjustment among older individuals. In early work performed by Havighurst and Albrecht, the Prairie City Study, religious attitudes of elderly persons were compared with their levels of personal adjustment. They found very little relationship between the two (Havighurst and Albrecht, 1953).

In Barron's review of several studies, mostly among familyless men in New York City, he concluded that the impact of religious attitudes on adjustment in old age was not conclusive. In particular, he pointed out the New York College Study, which found no difference between religiously and nonreligiously oriented subjects in levels of anxiety about getting older. Participants in this study, however, were all less than 65 years of age (Barron, 1958).

Covalt (1960), drawing upon her experience based on anecdotal cases limited to her private medical practice, declared that she had not observed elderly people asking for more spiritual help when they were ill. During the twenty-five years of her practice, she claimed that no patient had chosen to discuss religious beliefs or problems with her, or had asked for a minister. Furthermore, she noted that when a sick patient brings a Bible with him to the hospital and keeps it displayed, this is a sign of trouble for the physician from an insecure individual (Covalt, 1960).

Croog and Levine (1972) examined social and psychological factors in recovery from serious illness (myocardial infarction) in 324 men age thirty to sixty (Boston, Massachusetts). They interviewed patients at two times. The first interview was conducted two months after the medical event and inquired about religious attitudes and activities one month prior to the heart attack (T1) and at the time of the interview (T2). Followup was conducted one year later (T3). They were particularly interested in the impact that an experience of a serious medical event (heart attack) might have on religious attitudes. Self-rated importance of religion changed in 38 percent of patients between T1 and T3, with 22 percent showing an increase and 16 percent a decrease; church attendance changed for 27.2 percent of the group, with 10.4 percent showing an increase and 16.8 percent a decrease; 9.3 percent reported a change in religious feelings or views about religion, virtually all indicating an increase in strength of belief. Croog and Levine concluded that most persons did not have a change in religious feelings as a consequence of their life-threatening medical illness. The data, however, indicate that a significant minority did. Generalizing these results to populations comprised primarily of older women, however, should be done with caution; very different findings might arise from the study of such a population for which religion appears to play a more important role (Princeton Religion Research Center, 1982).

COPING WITH DEATH ANXIETY AND BEREAVEMENT

In addition to health problems, other major stressors in later life include thoughts of one's own death and the intense feelings of loss accompanying bereavement. As people age, thoughts of death may become more frequent and may represent a source of considerable stress (Jeffers and Verwoerdt, 1966; Wolff, 1970; Gubrium, 1973). As friends and family die and as the frequency of life-threatening illness increases, the older person may face persistent fears and anxieties about his or her own mortality, fears, and anxieties that were easily laid aside at a younger age. The inability to resolve such fears in later life may result in a state of anxiety or distress.

Numerous investigators have shown a positive impact for religious beliefs and commitment on feelings about death (Wolff, 1959; Jeffers, Nichols, and Eisdorfer, 1961; Gubrium, 1973; Wittowski and Baumgartner, 1977; Feifel and Nagy, 1981). Others, however, have shown no effect (Feifel, 1974; Kurlychek, 1976; O'Rourke, 1977) and some even indicate an increase in death anxiety among religious subjects (Feifel, 1959). Although the weight of the evidence points to a beneficial effect of religious beliefs and commitment on death anxiety, there continues to be controversy on this issue. Several investigators, moreover, have found that it is the *certainty* of belief, not the content (be it religious or irreligious), that is of primary importance in determining death anxiety (Hinton, 1967; Alexander and Adlerstein, 1959; Smith, Nehemkin, and Charter, 1988–84). Recent findings by Koenig (1988), however, are in contrast to earlier reports of lower death anxiety in the "certain nonbelievers." In a study of 282 elderly senior center participants (mean age seventy five), levels of death anxiety were found to decrease with stress. This was particularly true for the "older elderly" (< 74) and for women. In that study, the inverse relationship between religious beliefs/use of prayer, and death anxiety, was even stronger than that found between religious community activity and death anxiety, underscoring the importance of religious beliefs in allaying the anxiety associated with thoughts about death. There is still much that is unknown about the relationship between religious faith and fears concerning death. Until more uniform measures of death anxiety and religiosity are utilized in this research, comparison of results between studies will be difficult.

Smiley (1985) reported in a qualitative study done on fifty-six retired women religious, that rather than merely "coping" with death anxiety, these women, who had lived their lives for God, not only had low levels of anxiety, but looked forward to and accepted death as a face-to-face encounter with their God. Smiley also notes a comment by a medical student who accompanied the house doctor on his rounds. The future physician was impressed by the peace and serenity found among these religious women and exclaimed to the administrator "There is so much acceptance [of death] here, I have to contrast this to my regular nursing home experiences."

Moberg (personal communication) has commented on an important issue related to death and dying, and one that has received considerable press lately. This topic deals with the "life after life" accounts of pleasant experiences during clinical death (Moody, 1975; Kuebler-Ross, 1969). Moberg notes that Rawlings (1978, 1980), an instructor of resuscitation in medical schools, found that only about 20 percent of all who are revived volunteer any experience in a life beyond death's door; generalizing to all deaths from one-fifth is a bad error. Worse yet, about half recount horrible experiences immediately upon recovery, yet when questioned only a few hours later have so strongly suppressed them that they cannot be recalled, much less recounted, even to friends and family. Moberg notes that although no social or behavioral scientist has conducted comparative research on this subject, the older persons' beliefs about the afterlife are very significant to their conduct and sense of well-being.

A related issue, bereavement, may represent the most potent of all stressors for the older adult. That the loss of a spouse can predispose an elderly individual to serious mental and physical illness is well documented (Jacobs and Ostfeld, 1977). Heyman and Gianturco report in their observations of elderly persons during the course of the First Duke Longitudinal Study, that the elderly often adapt to bereavement through deep religious faith that helps stabilize their emotions (Heyman and Gianturco, 1973). In another longitudinal study of older women recently widowed, Vachon found that those who initially rated religion as not very helpful were significantly more likely to show poor adaption, indicated by continued high levels of distress two years later (Vachon et al., 1982). Similar findings with regard to the positive impact of religious faith on bereavement have been reported by several other investigators (Berardo, 1967; Mathieu, 1972; Peterson and Briley, 1977).

In conclusion, studies uncovered in this review have, in general, found a positive association between strong religious beliefs and successful adjustment and coping in later life, although reports on the strength of this relationship have been somewhat controversial. A few studies, in fact, have shown no relationship. It is therefore with some caution that such conclusions are stated.

RELIGIOUS COPING STYLES

A categorization of religious coping and an important theoretical framework has been outlined by Pargament and colleagues (Pargament and Hahn, 1986; Pargament et al., 1988; Pargament, 1988). Presented are three types of religious coping: self-directing, deferring, and collaborative. In the "self-directing" style, it is the individual's responsibility to resolve problems and stresses the power of the person rather than the power of God. In the "deferring" style, persons defer the responsibility of problem-solving to God; they wait for solutions to emerge through the efforts of God, rather than taking an active problem-solving stance themselves. In the "collaborative" style, the responsibility for the problem-solving process is held jointly by both the person and by God, neither of whom are seen as passive participants. The collaborative style has been related to increased prayer activity, salience of religion, intrinsic religiosity, and personal control and self-esteem (Pargament et al., 1988). Because of space limitations here, the reader is urged to refer directly to these works for a more extensive review of religious coping styles. Note should be made that certain styles of religious coping may be more effective than others in combatting the stresses of life change that older adults must face, yet few studies have examined the efficacy of specific religious styles in later life.

SUBJECTIVE WELL-BEING

As noted earlier, personal well-being may be considered the subjective component of adjustment or successful coping, and is reflected by indicators such as happiness, life satisfaction, and morale. Several studies have addressed the relationship between religious belief or commitment and these measures of subjective well-being.

Blazer and Palmor's longitudinal study of aging and religion, referred to in the previous section, did show a significant association between religious attitudes and adjustments, and feelings of usefulness, but not with happiness (Blazer and Palmore, 1976). Steinitz studied religiosity, well-being, and life satisfaction among 1493 elderly subjects using data for the 1972–77 NORC (National Opinion Research Center) Surveys. The four religious variables used were "confidence in organized religion," "strength of denominational affiliation," "belief in afterlife," and "frequency of church attendance." Only one of the above variables addressed personal religious beliefs (i.e., belief in an afterlife) and this was also the only religious measure that was significantly correlated with well-being; no similar association was found for the other three institutionally related religious variables. Steinitz (1980) concluded that no consistent pattern of association was seen between religiosity and well-being in the aged. The religiosity variable here is once again treated in a relatively superficial manner, with little attention given to religiosity as a multi-dimensional variable.

In a randomly selected sample of older persons (mean age 72) living in upstate New York, Tellis-Nayak (1982) examined the relationship between religion and the four mental health variables: death anxiety, meaning in life, loneliness, and psychic well-being. His religion measures consisted of four items based on Glock and Stark's dimensions of religiosity (1966) (belief, ritual, experience, and consequences). The items selected to measure the four mental health measures were not described, but were said to have come from a previously used survey instrument, "Social Indicators for the Aged." Tellis-Nayak entered the religion variable into separate regression equations, with different mental health measures as the dependent variable. Sex, age, marital status, and health were included along with religion as the predictor variables. Religion was significantly related to death anxiety ($r = -.145$, 32% of explained variance) and meaning in life ($r = .466$, 90% of explained variance), but not with loneliness ($r = -.065$, < 1% of explained variance) or psychic well-being ($r = -.11$, 12% of explained variance). Cameron (1975), likewise, did not find a positive relationship between religion and well-being in a study examining correlates of well-being in an older population.

In a national probability survey conducted by the Princeton Religion Research Center, the Gallup organization measured religious commitment (in terms of belief, ritual, and experience) among 1,485 Americans, 39 percent of whom were over 50 years of age. Twelve percent of the total sample were categorized as having a very high level of spiritual commitment (VHSC), based on responses to a seven-item religious commitment scale. Fifteen percent of the sample were categorized as having a very low level of spiritual commitment (VLSC). There were significant differences between these two groups in terms of life satisfaction and happiness. Sixty-three percent of the VHSC group compared to 30 percent of the VLSC group reported being very satisfied with life, while 68 percent of the VHSC and 36 percent of the VLSC claimed to be very happy (Princeton Religion Research Center, 1982).

Yates and his colleagues (1981) examined the impact of religious beliefs on life satisfaction of 71 elderly patients (mean age fifty-nine with advanced cancer. Religious belief was measured by a ten-item Religious Beliefs Index (RBI), which addressed issues of meaning, afterlife, existence of a powerful God, relationship with God, existence of heaven and hell, and prayer. High scores on the RBI were strongly correlated (r = .41, p < .005) with greater life satisfaction among participants, but were not associated with "happiness." Church attendance, however, was significantly related to both life satisfaction and happiness (r = .35 and .34 respectively, p < .005).

Hunsberger's study noted previously (1985), demonstrated a significant correlation between "happiness" and the three religious belief variables: degree of orthodoxy in Christian beliefs, agreement with beliefs taught while growing up, and importance of beliefs.

In a study of factors influencing the social-psychological well-being of older women, Beckman and Houser found degrees of self-professed religiosity (along with health, quality of social interaction, and degree of social support) to be significantly related to five major dimensions of well-being: attitude towards aging, amount of agitation, degree of loneliness/dissatisfaction, presence of depression, and extent of social isolation (Philadelphia Geriatric Center Morale Scale). All 719 subjects were aged 60 to 75. Correlations between religiosity and well-being were particularly notable for the widowed elderly (Beckman and Houser, 1982).

In Campbell's national survey addressing quality of life indicators among the general U.S. population, he reported that religion had little effect on life satisfaction (Campbell et al., 1976). Subsequently, an error in the analysis of the data was detected by Hadaway, who showed a significant impact for religiosity on life satisfaction (Hadaway, 1978). Several other investigators, although not dealing exclusively with elderly subjects, have provided data to support the importance of religious beliefs and attitudes on ameliorating the effects of stressful life changes and enhancing well-being (Clemente and Sauer, 1976; Denier, 1984; Cameron et al., 1973; Cantril, 1965).

Koenig and Blake (1986) investigated the relationship between life satisfaction and religion from a slightly different perspective. They examined the association between likelihood of using religious beliefs or prayer during stress, and life satisfaction among the aged. Recall that their sample consisted of 292 community-dwelling older persons (mean age 74), of whom 74 percent were women. Among participants age sixty to seventy-four, those highly likely to use religious beliefs/prayer during stress reported high life satisfaction considerably more often than did those unlikely to use religion (48 percent vs. 13 percent, respectively, p< .001). Although a similar trend was observed among those age seventy-four and over (35% vs. 28%), this difference was not statistically significant. Again, potentially important covariates were not controlled in the study.

Most recently, Koenig et al. (1988b) completed a study exploring the relationship between religion and well-being among 836 community-dwelling older persons of widely varying religious affiliations and levels of commitment. Recall from the earlier reference to this study that the Philadelphia Geriatric Center Morale Scale (Lawton, 1975) was used to measure well-being, while Hoge's (1972) validated intrinsic religiosity scale was used to measure intrinsic religious orientation or commitment (IR). A moderately strong relationship was found (see Figure 11) between IR and well-being for the sample as a whole (r = .24) and particularly for women (r = .28) and the "old old" (r = .29). In fact, among those age seventy-five and older, religious factors contributed more to the explained variance in well-being (25%) than any other predictor variable except for health. This was true even though religious variables had been entered into the regression equation after the other covariates (health, financial status, social support). Interestingly, a subsample of retired nuns in this study achieved the highest mean score on morale compared with other subgroups (Kvale et al., 1988).

The relationship between religious beliefs and attitudes, and well-being is a complex one. There likely exist many determinants of well-being that relate to hereditary factors, personality, early childhood and later experiences, social support networks, health, and financial status. The extent to which one has come to terms with existential issues and the meaning and "sense of coherence" (Antonovsky, 1979) that one finds in life, are other important factors. Religious beliefs and attitudes may interact with many of these variables in affecting well-being for the older person. Even more complex is the relationship of these factors over time in the older person's life. Unfortunately, longitudinal data are scarce in this regard but accumulating (Blazer and Palmore, 1976; Markides et al. 1987).

PSYCHIATRIC ILLNESS

With regard to the effect of religious beliefs and commitment on psychiatric illness, several studies are pertinent. Some investigators have shown an increase in personality maladjustments with increasing religiosity (Broen, 1955; Funk, 1956; Rokeach, 1960; W. Wilson and Miller, 1968; Bohrnstedt et al., 1968; Bahr and Martin; 1983), but only in younger age groups. Maranell (1974), after finding significant correlations between anxiety and religiosity among university sociology students, concluded that religious commitment involved a certain dependency, and that an increase in ego strength would lead to a decrease in religiosity. Furthermore, a bibliography of religion and psychiatry (*Bibliography on Religion and Mental Health 1960–1964, 1967*) is filled with articles that describe in detail the pathological aspects of religious attitudes and the aberrant behavior found in some strongly religious persons. Freud saw religion as an obsessional neurosis from which one might need to be cured (Spinks, 1963). Another eminent psychiatrist, Stanley Leavy, has noted that Freud followed a widespread trend that denied any authentic experience of a transcendent reality. Describing any faith in a personal God as unhealthy and neurotic, he felt obliged to interpret human existence and human health without, and even in opposition to, religion (Haring, 1985). Consequently, some writers from the psychoanalytic perspective have suggested that religious experience is a consequence of unresolved conflicts and therefore should be considered pathological (Ancona, 1961; Grollman, 1963; Schoenfield, 1962; Ellis, 1980).

Other studies have shown just the opposite. Williams and Cole (1968) tested Freud's hypothesis that religion was born out of insecurity, expecting a negative correlation between religiousness and anxiety. They found that their highly religious subjects had the *least* insecurity, as measured by three dimensions of anxiety, whereas those with the lowest religiosity had the highest insecurity scores. Bergin (1980) provided a comprehensive essay on the value of religious beliefs in psychotherapy, and notes several problems that arise when the views of patient and therapist conflict. He calls for the inclusion of religion in theories, research, and techniques bearing on personality and psychological disorders. Stark (1971) has suggested that much of the research that shows a positive correlation between psychopathology and religious commitment has used inappropriate samples, has not used comparison groups, and has employed less than competent methodology.

Again, the research cited above, and Stark's rebuttal, is in reference to *nonaged* samples, and any extrapolation from these studies to elderly populations must be done with caution. The religion of older adults, having matured over the years and having been tested in the trials of life's hardships, may be of a different character from that of younger adults or adolescents, whose religious experience and commitment may be new and unformed. For these younger persons, sufficient time may not have elapsed for religion to be infused into their lifestyles and life perspective. Consequently, the stabilizing effects of such beliefs and attitudes may not be as evident among the young as among older persons, in whom religion may be more fully integrated. The latter reasoning, however, is based on little research evidence and is highly speculative at this time.

DEPRESSION AND SUICIDE

Depression is one of the most common psychiatric illnesses in old age, and suicide among the aged is disproportionately higher (17%) than would be predicted from the percentage of the general population that the elderly comprise (11%) (Blazer, 1982a). Gianturco and Busse (1978) examined the occurrence of depressive illness in 264 normal elderly subjects over a twenty year period in the First Duke Longitudinal Study. During that period, 70 percent of the participants experienced one or more episodes of depression. They concluded that the "issue for older people may well be not just survival but *meaningful* and *purposeful* existence" (p. 6). The importance of beliefs and attitudes in maintaining a meaningful and purposeful existence should be underscored. Lazarus and Golden (1979) refer to the sustaining function of beliefs in noting that "if we are stripped of beliefs in which we are heavily invested, regardless of their validity, we may become deeply threatened, alienated, and perhaps even seriously disrupted in our capacity for involvement and satisfaction" (p. 285).

Self-esteem is another factor integrally related to depression. In a cross-cultural study utilizing participants from many countries with different cultural traditions, Zung (1972) found a high prevalence of depression in the over sixty-five age groups. He concluded that loss of self-esteem, possibly as a consequence of the multiple losses associated with aging, was the major depressive factor involved. Busse and colleagues (1954), over thirty years earlier, had also noted that depression in old age resulted from a loss of self-esteem, which came about because of the older person's inability to supply his needs or drives or to defend himself against threats to his security.

To what extent do religious beliefs and attitudes affect those factors integrally related to the onset of depression in old age? We have already noted the role that cognitions (derived from attitudes and beliefs) may play in the etiology of depression (Beck, 1976). Herein lies a potential mechanism by which religious beliefs may impact on the older person's affective state. Optimistic or hopeful ways of looking at life and the surrounding world may spawn cognitions that are protective against depressive states. Viktor Frankl (1975) has suggested that religious belief can supply purpose and meaning and, hence, affect one's entire satisfaction with existence.

Several investigators have, in fact, noted an inverse relationship between religiosity, and depression and suicide among the elderly. Wolff (1959) has reported that religious beliefs and strong faith were important in helping elderly state hospital patients who were disorganized to overcome grief and depression, illustrating the potential impact of such factors on mental health and level of adaptation to loss. In a study previously referred to, Koenig et al. (1988a) examined the relationship between depression, chronic anxiety, and intrinsic religiosity (attitudes and level of commitment) among a consecutive series of older patients attending a geriatic medicine clinic. They found that intrinsic religiosity was substantially lower among patients with depression or anxiety disorders; these findings were especially prominent among women, for whom differences were statistically significant. For both men and women, intrinsic religiosity was also considerably lower for patients who smoked or drank alcohol.

Recall also that Koenig et al. (1988b) examined the association between morale and religious factors in a sample of 836 community-dwelling elders. A moderately strong association between morale and intrinsic religiosity was found. The instrument used to measure morale, the Philadelphia Geriatric Center Morale Scale, has been shown by Morris et al. (1975) to closely correlate with depression scales such as the Zung Depression Scale (Zung, 1965). This suggests that depressive symptoms may be less common among older persons with an intrinsically oriented religious faith. Spilka (1977), studying a predominantly nonelderly population of 689 individuals, also found that an intrinsic religious faith was associated with a more favorable psychological orientation towards self and others.

Kivett (1979), in a study of religious motivation among middle-aged adults (age 45 to 65), found that persons with high intrinsic religiosity were significantly more likely to display an internal locus of control and maintain an ideal self-concept. Persons with an internal locus of control believe that they, not others, have direct control over their life situations. Such attitudes frequently correlate with psychological health. In other studies, persons with high intrinsic religious motivation have been found to be less prejudiced and better educated than extrinsically-oriented individuals (Allport and Ross, 1967; Strickland and Shaffer, 1971).

Hence, these studies suggest that intrinsic religiosity is both inversely related to depressive symptoms and is positively associated with psychological constructs that correlate with mental health. Intrinsic religiosity is an attitude towards religion that reflects a deep commitment and desire to implement beliefs into action in daily life (Allport and Ross, 1967). (See Appendix I for a more detailed description of this concept.)

Lower suicide rates have also been reported among more religiously oriented individuals. Nelson (1977) examined the quality of adaptation of fifty-eight chronically ill elderly hospitalized patients at the Wadsworth VA Hospital Center in Los Angeles. Looking at indirect life-threatening behaviors (i.e. refusing medications, pulling out IV's, other self-injurious behaviors), he found that the intensity of religious beliefs and commitment varied inversely with the extent of these behaviors. Nelson explained these findings in the following manner:

The importance of religiosity to the elderly, chronically ill patient centers primarily on the extent to which the patient's religious beliefs can provide a sense of continuity in established personal values, can maintain a supernatural dimension of support claiming to reward faith and good will rather than physical vitality and social utility, and can instill the conviction that a more satisfying form of existence may lie ahead in an afterlife if the patient follows the teachings of his faith. The overlay of such religious beliefs can nourish feelings of worthfulness and hopefulness that reduce the likelihood of self-destructive behavior. Moreover, the goal-directed behavior involved in attempting to follow the teachings of one's faith serves to reduce feelings of helplessess. While it is relatively easy to understand how strong religious beliefs can be of particular value to the individual whose life and future prospects are severely limited by age, illness, and personal loss, it is more difficult to deal with the issue of "religious experience" as a potential treatment mode in geriatric care. Secular professions such as medicine, psychology, and social work cannot prescribe religious commitment in the same manner as they prescribe physical or behavioral therapies. The dilemma facing us here is that, for the patient who has relatively little to live for and even less to look forward to, religious beliefs offer what may be the only means for transcending the existential limitations of life. (p. 73)

Others have likewise found inverse correlations between extent of religious commitment and suicide rates in large populations (Stack, 1983); however, it is the effect on suicide rates by involvement in church and related social activities that has received the most attention by researchers (discussed in a later section).

Studies on religious attitudes and the subjective state of "loneliness" are also revealing. Numerous investigators have found that loneliness is closely associated with depression and suicide (Breed, 1967; Payne, 1975). In a national survey by Harris and Associates (1975), loneliness was found to be ranked fourth among the twelve areas representing serious problems for older adults. Paloutzian and Ellision (1982) have shown that "religious well-being" is inversely related to loneliness. Likewise, Koenig et al. (1988a), in their survey of elderly patients attending a geriatric medicine clinic, found that over 80 percent of respondents either strongly or moderately agreed with the statement: "My relationship with God helps me not to feel lonely." Hence, religion may further buffer against depression by its impact on loneliness. This may occur by enhancing social networks through church participation and/or by conveying a sense of security through belief in an ever-present, all-powerful God who cares about them and is concerned with their well-being.

Finally, several investigators have shown a direct impact of religious faith on self-esteem. Gallup reports that his organization's national surveys have shown that self-esteem is closely related to "feelings of closeness to God." Although he found no relationship between frequency of church attendance, prayer, or religious program viewing and self-esteem, a significantly greater proportion of those with low self-esteem reported "feeling fearful of God" and "guilt, as a sinner" (Princeton Religion Research Center, 1982). Hence, religion may behave as a two-edged sword with regard to self-esteem: serving to enhance it through a feeling of a close relationship with God, or to decrease it through reinforcing a sense of low self-esteem by worsening feelings of guilt. These surveys, however, are cross-sectional and therefore say nothing about causality.

Wolff's study (1959a) of the effect of religious beliefs on a group of elderly psychiatric patients confined to a state hospital was conducted over three years and thus fulfills the criteria for a longitudinal study. Religious beliefs and faith helped these disorganized members to overcome loneliness and despondency. In fact, he reported that patients received greater "ego strength" from religion.

In summary, although the data are fragmentary, strong religious beliefs and commitment among older individuals are, in general, positively associated with personal adjustment and subjective well-being, and appear to have a moderating effect on psychiatric illness that is rooted in insecurity, loneliness, low self-esteem, and a sense of lack of purpose or meaning in life.

IMPLICATIONS FOR COGNITIVE AND BEHAVIORAL PSYCHOTHERAPY

Given that religious beliefs and attitudes are common among many persons in the present elderly cohort and that the world construct of these individuals may be at least partly determined by religious cognitions, important implications arise for a potentially fruitful approach to psychotherapy.

Cognitive and behavioral psychotherapies for the treatment of depression, anxiety, and adjustment disorders abound in today's psychology and psychiatry literature. Biological theories aside, it is hypothesized that dysfunctional thinking patterns are the major underlying psychological forces that maintain these adverse mood states. For example, the depressed person commonly dwells upon themselves and focuses intensely upon their problems. They may think "Oh, I'm not worth anything to anybody; I'm just a burden on my family; I'm never going to get well from this sickness; there is nothing to live for; what am I going to do about the hospital bill; I'm just no good, I can't even provide for my family anymore; I cannot survive in this world without my husband; I can't work anymore, or go fishing, or drive my car, or do anything anymore because of my physical condition; I need a drink in order to make it through the day." Such cognitions or thoughts frequently lead to progressively deeper and deeper dysphoric states that may interfere with the older person's ability to comply with their medical regimen, destroy motivation necessary to overcome disability, force the person into isolation, separate families, and in some cases lead to self-inflicted death. In cognitive therapy, an individual learns to become aware of their dysfunctional thought patterns, willfully interrupt these thoughts, and replace them with positive, healthy, optimistic cognitions.

The Judeo-Christian scriptures are full of references to the power of the thought life in affecting both emotional and spiritual states.

For out of the heart come evil thoughts, murders, adulteries, fornications, thefts, false witness, slanders. These are the things which defile the man. (Matthew 15:19–20)

For as he thinks within himself, so he is. (Proverbs 23:7)

There also may be found in scripture advice about how to avoid unhappiness that specifically refers to modifications in thinking and cognitive patterns.

Finally, brethren, whatever is true, whatever is honorable, whatever is right, whatever is pure, whatever is lovely, whatever is of good repute, if there is any excellence and if anything worthy of praise, *let your mind dwell* on these things. (Philippians 4:8, emphasis added)

The use of scripture in the counseling of religiously oriented older persons may assist in altering thought patterns that dwell upon and magnify problems, focus on the negative aspects of situations, arouse feelings of self-pity, worthlessness, self-centeredness, cause discouragement, and eventually lead to depression. Many of the Judeo-Christian scriptures encourage positive thinking and involvement with people. They often direct thoughts toward helping others in worse situations and discourage self-centeredness and isolation. The message of these religious writings is a positive one that could easily be incorporated into a brand of psychotherapy that may be particularly acceptable to the religious older person. It is also more likely that such therapy will receive the necessary reinforcement by the person's social support system (often centered in their church) in between treatment sessions. While pastoral counselors may be particularly well-suited to carry out such religiously based psychotherapy, other mental health professionals may also find this approach useful with certain patients.

From a behavioral perspective, Miller and Martin (1988) have published a book entitled *Behavioral Therapy and Religion* that discusses ways in which spiritual perspectives can be incorporated in modern behavioral therapies, in the training of therapists, and in behavioral psychology in general. They emphasize treatments of depression, anxiety, and pain with chapters by A. E. Bergin and E. M. Pattison. There is also a chapter on spiritual perspectives in cognitive therapy.

We recognize that the institution of religiously based cognitive or behavioral psychotherapy depends greatly on the religious perspective of the patient. Prior to embarking on religious psychotherapy, the therapist should clearly explain the approach that he or she is planning to take and obtain the fully informed consent of the patient.

4

RELIGIOUS BELIEFS AND PHYSICAL HEALTH

Given the generally positive association between religious beliefs and mental health, and a probable relationship between mental health and physical illness, one might likewise hypothesize a positive influence for religious beliefs on physical health. As noted earlier in the Introduction, investigators have repeatedly linked high stress states with various physical illnesses. Stress may often reflect poor social adjustment or unsuccessful coping with life changes. Herein lies a possible mechanism through which strong religious belief might impact on physical health through decreasing susceptibility to stress-related illness.

In the following paragraphs, we will examine the available evidence concerning the impact of religious beliefs and attitudes on physical health. Holmes' study (1962) of 200 tuberculosis cases in a Seattle, Washington, sanitarium found that these patients were more likely to be single or come from broken marriages, and 75 percent were found to have lost the religious beliefs of the tradition in which they had been reared. Hunsberger (1985) looked at the influence of five religious variables on happiness, adjustment, and health among eighty-five persons aged sixty-five through eighty-eight. Self-reported health was measured by a single question with four responses varying from poor to excellent. Among the five religiosity variables (Christian orthodoxy, childhood religious emphasis, agreement with beliefs taught, importance of beliefs, and church attendance), strength of childhood religious emphasis and importance of religious beliefs were significantly correlated with self-reported health ($r = .20$ and $.25$ respectively) (Hunsberger, 1985).

Simons and West (1985), however, did not find religion to moderate the effects of stress on physical health. They studied the impact of "the psychological variable religiosity" (as distinct from the social resources variable, i.e., church membership and attendance) as a buffer against the harmful effects of life stressors on the physical health of 308 community-dwelling elderly persons. Physical health was measured by a self-completed checklist of forty-nine diseases. Religiosity was measured by a four-item scale including questions about identity as a religious person, frequency of prayer and religious reading, and religious experience. In this study, however, neither social resources nor religiosity were found to significantly alter the impact of stressful life changes on health. Only income was found to serve this function. The sensitivity and validity of their physical health measure, however, may be challenged.

Koenig et al. (1988a) examined the relationship between intrinsic religious commitment, and both subjective and objective health in their sample of geriatric outpatients. Subjective health was rated by patients on a one-to-four scale varying from poor to excellent. Objective health was determined by a three-item index composed of physician ratings, chart review, and number of medications taken. Correlation between subjective and objective ratings were reasonably high (r = .49). Intrinsic religiosity was higher among patients in poorer health, regardless of whether subjective or objective ratings were used. Religiosity was more likely however, to be higher among patients with poor subjective health than among those with objectively measured poor health. Somewhat different patterns emerged when stratified analysis examined the effects of gender. Among men, intrinsic religiosity was consistently higher among those whose health was rated poor by both subjective and objective measures, the magnitude of the difference being equal regardless of measure chosen. Among women, intrinsic religiosity was higher among those objectively assessed to be in poor health; however, religiosity was slightly lower among those who assessed themselves as being in poor health.

The interpretation of these gender differences is difficult because of the small magnitude of the differences, and may be due to random error. The overall finding of higher religiosity in patients with poorer health, however, is interesting and consistent with the findings of other investigators (Jeffers and Nichols, 1961). Either religiosity in some fashion leads to physical illness, or older persons with poor health turn to religion for support. Based on the substantial evidence presented earlier in support of religion's vital role in coping, the latter hypothesis appears to be more tenable.

A report by Zuckerman et al. (1984) also supports this notion. Looking at mortality rates, he found an inverse relationship with religiosity—a finding that would argue against the idea that religious beliefs and at-

Figure 2

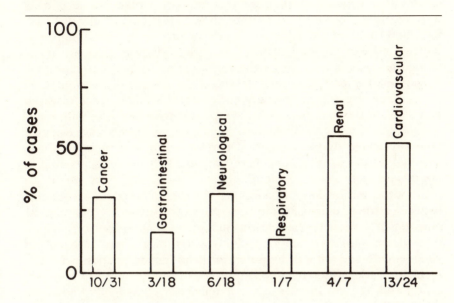

titudes lead to physical illness. In that study, Zuckerman examined the relationship between religious activities and attitudes, and mortality rates among four hundred elderly residents in New Haven, Connecticut. Religiousness was measured by frequency of church attendance, self-assessed religiosity, and the extent to which religion was a source of strength. Of these three variables, all of which were inversely related to mortality (especially among the medically ill), "strength from religion" was the best predictor of longevity. These findings suggest that benefits from religion are at least partly due to religious attitudes and beliefs rather than from increased social contact in the religious community.

Reynolds and Nelson (1981) examined various psychological, medical, and social variables that might be related to survival in the chronically ill, institutionalized elderly. Their sample consisted of 193 male veterans residing in a nursing home. At twelve months of followup, characteristics of patients who had died were compared with those still alive. Those who died were younger, had a poorer prognosis, greater cognitive dysfunction, lower life satisfaction, higher scores on a suicide potential scale, and were less religious.

The relationship of religious beliefs and attitudes to specific disease states and manifestations of disease (such as chronic pain) has also been examined. Studies in older populations, however, have been distinctly rare. Figure 2 presents unpublished data from the Koenig et al. (1988d) study of depression in the medically ill. The last 109 male patients admitted into that study (all age 70 or over) were asked the general question of how they coped with their medical illness; spontaneous responses were recorded. Responses were then dichotomized into "religious coping" (36%) and "non-religious coping." The proportions of patients employing religious coping behaviors for various disease states are given in Figure 2. Religious coping behaviors were more common than non-religious strategies among patients with cardiovascular disease and urologic or renal disease. Interestingly, patients with cardiovascular diseases had the lowest rate of depressive symptoms, whereas those with renal or urologic disease had the highest number. Overall, depressive symptoms (measured by the Geriatric Depression Scale) were slightly less common among the religious copers compared with nonreligious copers, but this difference was not significant.

In another recent study, Koenig et al. (1988a) examined the association between intrinsic religiosity and three physical diseases in older medical outpatients (cancer, hypertension, and dementia). Intrinsic religious commitment was lower among patients with cancer, about the same for patients with and without hypertension, and higher for those with dementia. Gender differences were present in the relationship between cancer and religion. In men, intrinsic religiosity was slightly higher for those with cancer than those without, whereas religiosity was clearly lower among women with cancer. Since there were only eight cancer patients in the study group (4 men, 4 women), random error could have again accounted for these differences. A lower rate of cancer, however, among religious groups (one-half to three-quarters that of the general population in some studies) has been demonstrated previously (Gardner, 1982a; Gardener, 1982b; Mayberry, 1982; Armstrong et al., 1977; Enstrom, 1975). These findings have generally been attributed to dietary and hygienic practices. Acklin et al. (1983) also found slightly lower levels of intrinsic religiosity among cancer patients (N = 26, mean age 48) than among medical controls (N = 18), although again these differences were not significant. Small sample sizes have made meaningful conclusions from such studies quite difficult. The relationship between religiosity and cancer may be confounded by cancer patients "turning to religion" as a source of comfort, and thereby negating any inverse relationship between religiosity and cancer that might be found prior to implementation of religious coping behaviors.

Epperly (1983) provided a good discussion on the spiritual needs of cancer patients and the role that religion may play in coping by enhancing meaning in suffering, relationships and communication with others, and by maintaining hope.

Although no relationship between religiosity and hypertension was found for their sample as a whole, Koenig et al. (1988a) found a strong trend suggesting lower intrinsic religiosity for older men with hypertension compared to that for men without hypertension. Other studies in younger populations have demonstrated a lower rate of hypertension among more religiously involved individuals (Scotch, 1963; Walsh, 1980; Graham, 1978). Kaplan (1976) has explained the protective effects of religion on the cardiovascular system as being mediated through mechanisms that maintain hope, regulate depression, fear, and anxiety, and enhance social-personal integration.

On the other hand, Levin and Markides (1985) found a higher prevalence of hypertension (43%) among a sample of 203 older Mexican-Americans (age 65 to 80) who rated themselves as highly religious than among those "less than very religious" (30%). Based on these findings, they concluded that religiosity might be a risk factor for stress-related illness (hypertension) due to increased levels of guilt arising from pressures to conform to high behavioral standards. Their sample included both men and women.

In a more recent study, Larson et al. (1988) examined the relationship between blood pressure, self-perceived importance of religion, and frequency of church attendance among a rural sample of 407 white men free from hypertension or cardiovascular disease. Analyses were adjusted for the confounding effects of age, socioeconomic status, smoking, and weight/height ratio (Quetelet Index; Tyroler et al., 1975). Diastolic blood pressures of persons with high church attendance and high religious importance were significantly lower than those in the low attendance, low importance group. These differences persisted after controlling for covariates. A dose-response effect was observed. The difference in diastolic pressures was particularly notable among persons age fifty-five and over (6 mm) and among those who smoked (5 mm). Note that this sample was all male and free of any detectable cardiovascular disease; Levin and Markides' sample, on the other hand, included women and persons in whom cardiovascular disease had not been ruled out.

With regard to dementia, Koenig et al. (1988a) found intrinsic religiosity higher among those with the disease than those without. This was especially true for men, but low numbers prevent meaningful comparisons (N = 2 for men, N = 5 for women). For most of these patients, questionnaires were administered by a spouse or child; the direction of bias that this may have had on patient responses is difficult to predict. There is no clear reason for the more religiously oriented person to suffer from dementia. Again, we doubt that religion leads to dementia; the more reasonable prospect is that these individuals had turned to religion to help them to cope with this frightening neurological disease. As part of the project examining the prevalence of depression and dementia among medical inpatients alluded to earlier (Koenig et al., 1988d), spontaneous coping behaviors were elicited for the final 109 consecutive patients admitted into that study. A comparison was made of dementia

scores between patients mentioning religious coping behaviors (39) and
those noting other coping behaviors (N = 70). Using the Folstein Mini-
Mental State Exam (1975) (score range 0 to 30) to measure cognitive
status (degree of dementia), no significant difference was found in mental status scores between religious copers and nonreligious copers (mean
scores 26.2 vs. 26.9, respectively, T value.90, p = .37). In conclusion,
the relationship between religious beliefs or attitudes and dementia remains unclear, and thus far no statistically significant association between the two has been reported.

Drug use, especially for the chronically ill, is another area in which
religious beliefs may have an influence. Less frequent use of alcohol and
drugs by religiously oriented subjects has been a common finding in
work done by several investigators (Zimberg, 1977; Parfrey, 1976). Khavari and Harmon (1982) found strong inverse correlations between the
degree of professed religious belief and the use of drugs. Although they
included older subjects (up to age 85), their study population consisted
predominantly of younger adults. Examining 4,853 subjects with regard
to self-professed degree of religiosity, and consumption of alcohol and
psychotropic medications, these investigators found a significantly
higher use of drugs among individuals considering themselves "not
religious at all" compared with those viewing themselves as very religious (Khavari and Harmon, 1982). As noted earlier, Koenig et al. (1988a)
found that older patients who smoked tobacco or drank alcohol reported
lower intrinsic religiosity. This finding was particularly true for men
who used alcohol.

While a direct effect of religious belief on physical health may in part
result from a discouragement of self-destructive behaviors (smoking,
alcohol abuse, psychotropic drug use) and an encouragement of healthy
dietary practices, other factors may be equally important. Kenneth Vaux
(1976), writing in *Preventive Medicine*, reports that religious belief may
also affect health by releasing the individual from obsessive self-concern,
given that hypochondriasis, narcissism, and neuroticism are integrally
related to physical and mental illness. In consulting physicians on this
subject, Vaux notes that the general feeling was that "the major imprint
of religion on health is at this point where anxieties and stress are diminished and where, even given a certain disease, the sense of morbidity
is diminished by an intact and integrated spiritual outlook" (p. 530).

For example, the perception of pain by persons suffering from chronic
illness is well known to be affected by psychological factors. In the Yates
et al. study (1981) of elderly patients with advanced cancer, the perception of pain by subjects with strong religious beliefs was significantly
less than among those patients with lower belief scores. A similar inverse
relationship was found between perception of pain and church attendance.

Personal religious beliefs among men have also been shown to modify perception of physical disability. Idler (1987), examining the relationship between religious involvement and health in 2811 elderly participants in the Yale Health and Aging Project, reported that at any given level of chronic medical illness men who said they received no strength or comfort from religion were more likely to see themselves as having greater disability compared with men at the same level of chronic illness who reported receiving a great deal of comfort from religion. For women, on the other hand, public religiosity (church attendance, etc.), rather than comfort from religion, was found to be inversely associated with physical disability and depressive symptomatology. For women at any given level of chronic medical illness, the more active they were in the religious community, the less they were likely to report themselves disabled and depressed. Idler concluded from these findings that—particularly among men—religious attitudes and beliefs may act to alter the individual's perception of illness and disability by providing comfort and an interpretive schema for extracting meaning in the midst of suffering ("theodicy hypothesis"). Bearing in mind that a major goal of geriatric medicine is to maximize functional status, these findings underscore the importance for clinicians to acquire knowledge about religion and other powerful cultural forces that may favorably modify the older adult's perception of their disability—and consequently impact on healthcare behaviors.

Vaux (1976), while emphasizing the potentially favorable effect of religion on perception of health and healthcare behavior, also notes concern about "distorting the belief of peace in existence," a situation often seen among poor minority groups wherein undue complacency or smugness is exhibited towards diseases such as chronic infection or presymptomatic hypertension, preventing these persons from seeking medical care. Again, little data have been collected in a systematic fashion to support either of these speculations or to suggest which forces predominate.

Regardless of the direct impact of religious belief on physical health, "indirect" influences may be considerable. Reldener and Scott have pointed out that the opposition between religious institutions and the traditional healthcare system, due largely to differences in ideas concerning the nature of sickness and its treatment, can ultimately lead to inferior clinical care of patients. This lack of mutual understanding becomes especially evident in cases where Jehovah's Witnesses have refused medical care in life-threatening circumstances (Redlener and Scott, 1979), and resulted in much disharmony and strife between patient, family, and healthcare providers. The truly best interests of the patient— always the physician's primary concern—may be difficult to discern where religious misunderstandings impede communication. Under these circumstances, health may indeed suffer.

FAITH

Belief and faith have been known for many years to impact on health and disease. Indeed, Sir William Osler (1910), one of the fathers of modern medicine, wrote about "the faith that heals" over seventy-five years ago. Biblical writings clearly document that faith and trust in God's power to heal plays a vital role in healing and cures in the Judeo-Christian religion. Throughout the Bible (New American Standard Version), references are made to God's role in healing:

> It is I who put to death and give life.
> I have wounded, and it is I who heal. (Deuteronomy 32:39)

> Bless the Lord, O my soul,
> And forget none of his benefits;
> Who pardons all your iniquities;
> Who heals all your diseases. (Psalm 103:2–3)

> And no resident [of Zion] will say, "I am sick";
> The people who dwell there will be forgiven
> their iniquity. (Isaiah 33:24)

> Go and report to John what you hear and see:
> The blind receive sight and the lame walk,
> the lepers are cleansed and deaf hear,
> and the dead are raised up . . . [These healings were
> considered proof of Christ's Divinity] (Matthew 11:4–5)

The study of psychosomatic processes—the influence of cognitions and emotional states on the body—has evolved into a recognized branch of psychiatry today with its own national organization and numerous publications (*Journal of Psychosomatic Research; Psychosomatics; Psychosomatic Medicine.*) The often dramatic effect of "placebos" in medical practice and scientific research testifies to the impact that faith can have on the course and outcome of physical illness (Goldman, 1985). Recall also, that the most common spontaneously reported coping behavior noted by older adults in the study of Koenig et al. (1988c) was religious in nature, and of religious behaviors, trust and faith in God were the most common.

What exactly is this entity "faith" that Osler refers to and that apparently has an influence on psychological coping and possibly even physiological processes? Webster's Dictionary (1983) defines *faith* as "the assent of the mind to the truth of what is declared by another, resting on his authority and veracity, without other evidence." Webster's theological definition is "the assent of the mind or understanding to the truth of what God has revealed." Faith means more than simple belief. It is more than hope. Faith requires action.

Even so faith, if it has no works, is dead, being by itself. (James 2:17)

Faith requires action on a belief in the absence of objective or empirical evidence. Unlike belief and hope, faith is substance (revelation) and itself may be considered evidence. From a theological sense, faith accepts God's word for things not seen. The religious person may not evaluate or appraise their situation on the basis of what they have seen, but rather on the religious teachings on which their faith rests. The older person who has just been told that he or she has cancer or who may have fallen and broken his or her hip might easily despair in the absence of faith, be it faith in him or herself; faith in his or her doctor, or faith in God. Faith results in a security that allows one to rest peacefully, and releases the natural recuperative processes of the body to take over.

Denying the facts is not faith. Faith is acknowledgment and acceptance of the facts, and a confidence and security in the outcome. Accepting the facts will not weaken real faith. The religious older person with faith might say to him or her "I am sick [acknowledges the fact], but I am fully persuaded that God will do what he said He will do." The Judeo-Christian scriptures are full of promises to the faithful. Consider Isaiah 46:4—

Even to your old age, I shall be the same, and even to your graying hairs I shall bear you! I have done it, and I shall carry you: And I shall bear you, and I shall deliver you.

As older persons with acute or chronic illness face situations that they and those around them are helpless to deal with, religious faith might serve to sustain hope and fuel their will to live. It might also assist people to accept those things that cannot be changed and save them from the frustration and internal restlessness that breeds depression and mental illness.

Hence, there is a need for clinicians to develop a better understanding of their patients' religious beliefs in order to enhance communication. It should be recognized that such beliefs may play an important role in assisting older persons to adjust and cope with life stresses, to accept circumstances when they cannot be changed, and to maintain a sense of emotional security in an unstable external environment. A few investigators have further maintained that religious faith may act directly to effect cures of physical illness through psychological or other unknown mechanisms.

An editorial (1985) in *Lancet* recently addressed the topic of faith healing in Great Britain. In that country, there exists a Confederation of Healing Organizations that represents over seven thousand healers who span a wide range of religious beliefs. It is concerned with establishing a code of conduct for members and certain legal restrictions to practice—such as the protection of children under sixteen years of age, assuring them proper medical care, and restrictions on diseases to which faith healing is applicable (i.e., exclusion of any serious illness that requires medical treatment). Clinical trials were planned to examine scientifically the efficacy of faith healing for five conditions: cataracts, cedeme bleu, child and adult cancer, rheumatoid arthritis, and pain. Protocols for these studies are described in the article.

Three responses to this editorial have thus far been printed that challenge protocol designs, and present cases of thyroid deficiency and epilepsy whose courses were adversely affected by discontinuation of medication related to faith healing (Goulder, 1986; Coakley and Mc-Kenna, 1986; Smith, 1986). The poor acceptance of such nontraditional healing practices by medical physicians, and the generally antagonist relationship between clinicians and faith healers, may create disharmony and distrust between religious patients and their physicians. On the other hand, encouragement of medically ill persons to stop taking their medications or not seek medical attention when necessary is clearly to be condemned.

Such overzealous religious practices, thankfully, are not a common occurence. The Judeo-Christian scriptures themselves encourage the following attitude towards physicians and medical care:

Honor a physician . . . for the uses which ye have of him, for the Lord hath created him. For from the Most High cometh healing . . . The Lord hath created medicine for the good of the earth . . . He hath given men skill, that He might be honored in His marvellous works. (Book of Ecclasiasticus, 190 BC)

Favazza notes that most influential faith healers encourage people to seek medical, including psychiatric help (Favazza, 1982). Piedmont has further observed that clergymen and religiously-oriented physicians may often engage in reciprocal referral patterns, each utilizing the expertise of the other (Piedmont, 1968). The subject of collaboration between medical professionals and the religious community is an important topic and will be discussed further in Chapter 13.

Although religious beliefs and attitudes may have an important influence both directly and indirectly on physical health, this issue remains largely unsettled and awaits definitive study. Studies with adequate sample sizes, that employ random sampling techniques and validated measures of religious and health variables, are necessary for acceptable research in the future.

5

RELIGIOUS RITUAL AND
MENTAL HEALTH

Maves (1960) has noted two major functions performed by religious institutions: first, to communicate a belief system and provide an opportunity for worship and expression of faith; second, to meet the social needs of their members. Hence, the focus of most churches is to address spiritual, social, and survival needs. The local church antedates current aging networks by thousands of years in providing services in the form of social support and practical assistance for living, and it has been only in recent history that this traditional role of the church has been assumed by government and social service professionals (Laporte, 1981; Marty, 1980). The healing of mental illness is historically embedded in religious rituals and practices (McNeil, 1951).

The importance of religious ritual and social activity in the lives of older adults has already been alluded to. Surveys conducted by the Princeton Religion Research Center have found that 45 to 50 percent of all Americans over the age of sixty-five *attend church* at least weekly (Princeton Religion Research Center, 1982; Princeton Religion Research Center, 1985). Several earlier investigators have reported that church attendance either declines or does not change as people age (Webber, 1954; Orbach, 1961; Riley and Foner, 1968). Recent studies by Young and Dowling (1987) and Koenig (1987b) have confirmed these earlier observations. Young and Dowling (1987), in a study of 123 adults (mean age 70) in Texas, similarly found an inverse relationship between age and organized religious activities (Beta = $-.13$, p $<$ .05); however, a positive association was found between age and private religious activity (Beta = .16, p $<$ .01).

Koenig (1987a) examined the frequency of church attendance, participation in other religious group activity (Bible study or prayer meetings,
Sunday school), and private religious activity (prayer, Bible, or other
religious literature reading) in a combined sample of two groups of older
adults: (1) a group of 106 consecutive geriatric medicine clinic patients
in Springfield, Illinois, and (2) 318 senior center participants from Springfield (central Ilinois), Burlington (eastern Iowa), and Columbia (central
Missouri). Response rates for these two groups were 78 percent and 70
percent, respectively. The results are presented in Figures 3 through 10.
Bear in mind that these are cross-sectional data and could represent a
cohort effect, rather than an effect of aging. Based on these data, the
following conclusions were made:

1. Church attendance and religious community activity tends to decline with
   age, especially among the sick. It is also lower among the young elderly (age
   55 to 64) (see Figures 3 and 4).
2. Religious TV viewing and radio listening remains stable with age, with a
   slight drop-off in extreme old age; health has little influence (see Figure 5).
3. Reading of the Bible and other religious literature steadily increases with age,
   until extreme old age, when a drop-off occurs; among the healthy, it remains
   remarkably stable with age; among the sick, it increases with age until late
   old age, when a drop-off is seen (see Figure 8).
4. Frequency of prayer remains stable with age, with a slight increase in extreme
   old age; this increase in late old age is particularly pronounced in the sick
   (see Figure 6).
5. The self-rated importance of prayer increases significantly with age, especially
   among the sick (see Figure 7).
6. There is little fluctuation of intrinsic religiosity with age; there is a slight
   increase, however, in the over seventy-five age group, compared with the
   under seventy-five; health makes little difference (see Figure 9).
7. At all ages, a remarkably high percentage of older persons' friends come from
   their church congregation (60 to 78%); over half the sample reported that four
   or five out of their five closest friends came from this source (Koenig et al.,
   1988a) (see Figure 10).

Supporting the findings above is the longitudinal work of Blazer and
Palmore (1976) (North Carolina), which demonstrated a relative stability
in church attendance up to about the age of seventy, after which a decline
was seen, whereas religious attitudes remained stable even into late old
age. The drop in church attendance in advanced age has generally been
attributed to declines in health, financial status, and transportation availability, all which limit accessibility to church facilities at this time in life
(Blazer and Palmore, 1976; Mindel and Vaughan, 1978).

Although organizational activities such as church attendance have

Figure 3

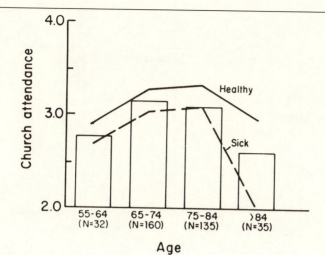

Figure 4

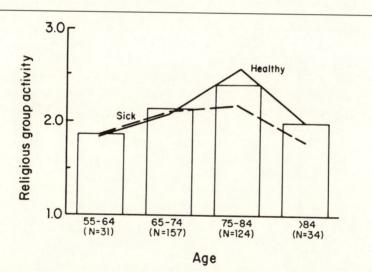

been shown to decrease in old age, nonorganizational activities appear to increase (Mindel and Vaughan, 1978; Young and Dowling, 1987; Fukuyama, 1961). In the following paragraphs, the prevalence and importance of personal religious activities (nonorganizational) will be discussed.

With regard to *prayer*, Gallup polls have shown that 95 percent of elderly Americans pray, and 84 percent reported completely or mostly true to the statement "I constantly seek God's will through prayer"

Figure 5

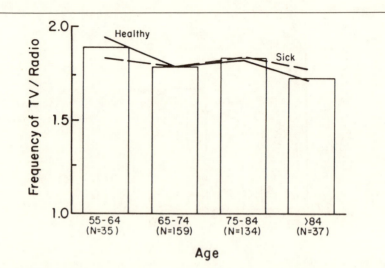

Figure 6

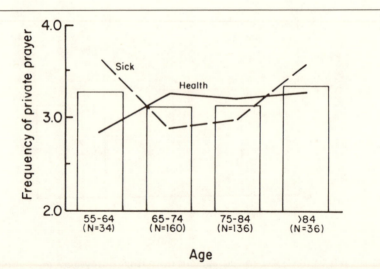

(Princeton Religion Research Center, 1982). One out of every five (19%) older Americans is involved in a prayer group (Princeton Religion Research Center, 1982). Among patients attending a geriatric medicine clinic for health care (mean age 74), 72 percent prayed at least once a day, and 82 percent moderately or strongly agreed that "prayer is important in my life" (Koenig et al., 1988a). In the multi-state survey of senior center participants (Burlington, IA; Columbia, MO; Springfield,

Figure 7

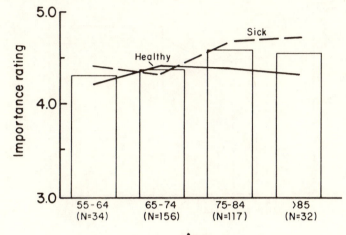

Figure 8

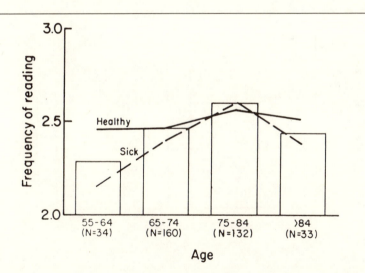

IL) noted earlier, 63 percent reported praying at least once a day and 89 percent moderately or strongly agreed to prayer's importance (Koenig, 1987b). There can be little doubt of the salience of prayer in the lives of most older adults in this country.

   Bible reading is also more frequent among the elderly than any other age group. More than one out of four (27%) people over age sixty-five read the Bible at least daily (Princeton Religion Research Center, 1982),

Figure 9

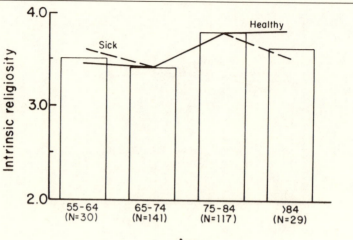

Age

Figure 10

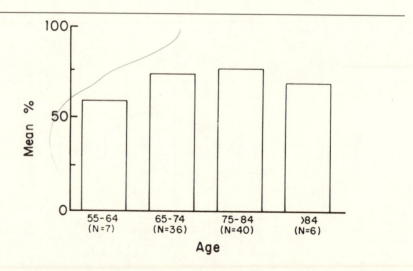

Age

and nearly the same percentage (23%) are involved in Bible study groups. Likewise, 28 percent of geriatric medicine outpatients admitted to reading the Bible or other religious literature at least once a day (Koenig et al., 1988a), and 38 percent of senior citizens in the multi-state survey (Koenig, 1987b) did the same.

The elderly frequently read other religious literature as well. In a survey conducted of subscribers by *Guideposts*, America's largest paid circulation inspirational publication, it was discovered that the average age of readers was over fifty (Trost Associates, Inc., 1984). *Guideposts* readers were also found to have both a higher annual family income $23,048 vs. $20,171) and more college education (53% vs. 33%) than the average American adult. As with Gallup's surveys of Bible readers, a significantly higher percentage of subscribers were women (90%) (Trost Associates, Inc., 1984).

Turning to the importance of *religious TV program* viewing for older adults (the "electronic church"), some interesting data have been recently uncovered. According to recent Nielsen ratings (Nielsen, 1985), approximately 61 million Americans (representing 40% of the 84.9 million TV households in the United States) watch one or more of the top ten syndicated religious broadcasts each month. These figures do not include the audiences of the other fifty-two nationally syndicated religious programs along with those of many other locally produced programs. At the top of the syndicated religious program is "The 700 Club," which attracts 28.7 million viewers each month. As with readers of *Guideposts*, the majority of viewers of the 700 Club are women (59%) and over fifty-five years of age (55%) (Nielsen, 1985).

Most *religious radio* programs do not conduct surveys of the demographic characteristics of their listening audiences (National Religious Broadcasters, Ambassador Advertising Agency). We were, however, able to locate one religious broadcasting organization that does demographic surveys of its listeners. The Good News Broadcasting Association, located in Lincoln, Nebraska, is the largest international broadcasting organization and one of the largest and oldest in the United States (broadcasting since 1939). In their 1984 survey, 68 percent of their listeners were over fifty years of age and 27 percent were over age seventy (Schinder, 1984). In other surveys, 38 percent of geriatric clinic patients (Koenig et al., 1988a), and 47 percent of midwestern senior center participants (Koenig, 1987b) reported watching religious TV or listening to religious radio at least several times a month.

Private activities such as prayer, Bible reading, listening to religious music or radio programs continue to flourish throughout the individual's later years. It is hypothesized that such activities are independent of functional status and accessibility concerns that may limit involvement in religious community activity. In a sample of 127 AARP members (mean age 71) from El Paso, Texas, Young and Dowling (1987) also found that the more active in general that older people were, the more actively they participated in organized religious activity. The younger elderly participated more in formal religious activities, whereas the older elderly were more involved in private devotions. They did not, however, find that poor health, low income, reduced activity, and living alone predicted higher levels of private devotional activity.

Clearly, the older adult is very likely to be engaged in some type of religious activity, be it church-related or more private in nature. The current predominantly cross-sectional evidence suggests that on the average, religious activity either stays constant or increases into advanced age. Does this activity simply represent a cultural phenomenon, or does religion play a specific role among older people to enable them to cope more effectively with the stresses that they experience? What effect does religious activity, either organizational or nonorganizational, have on the mental health of the mature adult?

ADJUSTMENT AND COPING

Numerous studies in the 1940s and 1950s addressed the impact of religious ritual in the lives of elderly people. For the most part, these studies supported the positive influence of religious activity (church attendance, involvement in religious community, reading religious literature, etc.) on personal adjustment in old age (Lawton, 1943; Lardis, 1942; Pressey and Sumcoe, 1950; Schmidt, 1951; Britton, 1949; Moberg, 1953; Lloyd, 1955). In the majority of these studies, personal adjustment was measured by use of the Burgess-Cavan-Havighurst Attitudes Inventory and was defined as satisfaction with activities and status, general happiness, and a feeling of usefulness (Burgess, Cavan and Havighurst, 1948). Although limited in research design and data analysis, this work provides important information—even if relevant only to a cohort nearly forty years distant from the present elderly population.

A closer examination of a select number of these studies is revealing. Moberg (1953, 1956), after rigorously controlling for other factors related to adjustment, found that church membership alone was not correlated with personal adjustment among 219 elderly residents living in a northern metropolitan area. As a possible explanation for this finding, he suggests that membership alone does not indicate anything about the "quality" of that membership or the intensity of commitment. Religious activity (such as church attendance), on the other hand, was significantly related to good personal adjustment, as was the holding of conservative orthodox Christian beliefs. The Burgess-Cavan-Havighurst Attitudes Inventory was used to measure personal adjustment in this study.

Scott (1955) examined personal adjustment and religious activities in a population of nursing home residents and among persons over age sixty living in a community located in a southern urban area. Adjustment was also measured by the Burgess-Cavan-Havighurst Attitudes Inventory. In both samples, those persons attending church frequently had higher levels of adjustment. Frequent Bible reading was also significantly associated with better adjustment in the noninstitutionalized sample, but not in the nursing home population.

In a recent study, Hunsberger (1985) also found significant correlations between church attendance and both happiness and adjustment, but not with health. Argyle and Beit-Hallami (1975) found that church members and frequent attenders had less psychiatric impairment, greater positive adjustment to old age, were less likely to abuse alcohol and commit suicide, and had better physical health.

Koenig et al. (1988b) found a low but significant correlation between subjective coping and both organizational ($r = .11$) and nonorganizational ($r = .15$) religious activity, after controlling for health, financial status (objective and subjective), social support, sex, and age. A single item was used to measure coping: agreement or disagreement on a four-point scale with the statement, "I handle tension in my life very well." In another study, Koenig and Blake (1986) found that the younger old (age 60 to 74), with high levels of religious community activities, were significantly more likely to report that they handled stress very well (42%) than did those with low religous activity (24%). This relationship, however, did not hold up among participants age seventy-five or older for which, regardless of the level of religious activity, about 40 percent reported that they coped very well with stress.

In their longitudinal study, Blazer and Palmore (1976) found religious activities (church attendance, listening to church services on TV and radio, reading religious literature), more than attitudes, to be significantly related to happiness, usefulness, and adjustment. Interestingly, their highest correlations were seen among men age seventy years and over, and persons engaged in manual occupations. At the same time, frequency analysis of their data showed that women were much more likely to be involved in religious activities than men. Apparently, among the men who were actively involved, the effect of religious activity on well-being was quite pronounced. It has been well established that suicide rates among single white elderly men are the highest of any segment of the population (studies performed in the late 1970s). Indeed, after age eighty-five, the male : female suicide rate is twelve : one (Osgood, 1985). There is considerable evidence to suggest that religious activity such as church attendance is significantly associated with lower suicide rates among elderly populations (Nelson, 1977; Argyle and Beit-Hallami, 1975). Taken together, these findings are provocative and underscore the need for future studies to address the potential impact of involvement in the religious community on the mental health of elder males in this society.

How might religious community involvement impact positively on mental health? Gray (Gray and Moberg, 1962) provided interview evidence to support the notion that frequent church attendance and involvement in the religious community provides companionship and friends, helps to alleviate anxiety about death, exposes the person to a social environment of age-matched peers, places them in a supportive atmosphere to buffer stressful life changes, and provides practical assistance when needed. He also presented problems encountered in religious organizations, including age discrimination and conflicts with younger members over roles of the elderly in church government.

In discussing "primary groups" that provide social support that buffers and cushions the individual from physiologic and psychologic consequences of exposure to stressors, Kaplan et al. (1977) included religion along with family and work relationships as major examples. The church has also been characterized as a social support system by others (Anderson, 1979; Williams, 1974). Delgado (1982) discusses the value of natural support systems in helping elderly Hispanics to deal with a variety of problems, such as short-term crisis and life transitions. He includes religious support systems, along with family, folk healers, and social clubs as examples. Delgado claims that religious groups provide support to the elderly through provision of concrete services such as jobs, housing, counseling, information referral, and day care, as well as through prayer.

Several authors have suggested that church membership and attendance offer a strong source of social support and participation that is associated with successful adaptation to bereavement (Yates et al., 1981; Berardo, 1970). Active religious elderly have been shown to have a more positive attitude toward death than those uninvolved in religious activity (Swenson, 1961; Feifel, 1964; Stark, 1968; Feifel and Nagy, 1981; Smiley, 1985). Furthermore, religious groups may also serve as an effective source of social support for families coping with the demands of caring for demented family members or those with other chronic illnesses (Steele, Lucas, and Tune, 1982).

In summary, then, involvement in organized religious community activity tends to be associated with higher levels of personal adjustment and coping. The extent to which these findings reflect the religious nature of such activity, above and beyond the benefits gained from social interaction, is uncertain. Further clarification of this issue will be sought in the next section dealing with subjective well-being and religious activity. What limited data exist also suggest a positive relationship between personal adjustment and nonorganizational activities such as prayer and Bible reading.

SUBJECTIVE WELL-BEING

Church attendance or church-related activities have been reported to be significantly related to both "happiness" and "life satisfaction" by a number of investigators (O'Reilly, 1957; Palmore, 1969; Scott, 1955; Shanas, 1962; Edwards and Klemmack, 1973). Edwards and Klemmack

(1973) found that after examining the impact of twenty-two variables on life satisfaction among 507 older adults, income level and perceived health were the two strongest indicators. Church-related activity, however, was the next strongest predictor of life satisfaction. This association remained positive after controlling for the remaining variables.

Guy (1982) examined life satisfaction and frequency of church attendance among 1,170 elderly adults residing in a southern metropolitan area (Memphis, Tennessee). She found that aged individuals who had decreased their church attendance from earlier years had lower life satisfaction than those individuals increasing their church attendance or maintaining the pattern of their earlier years. Life satisfaction in this study was measured by Neugarten et al.'s (1961) Life Satisfaction Index A, which addresses five dimensions of life satisfaction.

Age has been shown to be an important factor in the well-being church activity relationship. Spreitzer and Snyder (1974) examined 11 predictors of life satisfaction in a sample of 1,547 persons from data collected in the 1972 and 1973 NORC surveys (National Opinion Research Center, at University of Chicago). In their sample were 224 persons age sixty-five and older. While finding a positive and significant correlation between church attendance and life satisfaction among the population less than age sixty-five, they found no such association among those sixty-five and over. The strongest predictors of life satisfaction in the latter group were again self-assessed health and economic sufficiency (same as with Edwards and Klemmack). Response categories for church attendance were not mentioned for this study.

Along these same lines, Graney (1975) found that religious activities were positively correlated with happiness (measured by Affect-Balance Scale; Bradburn, 1969) among the "young old" (age 66 to 75, N = 16), but not the "old old" (age 82 to 92, N = 17). Categories of religious activity were "never," "sometimes," and "at least once per week." Given the high level of religious activity older adults in this country are involved in, such categories show little discriminatory capacity; over half of the sample is likely to fall into the highest category and the other half in the second highest category, the result being a variable with only two response levels for analysis. In examining the religious activity variable among older adults, response categories must be structured to distinguish differing grades of high response where "once a week" is the middle of a range of possible responses, not the end of the range. Not doing so might *underestimate* the correlation between religious attendance and life satisfaction, particularly when parametric methods of analysis are used (Levin and Vanderpool, 1987). Koenig and Blake (1986), while also employing weak response categories for their religious activity variable, confirmed Graney's findings of a significant association between religious activity and life satisfaction in the young old (age 60 to

74), and likewise found no association among the old old (age 75 and over).

Why should religious activity be associated with life satisfaction among the young elderly and not in the old? The answer to this question is not entirely clear. It may, of course, be due to simple random statistical error or unknown biases in sample selection. The consistency among studies, however, is notable. One explanation might be the following: Because religious activity is lower among the old old for reasons due to health and transportation problems rather than to "lower religiosity," the correlation between life satisfaction and church attendance mediated by a "religious factor" may be obscured in such analyses.

Evidence for a "religious factor" being the mechanism behind the association between life satisfaction and church attendance has been demonstrated. Cutler (1976) studied the impact of participation in voluntary associations on well-being among a representative national sample of 438 older adults (mean age 72). Data were obtained from the NORC general social surveys of the United States population 1974–75, and thus represent cross-sectional data. He found that church membership was by far the most common among all organizations participated in by the elderly (49%). It was also the *only* organization whose membership was associated with well-being. The latter finding does suggest that religious community activity conveys more to its members than the benefits derived from simple group social activity, and this "something more" may be the "religious factor" alluded to previously. Both Edwards and Klemmack (1973), and Pihlblad and Adams (1972), had also previously demonstrated the seemingly unique association between church attendance and life satisfaction in older adults that was not found for other social activities.

Cutler (1976) explained this phenomenon by pointing out that church-affiliated groups to which the older persons belonged were characterized by a greater degree of age homogeneity than is the case with other types of associations. Other research has shown that well-being is associated with high concentrations of aged peers in a community (Bultena, 1974). As an alternative to the social hypothesis, Cutler also suggested a possible association between psychological well-being and religiosity in general.

Satisfaction with Health

To health professionals, even more relevant than general life satisfaction, are older persons' feelings of satisfaction with their health. Singh and Williams (1982) examined survey data on 1,459 elderly persons (age 65 and over) to determine those variables explaining satisfaction with health and physical condition. The importance of the individual's perception and satisfaction with their health was stressed because of its value as a determinant of health-related behavior (Cluff and Cluff, 1983; Downey, 1984). Multiple regression models that included possible confounders such as sex, age, race, education, marital status, working status, alcohol use, smoking, hospitalization in past five years, and religious attendance, revealed that religious attendance was the most important factor explaining satisfaction with health and physical condition. These findings have vital implications for studying healthcare utilization by older adults. Religion may impact on the likelihood that an older person will seek medical attention for physical symptoms.

Negative Studies

Not all studies show a strong association between subjective well-being and religious activity (Ray 1979). Toseland and Rasch (1979–80) examined thirty-one predictors of life satisfaction in a national sample of 871 adults fifty-five years and over. Included among these predictors was "religious participation." Life satisfaction was measured using a single item self-rated scale (validity and reliability absent). Religious participation was not one of the nine variables that contributed significantly to life satisfaction. Their regression model, however, predicted only 21 percent of the variance in life satisfaction.

Barron (1961) reported that church and religion were noted less frequently as sources of comfort and life satisfaction than were such activities as "being at home with the family," "keeping house," "doing things that I like doing by myself at home," "having relatives visit," and "spending time with good friends." This nation-wide study sample consisted of 1,206 urban-dwelling elderly who were mostly male. Generalization of these results, therefore, should be made with caution, since the majority of elderly are women (about two-thirds after age 75, 1980 U.S. Census), who have been repeatedly shown to be more inclined toward religion than men.

Longitudinal Studies

Only two major longitudinal studies have examined the relationship between religious activities and attitudes, and well-being over time: the First Duke Longitudinal Study of Aging completed in 1975 and an ongoing study begun in 1976 by the University of Texas Medical Branch in Galveston, Texas. Three major reports have come out of these studies thus far. Blazer and Palmore (1976) reported the results of eighteen years of followup on 272 older, white, southern Protestants (mean age 71) involved in the Duke study. Markides reported the results after four years (Markides, 1983), and eight years (Markides et al., 1987) of followup on 336 older (mean age 70), predominantly Catholic, Mexican-American participants (70%) in the Texas study.

The study that has followed subjects the longest thus far is that of Blazer and Palmore (1976), who report on the results of the First Duke Longitudinal Study of Aging. Examining the change in the relationship between religious activities and attitudes and well-being over an eighteen year time span, they found that religious activities were significantly related to happiness ($r = .16$), especially among men ($r = .26$), and among participants over age seventy ($r = .25$). Feelings of usefulness were also associated with religious activity ($r = .25$), especially among persons with manual occupations ($r = .34$), and among those over age seventy ($r = .32$). Significant relationships were also found between religious activity and adjustment ($r = .16$), especially among older adults with manual occupations ($r = .33$), and among men ($r = .28$). While significant correlations did occur between religious attitudes and adjustment and well-being, those noted for religious activities were considerably stronger. These findings prompted Blazer and Palmore to state that religious activities were more important than attitudes in influencing adjustment. Finally, they noted that correlations between religion and adjustment did increase over the eighteen year span of the study, suggesting that as people age, religion takes on a greater role as a predictor of well-being.

Consistent with the latter observations are recent findings (cross-sectional) by Koenig et al. (1988b). In a sample of 836 older adults, church attendance and involvement in religious community activities were significantly related ($r = .26$) to well-being for the group as a whole (see Figure 11). Involvement in religious community activities accounted for 20 percent of the explained variance in well-being among persons age seventy-five and over, after health, social support, and financial status were controlled. Among older persons age seventy-four and younger, however, organized religious activities accounted for only 5 percent of the explained variance in well-being. Note that the findings of Blazer and Palmore (1976) and Koenig et al. (1988b) are in contrast to those others that have noted higher correlations between well-being and religious activity among the younger old than the old old (Graney, 1975; Spreitzer and Snyder, 1974; Koenig and Blake, 1986). Bear in mind, however, that the quality of the data—based on sample sizes and study design—is considerably higher for the Blazer and Palmore (1976) and the recent Koenig et al. (1988b) studies.

In the Texas longitudinal study, Markides (1983) used the Neugarten Life Satisfaction Index to assess well-being, and three variables to assess religiosity (church attendance, self-rated religiosity, and private prayer). Each of the three religion variables was measured by a single question with four to six response options. At four years of followup, among

Figure 11
Well-being among quartiles of the sample divided up by scores on religious variables. ORA = organized religious activity, NORA = nonorganized religious activity, IR = intrinsic religiosity. From Koenig et al. (1988b). *indicates standard error of the mean. PGCMS = Philadelphia Geriatric Center Morale Scale. N = 836.

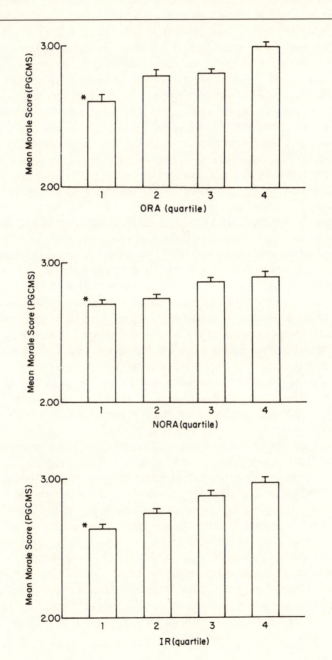

Mexican-Americans the correlation between life satisfaction and church attendance decreased slightly (.14 to .12), remained unchanged (.09) with self-rated religiosity, and increased for private prayer (.06 to .15). For the Protestant Anglos (30% of the sample) correlations between life satisfaction and church attendance increased (.19 to .38), decreased for self-rated religiosity (.23 to .12) and private prayer (.33 to .11). The short followup period presented in that report (4 years) leaves some questions about the meaning of the above correlations.

Markides et al. (1987) have recently reported the results of an eight year followup on their sample. As previous studies have demonstrated, little evidence was found to support a turning to religion with aging. Associations between religious variables and life satisfaction were weak and often lost significance once variables such as subjective functional health, ethnicity, sex, education, age, and marital status were controlled. These associations did not increase over the eight year course of the study, as was reported earlier by Blazer and Palmore (1976) in their eighteen year study.

Careful analysis of Markides and colleagues' sample and methodology, however, brings up questions that challenge their results. First of all, let us consider the validity and specificity of variables employed to measure religiosity. Church attendance (measured on to point scale) achieved mean response scores ranging from 4.3 to 4.6 over the three waves of the study; responses to self-rated religiosity (rated on a 1 to 3 scale) achieved a range of mean scores from 2.3 to 2.5; and mean scores on private prayer (rated on a 1 to 5 scale) ranged from 4.1 to 4.2. The deviation of responses from a normal distribution, and consequent asymmetric distribution near the high end of the response range, would result in correlations that underestimate the true strength of the association with life satisfaction, health, and other variables. This point has been noted in a recent paper by Levin and Vanderpool (1987) with regard to church attendance.

Other concerns include the limited range of response options for the religious variables employed, and the use of single items to measure the highly complex notions of group-related and personal religiosity. Organized religious activity was measured using a single item (church attendance), a somewhat restrictive variable in that other church-related group activities were not measured. Also, church attendance may not be the best indicator of social-oriented religious activity among a sample composed predominantly of Mexican-American Catholics, for whom frequency of church attendance may be more a reflection of culture and tradition, rather than a choice to be involved and interact socially with other church members. Bible or other religious reading and religious TV viewing or radio listening were important aspects of private religious activity that were not measured.

Note should also be made on the relatively small number of response options for each of the religious variables that may have limited their discriminatory capacity. Many older adults may have attended church more frequently than once a week; these, however, were lumped into a single category with the weekly attenders—a consequence of the restricted response options used for this variable. Similarly, the single item subjective religiosity variable—self-rated religiosity—with response options of "very religious," "somewhat or not very religious," and "not at all religious," is unlikely to yield much specificity among the majority of older adults, most of whom are quite religious. Private religious activity was also measured by a single item, private prayer, which despite having a wider range of response options, still was minimally discriminatory due to the very high prevalence of prayer in this population (whose mean prayer scores were 4.1 to 4.2 out of 5.0).

Next is the issue of the generalizability of these results. Almost three-quarters of their sample were Mexican-American Catholics whose religious expression is likely to be influenced heavily by social and cultural forces that may be different from those influencing the majority of older white or black Protestant Americans. Consequently, the comparison of their results with those from the Duke Longitudinal Study (a sample composed predominantly of white Protestants) should be done with great care—if at all.

One must also contend with the question of whether even eight years is long enough for significant changes to occur in a durable, deeply rooted social and cultural variable such as religion—particularly life-long patterns of church attendance and religious attitudes (often instilled in childhood and molded throughout adulthood). Life satisfaction, as well, is a construct that is relatively stable and differs distinctly from happiness, a more transient, mood-dependent state. The First Duke Longitudinal Study covered almost two decades, possibly a more optimal time period for important changes to occur in stable characteristics such as religion and life satisfaction.

Finally, leading off the discussion section of their report, Markides et al. comment about the impact of dropouts in longitudinal studies on the relationship between church attendance and life satisfaction (Markides et al., 1987). They found that when dropouts were excluded from the analysis, the effect of religious attendance was no longer significantly related to life satisfaction. This loss of association, they explained, was due to the composition of the dropout group, who were often physically ill, lower in functional status, attended church less frequently, and had lower life satisfaction. They hypothesized that increasing associations found between religious attendance and life satisfaction over time in longitudinal studies (Blazer and Palmore, 1976) might be "due in part to the removal of a disproportionate number of individuals concentrated at the low end of the religious attendance-life satisfaction distribution." This speculation, that dropouts in longitudinal studies may leave a rather select group of survivors present for the later analyses (who in this case may be persons with high life satisfaction and high church attendance) is not unreasonable. They do in fact present some data to support this hypothesis. Below is a comparison of mean rates of church attendance and life satisfaction between respondents available at the time of (A) each observation, (B) the dropouts, and (C) respondents available at all three times of observation. Standard deviations are in parenthesis.

Comparison of Mean Rates of Church Attendance (N=230)

Time	Respondents A	Dropouts B	Respondents C
Church Attendance			
1976	4.3 (1.8)		4.6 (1.7)
1980	4.3 (1.9)	4.0 (N = 123)	4.5 (1.8)
1984	4.3 (1.9)	4.0 (N = 108)	4.3 (1.9)
Life Satisfaction			
1976	14.4 (4.6)		15.0 (4.2)
1980	13.9 (5.9)	13.9	14.5 (5.0)
1984	13.3 (5.3)	12.6	13.3 (5.3)

The differences here are small, and hardly provide solid proof of their hypothesis. Hence, before the increasing correlations between life satisfaction and church attendance with aging can be attributed to the effects of dropouts, it would be wise to have further evidence that such effects really are both satistically and clinically significant. The use of a larger sample size and longer followup, with careful objective measures of physical health and more comprehensive and specific measures of religious community activity, would go a long way to provide the solid type of evidence needed. Despite the rather critical comments above, we believe that this study of Markides et al. has contributed important new information that challenges many previous findings in this area.

RACIAL FACTORS

The importance of religion in the lives of older blacks has recently been underscored by Taylor (1986). He also demonstrated the effect of gender, marital status, age, and urbanicity on religious participation by this group. Several studies have noted the strong relationship between life satisfaction and church attendance in blacks. St. George and Mc-Namara (1984) examined the relationship between psychological well-being and religious measures among 1,353 men and 1,570 women age twenty-five to fifty-four in the NORC 1972–82 national surveys. The religious measures frequency of church attendance and strength of religious preference were reported to be good predictors of well-being, especially among blacks.

Ortega et al. (1983) have also contributed significantly to our understanding of the powerful role played by religious factors in enhancing well-being among minority groups. They speculated that despite being much more likely to suffer from inadequate housing and low income, racial minorities are at least as well-off as older white adults in terms of subjective well-being. In a survey of 4,522 older adults in Alabama, a substantial proportion of whom were black, life satisfaction was entered as the dependent variable in a model with several social interaction variables. They found that the critical factor in accounting for race differences in well-being was the frequency of contact with church-related friends. Explanations given for this include that, (1) the church is the center of a moral community, (2) it is a community of faith where members share common beliefs that impact positively on their sense of well-being, and (3) the black church serves as an extended family for its participants.

Recall that Koenig et al. (1988a), in a central Illinois study located far from the heavily religious Bible Belt of the South, found that over half of their consecutive sample of geriatric patients reported that almost all of their closest friends came from their church congregations. Since the sample was predominantly white (92%), such findings underscore the importance of the church as a powerful source of social support for older persons, regardless of race.

INFLUENCE OF SOCIAL FACTORS

Social support has been shown to buffer the impact of stress on mental health. Brown and Prudo (1981) examined the social factors (including church attendance) related to depression (absence of well-being) among a random sample of English women residing in an urban area, London (N = 458), and a random sample of women located in a rural area, Outer Hebrides (N = 355). These samples were not elderly, in that the age range was eighteen to sixty-five; however, their results may provide clues to a better understanding of similar issues among the aged. They found that in rural areas where church attendance was in general high (63%), there was a much lower prevalence of depression among churchgoers (6%) than among nonchurchgoers (20%). On the other hand, in the urban environment of London where church attendance was low (14%), no difference was seen in prevalence of depression between churchgoers and nonchurchgoers. The question raised by these results is what are the social factors at work in determining whether or not church attendance is positively related to well-being. In other words, if a person resides in an area where everybody goes to church and he or she does not go to church, the failure to join in with the rest of the crowd may mark that person as a social outcast and result in depression and loss of well-being on social grounds alone.

Using data from the Koenig et al. (1988b) study of the relationship between well-being and religiosity in the aged, Koenig examined the correlations between morale and religious variables within various subgroups of the sample (unpublished data) in order to test the above hypothesis. Since morale measures correlate strongly with measures of depression (Morris et al., 1975), there is validity in comparing results from a morale study with that of Brown and Prudo. The subgroups were divided into: (1) a group of retired nuns and elderly church members, in whom the social pressure to attend church would be high (as in the Outer Hebrides population), and (2) a group of senior center participants and geriatric clinic patients, in whom there would be fewer social forces favoring church activities and religious attitudes (as in urban London). The results are noted in Table 2.

With regard to church attendance among *women*, the strength of the correlations with morale was roughly equal between the "religious" subgroup (retired nuns and church members) ($r = .18$), and the "other" subgroup (geriatric clinic and senior centers) ($r = .19$). Similarly, little difference was seen in this relationship between organized religious activity (church attendance, etc.), and morale among the male church member subgroup and the male geriatric or senior center subgroup. The same held true for nonorganizational religious activities (prayer, Bible reading, religious TV, and radio). The strength of the relationship between intrinsic religiosity (attitude or commitment) and morale, however, was quite different depending on the subgroup examined. Among those with strong religious social influences (the retired nuns and church members), correlations between intrinsic religiosity and well-being were relatively high ($r = .27$ for women, $r = .24$ for men), compared to correlations between religiosity and well-being among the geriatric clinic patients and senior center participants ($r = .15$ for women, $r = -.02$ for men).

While these findings fail to support those of Brown and Prudo with regard to church attendance and well-being, they do support an influence of social forces on religious attitudes/orientation and well-being. In other words, if a person is a member of a social group in which a high

Table 2

Intragroup Zero-order Correlations between Religious Variables and Morale (PGCMS) Scores

N	Group	Organized Religious Activity (ORA)	Non-Organized Religious Activity (NORA)	Intrinsic Religiosity (IR)
721–43	Entire Sample[1]	.26***	.16***	.24***
166–79	Men	.27***	.11	.18
525–43	Women	.27***	.19***	.28***
407–24	Under age 75	.24***	.14**	.25***
277–94	75 and over	.32***	.22***	.29***
350–75	Geriatric Clinic Patients and Senior Center Participants	.15**	.08	.10*
88–101	Men	.09	-.04	-.02
230–50	Women	.19**	.11*	.15**
168–85	Under age 75	.15*	.07	.08
144–59	75 and over	.17*	.11	.20**
352–85	Retired Nuns and Church Members	.15**	.04	.26***
70–72	Men	.03	.02	.24*
274–301	Women	.18**	.09	.27***
227–232	Under age 75	.11*	.00	.29***
121–44	75 and over	.24**	.13	.22**
145–75	Retired Nuns	.35***	.09	.21**

[1] Includes Jewish sample (N=16); data for Entire Sample from Koenig et al. (1988b)

*	$\leq .05$
**	$\leq .01$
***	$\leq .001$

priority is placed on one's religious commitment and he or she is not very religiously committed, then low morale or unhappiness may result. If that person were a member of a nonreligious group, however, the forces to conform to religious expectations would be less intense and less likely to arouse feelings of guilt or dysphoria that might occur in a religious setting; a sense of failure or inadequacy in meeting high religious expectations would then be less likely to occur.

The latter hypotheses, however, are based entirely on the results of a single study and alternative explanations may well exist. It is widely known that social and cultural forces may impact on well-being in a variety of ways other than through religion. Clearly, much further research is needed to elucidate ways in which social forces either enhance or diminish the impact of religion on well-being and mental health.

PSYCHIATRIC ILLNESS AND RELIGIOUS ACTIVITIES

To what extent does religious activity act as a buffer against psychiatric illness? Stark (1971) noted that common sense would dictate that involvement in stable social groups, such as well-established religious organizations, would be inversely related to psychopathology. Several studies have reported positive correlations between involvement in religious community activities and mental health (Lindenthal et al., 1970; Galanter and Buckley, 1978; Griffith and Mathewson, 1981; Griffith, English, and Mayfield, 1980; Ness and Wintrob, 1980). Other investigators, however, have shown little or no association (Kranz et al., 1968; Carr and Hauser, 1976).

RELIGIOUS DENOMINATIONS AND
PSYCHIATRIC DISORDERS

In general, the data indicate that religion has a positive impact on mental health in later life. So far the word "religion" has implied the Judeo-Christian tradition in a broad sense. What about specific religious denominations? Are certain religious denominations associated with a lower or higher prevalence of psychiatric disorders among the aged? Unfortunately, very little data exist for older populations. Koenig et al. (1988b) did find that elderly church members of Assembly of God, Baptist, and Nazarene congregations scored significantly higher on subjective well-being (morale) than either senior center participants or outpatients of a geriatric medicine clinic. Although no data presently exist on the clustering of specific psychiatric diagnoses among older members of different religious denominations, some information is available on this particular question for the general population.

MacDonald and Luckett (1983) studied the relationship between re-

ligious affiliation and psychiatric diagnoses (DSM II) among 7,050 patients attending a community mental health clinic in a midwestern
community between 1977 and 1980. The sample was equally divided
between men and women, but no age characteristics were given. Forty-
four psychiatric diagnoses were examined across the following seven
major religious groups: mainline Protestants (N = 1,116) (United Church
of Christ, Presbyterian, Lutheran, United Methodist, Episcopal, Christian), nonmainline Protestants (N = 1,797) (Church of the Brethren,
Amish, Mennonite, Assembly of God, Bible Church, Missionary Church,
Chapel, Church of God, Pentecostal, Nazarene, Free Methodist), other
Protestants (N = 277), Catholics (N = 554), Sects (N = 61) (Christian
Science, Jehovah Witness, Church of Jesus Christ of the Latter Day
Saints, Seventh Day Adventist), unknown (N = 194), and no religious
preference (N = 2,999).

One finding of importance was that of all the patients with psychiatric
illness noted in this sample, a striking 43 percent reported no religious
preference. This figure is in marked contrast to the 7 to 8 percent reported
by the Gallup organization in 1977–80 for the general U.S. population
(Princeton Religion Research Center, 1982). Furthermore, the Mac-
Donald and Luckett study took place in the Midwest, a region of the
United States noted for religious fervor (only 5% no religious preference
in 1979 Gallup survey) (Princeton Religion Research Center, 1982). These
findings suggest that either, (1) the religiously unaffiliated preferentially
seek assistance from mental health professionals in dealing with their
psychiatric problems (whereas the religiously affiliated seek help from
other sources, such as within their church), (2) there is a higher prevalence of psychiatric disorders among the religiously unaffiliated compared with church members, or (3) those with psychiatric illness may
drop their membership as a consequence of it, or they may be excom-
municated because of its symptoms and effects. Other selection factors,
of course, may have been operative but are difficult to predict.

With regard to specific clusters of psychiatric diagnoses found within
each of the above religious groups, MacDonald and Luckett found the
following. Among persons with no religious preference, there was a
clustering of patients with alcohol and drug abuse—diagnoses that were
remarkably absent from the religiously affiliated groups. Nonmainline
Protestants had a much higher rate of adjustment reactions in childhood,
depression, and obsessive compulsive personality disorders. Mainline
Protestants suffered from marital maladjustment and hysterical personality disorders more frequently than others. Inadequate personality and
hysterical neuroses were more common among the "other" Protestant
group. Catholics were notable for obsessive compulsive neuroses and
hysterical personality disorders. Those persons in the unknown group
were more frequently associated with alcohol and drug problems as well

as psychotic disorders. Psychoses were also more prevalent among sect members. It would be unwise to generalize the above findings to populations in later life, since study participants above were mostly non-aged. As noted earlier, this subject has yet to be investigated more specifically among adults in later life.

DEPRESSION AND SUICIDE

Durkheim (1951) noted around the turn of the century that suicide rates were highest among socially isolated individuals and that membership in groups whose participants shared a common identity and tradition was protective against suicide. With the greatest proportion of suicides occurring in the over sixty-five age group (Osgood, 1982), examination of the impact of such universally prevalent and assessable social institutions as churches and synogogues on life satisfaction and well-being becomes particularly relevant. Stack compared suicide rates in twenty-five different countries with their religiosity (Stack, 1983). Religiosity of each country was measured by religious book production rates, which have been found to be highly correlated with church attendance. He found that suicide rates were inversely proportional to religiosity. When broken down by age group, these findings held true for women over sixty-five years of age and men in the sixty-five to seventy-four year age range. Surprisingly, no significant correlation was found among men over age seventy-five, the group that may have the highest suicide rates of all (Osgood, 1985).

Krantz examined the frequency of church attendance among twenty suicide attempters and twenty controls, while matching for religious affiliation, marital status, and race. No significant differences were observed (Krantz et al., 1968). This study was not, however, restricted to older adults. On the other hand, Goldberg et al., in a study of 1,144 women aged sixty-five to seventy-five, examined the frequency of depressive symptoms among participants, and various aspects of the social networks that provided them with social support. They found a significantly lower number of depressive symptoms among elderly women having social networks of greater homogeneity in terms of age, sex, and religion. *Church groups* were felt to be an easily accessible social group particularly suitable in terms of providing a homogeneous social network of support (Goldberg, VanNatta, and Comstock, 1985).

Several investigators have found a high correlation between religious group participation, commitment, and prayer, and relief of psychiatric symptoms such as depression and anxiety among Protestant fundamentalists and others (Pattison, Labino, and Doerr, 1973; Galanter and Buckley, 1978). Such expressions of religiosity have also been found to be advantageous for success with outpatient psychotherapy (Shapiro et al., 1976). Yale psychiatrists Griffith and Mahy (1984) interviewed twenty-three members (age 19 to 71) of the Spiritual Baptist Church in the West Indies to examine the mental health effects of a ritual called "mourning" that involved prayer, fasting, and the experience of dreams and visions while in isolation. Six benefits were cited by mourners: relief of depressed mood, attainment of the ability to foresee danger, improved decision-making ability, enhanced ability to communicate with God, clearer understanding of their racial origins with increased self-esteem and higher self-confidence, identification of their role within the church, and physical cures. Griffith and Mahy validated the psychotherapeutic effects of such practices. These reports must be interpreted with caution if they are to be generalized to older age groups, since participants consisted of mostly younger adults.

Favazza (1982) remarks that religious communities offer life-long support systems for their members. In general, he noted these groups offered a sense of fellowship, an atmosphere of acceptance, and an emphasis on forgiveness and hope, and he compared them to organizations like Alcoholics Anonymous. Small group meetings for prayer, Bible study, fellowship, or sharing activities may further provide psychological support for members through prayer, through direct practical advice from other members based on personal experiences, and by exposure to models of handling stress provided by Biblical characters.

An activity that falls between religious community and private religious behaviors is the ritual of going on a *religious pilgrimage*. Whereas this tradition is firmly entrenched among the Moslem people in their yearly journey to Mecca, it is less common today among people of the Judeo-Christian tradition. The effects on mental health of such a trip are of interest. Morris (1982) examined the effect of a religious pilgrimage to Lourdes on depression and anxiety among a group of twenty-four medically ill older persons (mean age 60 years). Eleven patients suffered from neurological diseases, including four with multiple sclerosis, two with stroke, and one each with Parkinsonism, spastic diplegia, spinal injury, and muscular dystrophy. Four persons had cardiovascular conditions, and the remaining seven had leukemia, bronchiectasis, carcinoma of the breast, gout, rheumatoid arthritis, ulcerative colitis, and endogenous depression. Two of the men were frail and elderly (ages 86 and 84). Anxiety was measured using the State-Trait Anxiety Inventory (Spielberger et al., 1970) and depression by the Beck Depression Inventory (Beck et al., 1961). Participants were interviewed one month prior to departure, one month following their return, and again ten months later. Following return from the religious pilgrimage, Morris found a significant decrease in symptoms of anxiety (33.4 to 26.8, $p < .01$) and symptoms of depression (7.2 to 1.0, $p < .01$). The decrease in symptoms persisted at the tenth-month followup evaluation for both anxiety (24.8) and depression (.8). Morris acknowledges that any holiday or vacation can improve emotional health; however, for this group of elderly, sick persons, there was considerable stress involved in travel by air and coach to Lourdes, and while some of the initial benefit could have been attributed to a vacation effect, it was unlikely that this could have explained the sustained benefits observed. Recall also that these were a group of people with chronic medical illness and their physical condition would have probably worsened over time, leading to even greater emotional stress. Morris notes that the visit for most had strengthened their religious faith and made them more relaxed and capable of accepting their physical conditions.

PRAYER

Parker and Brown (1982) studied coping behaviors that mediate between life events and depression in 176 patients coming in to see their general practitioner. *Prayer* was ranked seventh in effectiveness in a field of twenty-five possible coping behaviors. Stark (1968) has shown that private devotionalism, measured by frequency of prayer and the importance that the individual places on that activity, increased greatly with age in a cross-sectional study of religious commitment among a sample of three thousand people of all ages. The greatest increase was noted among conservative Protestants, where a near linear increase was found between persons in their twenties compared with those over age seventy (from 62% to 96% scoring in the high category).

Francis MacNutt is one of the persons most responsible for the importance of prayer-healing in the new charismatic movement, and has authored several books on this subject (MacNutt, 1974; MacNutt, 1977). He stresses the interrelatedness of physical, emotional, and spiritual sickness, and his approach focuses on delving into the psychological orgins of illness, as well as using prayer as a therapeutic tool. MacNutt notes that the most common type of healing associated with prayer results in a speeding up of the natural recuperative forces of the body, rather than a miraculous, instantaneous recovery from illness (MacNutt, 1974). According to Favazza, religious counselors have begun to use psychodynamic principles incorporated into a religious framework, making good use of religious symbols (Favazza, 1982). This type of religious psychotherapy may in fact be more acceptable to and effective in older persons, whose religious beliefs may be elemental to their view of the world around them and the problems they are facing in it.

At a time when financial resources for physical and mental health care are a target of the Reagan administration's budget balancing strategies, some investigators have suggested a cooperative model between medicine/psychiatry and religious institutions that would serve the comprehensive health care needs of the population (Anderson, Robinson, and

Ruben, 1978; Griffith, 1983). The practical details involved in implementing such a model remain to be worked out.

In conclusion, the literature in general supports the contention that religious activity, particularly group-related, is inversely associated with mental illness such as depression and its consequences (i.e. suicide), and positively correlated with well-being and adjustment. Once again, because of the cross-sectional nature of many of these studies, direction of causation is indeterminant. Still unanswered is the question of whether religious activity *leads to* lower rates of mental health problems. Alternatively, those individuals who for other reasons are less likely to be psychologically ill, may be more likely to be involved in the religious community. Which of these explanations (or another explanation) is the cause for this association awaits studies that include a temporal perspective in their design.

6

RELIGIOUS RITUAL AND PHYSICAL HEALTH

To what extent, if at all, do religious activities buffer against harmful stressors in later life, moderate their impact on physical health, and protect older persons against stress-related illness? Few studies directly address this question, but some investigators have uncovered notable associations between religious activities and stress-related diseases, as well as with various health practices.

Levin and Vanderpool (1987) present an excellent, critical, updated discussion of the issues surrounding the relationship between physical health and church attendance. They note that the value placed by different religious traditions on church attendance may critically affect its relationship to health. Emphasis is placed on the possible confounding influence of physical disability on the church attendance-health relationship. They confirm the need for multi-dimensional religiosity scales and emphasize that the church attendance variable should be measured more precisely (including such categories as more than three times per week, three times per week, twice per week, once per week, etc.), to allow for a greater response spread among populations where church attendance is very common. Furthermore, these authors present the case for an "epidemiology of religion" encouraging collaboration between religion scholars, sociologists, psychologists, gerontologists, and epidemiologists in research efforts to examine the relationship between religion and health.

Some studies have related involvement in religious activities with lower blood pressure. Scotch (1963) found dramatic increases in blood pressure among Zulu people of South Africa moving into an urban environment, compared to that of persons remaining in a rural setting. Church membership among the adult women who moved to the city, however, was shown to be significantly associated with no increases in blood pressure. Walsh (1980) investigated the impact of the process of immigration on blood pressure. Studying seventy-five immigrants of varying ages from nineteen countries, he found that blood pressure increased significantly less for those with high levels of church attendance. This finding confirmed the earlier work of Scotch. Benson and colleagues (1977) reported that meditative prayer, possibly acting through decreasing sympathetic nervous activity, may have a dramatic effect on lowering blood pressure.

Looking at blood pressure changes with aging, Timio (1985) followed the blood pressures of a group of cloistered nuns for twenty years. These women spent most of their time in prayer and worship. A comparison group was chosen from a nearby community. Over the twenty year observation period, blood pressure in the nuns remained virtually unchanged, while that of the community-dwelling women increased progressively over time. Age-related increases in blood pressure found in community surveys may not represent an inevitable accompaniment of aging. As with these nuns, if persons could be protected from the harmful effects of daily life stressors, such elevations of blood pressure commonly seen with aging might be preventable. The definitive study to test this hypothesis, however, would be difficult and time consuming— though immensely relevant to public health concerns.

Among the elderly, blood pressure may represent the most important of all cardiovascular risk factors (Gavras and Gavras, 1985). Hence, any effects that religious behaviors may have on blood pressure could easily be translated into lower mortality rates and deaths from cardiovascular and cerebrovascular disease.

Studies of rates of coronary artery disease have also examined religious influences in terms of broad categories of religious denomination. Where differences have been found, Catholics tend to have lower rates of CAD than Protestants or Jews (Wardwell et al., 1963; Ross and Thomas 1965; Yater et al., 1948). The provision and encouragement of regular confession and absolution from guilt has been presented as a means by which practicing Catholics might be protected from pent-up tensions and stresses that hasten the development of CAD.

Mortality rates, in general, have been shown to be significantly lower among church attenders (Berkman and Syme, 1979; House et al., 1982; Zuckerman et al., 1984; Comstock and Partridge, 1972; Wingard, 1982). Berkman found that individuals belonging to a church or temple have lower mortality rates than those who do not. This was true for both men and women. The effect on mortality, however, was not as great as that for other social contacts—i.e. spouse, relatives and friends (Berkman and Syme, 1979).

This section would be incomplete without mentioning the seminal work of Comstock and Partridge (1972), who reported on the effects of frequent church attendance on mortality rates from selected diseases in Washington County, Maryland. Among white males age forty-five to sixty-four dying from arteriosclerotic heart disease, frequent church attendance (once a week or more) was substantially lower than among a control group of 378 persons matched for race, sex, and age. The risk for frequent church attenders was only 60 percent of that for men who attended infrequently. For women, the relative risk of dying from arteriosclerotic heart disease among infrequent attenders (less than once per week) was over twice (2.1) that of frequent attenders. In the general population, rates of death from pulmonary emphysema (relative risk 2.3), cirrhosis (3.9), and suicide (2.1) were similarly higher among infrequent church attenders.

The lower mortality of persons involved in the religious community has, in general, been attributed to the ability of churches as "social networks" to provide social support for their members. As noted earlier, however, additional benefits from the "religious nature" of such activity have also been proposed. Zuckerman et al. (1984) investigated the effect of religiousness on mortality rates of four hundred elderly residents of New Haven, Connecticut. He measured religiousness by frequency of church attendance, self-assessed religiosity, and extent to which religion was a source of strength. Although all variables were significantly associated with lower mortality rates (especially among the elderly in poor health), strength from religion was the greatest predictor of low mortality—greater even than church attendance. He concluded that these findings made it unlikely that the benefits of religiousness were predominantly due to social contacts associated with church attendance. The results of this study are consistent with those that have investigated life satisfaction among elderly persons involved in religious versus nonreligious community organizations. As noted earlier, social activity in religious organizations was found to have a significantly greater impact on life satisfaction than did involvement in nonreligious groups (Edwards and Klemmack, 1973; Cutler, 1976; Pihlblad and Adams, 1972).

Recent studies, however, have challenged the hypothesis that religious community activity leads to better health. Levin and Markides (1986), studying a sample of older, predominantly Mexican-American Catholics in southern Texas, have reported that the well-established association between church attendance and physical health may be either partially or entirely accounted for by functional status. Examining the problem from a different perspective, Idler (1987) reported that the number of chronic health problems (physical health) accounted for much of the inverse relationship between group-related religious activity and physical disability (functional status). In other words, older people who are sick may not be capable of getting to church because of their low functional status and vice-versa; consequently, the positive correlation found between church attendance and health or functional status might be explained on these grounds, rather than by being attributed to favorable effects of church attendance itself on health.

Idler, however, found that even after controlling for chronic health problems in a regression model, public religious activity was still inversely related to disability (and depressive symptomatology), especially for women; Markides et al. (1987) likewise reported that the relationship between religious attendance and life satisfaction remained significant despite controlling for functional status. Idler further noted that over a quarter (98/358) of her sample's most severely disabled women reported a frequency of church attendance of once a week or more, and therefore concluded that disability did not entirely determine behavior.

Finally, caution should be advised in choosing a variable to measure functional status in studies that attempt to sort out its confounding influence on the complex relationship between church attendance and physical health. Levin and Markides (1976) measured functional status by self-assessment, utilizing the following question: "How much of the time does bad health, sickness, or pain stop you from doing things you would like to be doing?" This variable is not an objective measure of functional status or health, but mostly reflects how a person *perceives* their functional status (which already may include an impact from church attendance on this perception). In fact, Idler (1987) has reported that at a given level of chronic illness, frequent church attenders and those for whom religion was more of a comfort perceived their functional status as higher than infrequent attenders or those receiving less comfort from religion. Hence, future efforts utilizing objective measures of functional status (independent of self-perception) are needed to truly sort out the confounding influence of this variable on the church attendance-functional status-physical health relationship.

RELIGIOUS ACTIVITY AND PHYSICAL SYMPTOMS

In a longitudinal study of 133 elderly New York City residents, Cohen and colleagues (1985) have recently shown that social networks—through providing social support—exert a direct effect on reducing physical symptoms. They concluded that *intervention to reinforce a network can be as clinically significant as implementing a medical procedure*. For the elderly person, the church represents a powerful, pervasive, and accessible social network.

Hannay (1980) studied the relationship between religious alliance and mental, social, and physical symptoms among 926 adults in Glasgow, Scotland. Religious alliance was categorized as either active (taking part at least 1 time per month in a religious service or activity) or passive (less than 1 time per month). Among those with an active alliance, he found a decrease in number of mental symptoms (5.53 to 4.63, $p < .005$), social symptoms (.35 to .21, $p < .001$), and physical symptoms (1.24 to .90, $p < .001$), after controlling for age and sex. He concluded that "assurances of an active religion protect against instabilities of urban living" (p. 685).

Yates et al. (1981), in a prospective study of religious attitudes and activities among terminally ill elderly cancer patients, found that church attendance was significantly associated with lower levels of perceived pain; no signficant correlations were found between religious involvement and the actual presence or absence of pain or the time interval before death. The mechanism by which church attendance may lower the perception of pain is unclear. Perhaps the social support conveyed by such activity is the influential factor. This study did not examine the impact of nonreligious community activity on pain level, and leaves open the possibility that this effect represents that of increased social contact and activity in general. As noted previously, however, the high inverse correlation found between intensity of religious belief and pain level is not so easily explained by such reasoning, and suggests that the effect of frequent church attendance may originate at least in part from the religious nature of such activity. This finding, then, is consistent with studies noted earlier that found a more positive impact on mortality rates and life satisfaction for involvement in religious compared with nonreligious social groups.

RELIGIOUS ACTIVITIES AND
HEALTHCARE BEHAVIORS

With regard to the association between religious activities and health-related behaviors, several studies have reported church attenders to have a lower prevalence of self-destructive behaviors and to pay more attention to healthcare maintenance. Berkman et al. (1979), in the Alameda County Study, showed that the existence of social networks, such as those provided by religious institutions, was positively related to good health practices: no smoking, lower alcohol intake, better eating habits, regular exercise, and normal weight maintenance. They suggested that "social ties" might prevent disease by psychological processes that facilitate coping.

Cahalan et al. (1969) examined the drinking behavior of adults in a nationwide probability sample. Only 10 percent of frequent churchgoers were heavy drinkers, compared to 22 percent of nonchurchgoers. Participants included but were not restricted to the elderly. Naguib et al. (1968) have shown that both church membership and frequency of church attendance by middle-aged women were highly predictive of participation in a cervical cancer screening program. This finding suggests a possible correlation between medical compliance and degree of religious community involvement. American religious traditions, in general, emphasize the importance of caring for the physical body (Favazza, 1982), which represents the temple or dwelling place of God (Corinthians I, 3:17).

THE CHURCH AS A MEDIATING STRUCTURE

Levin and Idler (1981), in their book *The Hidden Health Care System*, describe the "mediating structures" in our society that act to buffer and cushion the individual from physiologic and psychologic consequences of exposure to the stressor situation. These mediating structures included the family, neighborhood and ethnic community, voluntary associations, and religious groups. They note that social epidemiologists have repeatedly found that the presence of close knit social groups in an individual's life has a strong beneficial effect on physical and mental health.

Approximately one-third of individuals over age sixty-five live alone; of these almost two-thirds are women (1980 U.S. Census). With age there often comes loss of family and friends through death or geographical relocation. This may leave the elderly person with a deteriorating social support system and a greater need to find a substitute support system in local community groups. Among voluntary social organizations in which the elderly participate, as noted earlier, religious institutions are by far the most common. Church affiliated groups are characterized by a greater degree of age homogeneity than is the case with other types of associations (Cutler, 1976); high concentrations of aged peers in a community, in turn, have been shown to be associated with significantly greater well-being (Bultena, 1974). Hence, for these reasons alone—independent of any beneficial impact from its religious nature—involvement in church-related activities would be expected to have a positive effect on mental health and well-being, and indirectly on certain aspects of physical health.

7

RELIGIOUS EXPERIENCE, MENTAL, AND PHYSICAL HEALTH

PREVALENCE OF RELIGIOUS EXPERIENCE

Religious experience is different from either religious belief, or religious activities or rituals. Stark and Glock (1970) define religious experience as constituting "occasions defined by those undergoing them as an encounter—some sense of contact—between themselves and supernatural consciousness" (p. 127). They further divided religious experience into four types: (1) Confirming experience—where a person feels or senses the existence or presence of a Supreme Being, yet that Being is not perceived as specifically acknowledging the person in return, (2) Responsive experience—where the Supreme Being specifically notes and responds to the person (i.e. answer to prayer), (3) Ecstatic experience—where a relationship characterized by love or friendship is experienced between a person and the Supreme Being, and (4) Revelational experience—a person perceives himself or herself as being a confidant or fellow participant in action with the Supreme Being.

How does aging affect the likelihood of having religious experience? In a review of research on the experiential dimension, Moberg (1970) notes that religious feelings in the later years have seldom been studied systematically, resulting in a dearth of empirical data on the subject. Nevertheless, some researchers have demonstrated that religion "means more" to most people as they grow older (Jeffers and Nichols, 1961; Moberg, 1965). Swenson reported that the highest proportion of people who had experienced unusual religious experiences were age seventy and older (more time over which to accumulate such experiences?). This group more often also reported feeling very religious than younger individuals (Swenson, 1961). Stark (1968), studying a sample of 2,771 Americans of all ages, found the tendency to have religious experiences did not increase with age except among conservative Protestant groups. He hypothesized that, among conservative Protestants whose churches maintained organized social situations aimed at producing such religious encounters, the proportion of people who "succeed" in fulfilling this expectation rises with age. Bowman (1982) measured change in twelve areas of spiritual and religious awareness in one hundred elderly people in the north central United States. The highest reported change in awareness, compared to earlier years, was an increase in "feelings of experiencing God's closeness;" although no one reported decreased awareness, most subjects reported no change.

Hence, the evidence suggests that except among more fundamentalist, conservative Protestant groups, the frequency of religious experience remains relatively stable with aging; however, the experience of closeness to God may increase.

The "Born Again" or Conversion Experience

In 1976, a Gallup survey's results were printed in *Newsweek* (October 25, 1976) as the cover and lead article entitled "Born Again." Nearly a third of the United States population or more than fifty million Americans were reported to have had a significant religious experience. A more recent survey by the Gallup organization (Princeton Religion Research Center, 1982) has revealed that as many as 40 percent of Americans age sixty-five or older consider themselves "born again." In a study of 304 senior center participants (mean age 75) in seven small midwestern communities (Missouri), Koenig and Blake (1986) reported that 64 percent considered themselves "born again." Use of religious beliefs and prayer during stress, and religious community activity was particularly high in this subgroup.

What percentage of people have conversion experiences in their later years, i.e., over age fifty? We are aware of no study that has examined precisely this question. There are some data available on what percentage of older adults experience a change of faith. In a 1985 national Gallup survey of 1042 adults (Princeton Religion Research Center, 1986), the following question was asked: "About how old were you when your faith changed significantly?" Thirty-nine percent of this sample was over age fifty. Eight percent (20% of those over age 50) noted a significant change in faith in the later years.

One might argue rightly that a "significant change" in faith is not the same as a conversion experience; however, over 80 percent of the respondents in the above study did note that the change in faith was a positive one that strengthened their religious beliefs and made them more meaningful. In any event, it appears that by the time people reach their later years, the majority have already had a change of faith, and significant changes in faith at this time in life are probably not common. The latter statement, however, is made with a great deal of uncertainty in the face of little data. Changes in faith that occur when older persons are severely ill or at their deathbed would be very difficult to measure, and could dramatically alter the hypotheses noted above. Recall that the Gallup surveys in general do not include such persons, but rather the community-dwelling elderly who are in reasonably good health. On-going studies to examine this question are being done in the southeastern United States and need to be initiated in other geographical locations as well (especially the west and northeast).

To what extent do older persons have religious experience in their daily lives on a regular basis (as opposed to a significant single experience that changes their faith)? Koenig et al. (1988a), in their survey of older adults seeking medical care, reported that over half (51.1%) of their patients noted "definitely true" to the statement: "In my life, I experience the presence of the Divine (that is, God)." Responses given to this question by senior center participants in three different midwestern states were comparable to those reported by geriatric clinic patients (central Illinois, 53.4%; eastern Iowa, 43.7%; central Missouri, 60.0%) (Koenig, unpublished data). Note that the general health of both the geriatric clinic patients and senior center participants was similar (44% and 48%, respectively, claiming relatively poor health). These findings suggest that a majority of older adults have ongoing religious experiences in their daily life, even if they do not have a major religious experience that suddenly changes their faith at this time.

Religious Experience and Mental Health

Does religious experience have a positive or negative effect on mental health in older adults? The data available on this subject, again, are fragmentary, and much of what is available has been acquired from nonelderly samples. William James (1902) described the benefits of the salvational experience as conferring a decreased sense of worry, a sense of greater understanding, and a fresher, more positive view of the world. Psychiatrists, however, have viewed these changes with mixed feelings. Some have looked upon them as being pathological (*Bibliography on Religion and Mental Health 1960–1964, 1967*), while others have observed that such experiences can be an asset in psychotherapy (Pattison, 1965; Griffith, Young, and Smith, 1984; Griffith, English, and Mayfield, 1980; Galanter and Buckley, 1978).

W. P. Wilson (1972) (professor of psychiatry at the Duke University and Durham VA Medical Centers), studied the effects of religious experience on sixty-three subjects—a sample including, but not restricted to older persons. He found that strong religious experience ("salvation" or "conversion") altered both the affective state and the behavior of these individuals to the degree that they became more beneficial to family, friends, and community. The changes brought about by these experiences were remarkably stable and had lasted an average of eleven years (range 2 to 56) at the time the participants were interviewed.

Yale psychiatrists, Griffith, Young, and Smith (1984) examined the effects of religious experiences such as "possession," "testimony," "dancing," and "speaking in tongues" among twenty members of an urban black church during a Wednesday night church service. Elderly subjects were included in the group examined. These investigators concluded that participants' responses corresponded to several curative factors associated with group psychotherapy, and suggested that the church service was functioning as a community mental health resource for its participants. The latter findings confirmed earlier work done by these investigators with regard to the therapeutic effects of religious experience on mental health (Griffith, English, and Mayfield, 1980). Pattison (1965) had also observed that religious faith could be an asset to psychotherapy and that certain mystical religious experiences could benefit individuals in terms of personality growth.

Unpublished data from the Koenig and Blake (1986) study of religious practices of senior center participants in central Missouri, reveals a significant association between life satisfaction and being "born again" (p value for $X^2 < .05$) among senior center participants (N = 217). Life satisfaction in that study was measured by a two-item index consisting of questions about life satisfaction now and life satisfaction over one's life-span. Older persons who considered themselves born again were much more likely to use religion and prayer during times of stress (p value for $X^2 < .005$), and to be involved in religious community activities (p value for $X^2 = .01$). These findings suggest that persons who experience religious conversion or consider themselves "born again" have integrated their beliefs more fully into their daily lives and generally claim high life satisfaction.

Although the long-term effects of religious conversion appear to be beneficial, the period immediately surrounding the religious experience may be one of psychological instability, particularly when occurring in the setting of mental illness. Cavenar and Spaulding (1977) note that in their clinical experience as psychiatrists practicing in the Bible Belt region of the United States (Durham, N.C.), they were impressed by the frequent association between religious experiences and depressive disorders. They presented four cases, two of whom were men ages fifty and fifty-three with major depressive disorders, who reported dramatic religious experiences followed by the immediate resolution of depressive symptoms. Both of these men soon relapsed into depression and consequently committed suicide. The two other cases presented were a man age thirty-three and a woman age forty-three who also had major depression and a religious experience that was immediately accompanied by resolution of depressive symptoms. No relapse, however, was evident, and depressive symptoms had not returned by four months to three years of followup. Cavenar and Spaulding noted that in depressions with hysterical components, religious conversion helped to strengthen repression, a psychodynamically favorable effect. With depression occuring in the obsessive-compulsive personality, however, repression does not facilitate healthy psychodynamic processes, but simply leads to the denial of the depression, which may be quickly overcome once the initial thrill of the religious experience has passed. They encouraged careful followup of patients with depression and obsessive-compulsive personality traits who have religious experiences.

In an empirical study, Gallemore et al. (1969) examined the prevalence of religious experience among a sample of sixty-two depressed psychiatric patients compared with forty controls. Thirty-two percent of the patient group was over forty years of age. Only 20 percent of the control group, compared with 52 percent of the patient group, reported having had a religious conversion experience. They observed that many patients with affective disorders have a basic personality trait of "increased affective responsiveness" that may both predispose them to depressive disorders and confer upon them a sensitivity to experience religious phenomena (W. P. Wilson et al., 1969).

Besides the association with spontaneous resolution of depressive symptoms, religious conversion has also been related to the cessation of drinking among alcoholics (Larson and Wilson, 1980). Prior to Alcoholics Anonymous, 28 percent of alcoholics died prematurely from this disease, 51 percent drank the rest of their lives, and 31 percent recovered. Of those recovering, 35 percent did so spontaneously, and 23 percent as a consequence of a religious experience (Lamere, 1953). The dismal future of alcoholics has changed substantially since the appearance of Alcoholics Anonymous. Much of the latter group's success, in fact, has been related to the spiritual dimension that is central to its twelve steps to recovery (B. Wilson, 1968).

With regard to schizophrenia, W. P. Wilson et al. (1983) examined the early life of a group of seventy-two psychiatric inpatients with this diagnosis compared with 104 controls. They found that the early home lives of such patients were often characterized as having a limited religious emphasis that was often based on obligation and threat, with less paternal religious commitment and participation. They also report that the schizophrenic seldom indulged in personal religious practice.

There have also been reports of religiously mediated changes in sexual orientation among homosexuals as a result of religious experience. Although once again most studies have examined this issue only among younger individuals, it is well known that there are a significant number of older homosexuals. It is likely that this proportion will grow as our society ages. Pattison and Pattison (1980), reviewing the records of a Pentecostal church-sponsored crisis program over a five year period, identified thirty cases of individuals who claimed to have a change in sexual orientation from homosexuality to heterosexuality. Of these thirty cases, the investigators personally interviewed eleven cases and confirmed a definite change in sexual orientation to heterosexuality among these cases. Self-identified change to homosexuality occurred at the mean age of eleven and the change back to heterosexuality occurred at a mean age of twenty-three. As homosexual identity becomes fixed with aging, however, change may become progressively more difficult. Pattison and Pattison concluded that "change has occurred through significant longitudinal experiences in 'folk therapy' provided within a supernatural framework and utilizing generic methods of change common to folk therapy" (P. 1562). This is the only empirical study that we are aware of that has examined this issue.

Religious experience, in some circumstances, has been linked with psychiatric illness. Galanter (1982) discusses psychopathology among members of religious sects such as Divine Light Mission, Hare Krishna, Unification Church, Soka Gakkai, Devotees of Baba, the Subud, and Erhard Seminars Training (EST) groups. There is clearly a need to carefully consider the particular religious group that a person is a member of before concluding it has either psychotherapeutic or psychopathologic influences. Most older adults find their religious experiences in the context of traditional, conservative Judeo-Christian groups that have little similarity to the religious sects considered by Galanter.

Religious experience, then, appears to be common among older adults. Although most research concerning the effect of such experience on mental health has not concentrated on older age groups, they have included elderly persons. In general, religious experience in the context of well-established religious traditions—particularly among Judeo-Christian groups—may serve a psychotherapeutic function, and for some individuals, results in a new, positive outlook on life. For the older person bearing the burden of chronic illness and struggling with losses over which he or she may have little or no control, religious experience in a closely knit social group of supportive age-matched peers might be quite positive. No systematic studies have yet addressed this issue, however, and caution must be exercised in extrapolating findings in one age group to another.

Religious Experience and Physical Health

With regard to religious experience and its effects on physical health, even less data are available. Anecdotal reports of faith healings have commonly been described in religious literature. Kelsey (1973), in his book *Healing and Christianity*, remarks that more than any other world religion, the Judeo-Christian tradition places value on the physical body and human relationships, giving it the potential to deal most fully with problems of illness. The most famous of all healing shrines is at Lourdes in southern France. The Catholic church maintains a "rigorously scientific" medical bureau at the shrine that has certified only approximately fifty cases as genuine "miracles" over the 130 years (Cranston, 1955). Of interest here is the nature of the illnesses that are reported to be healed through religious methods. Most of the healings noted in Kuhlman's book, *I Believe in Miracles* (1962), tended to be *chronic illnesses* (Braden, 1954). Although these reports are intriguing, medical documentation of such healings has not been performed in any long-term, systematic fashion to substantiate such claims (except at Lourdes).

Whether or not scientific proof exists for such healings, personal testimonies have been abundant. A significant proportion of the older Americans, at least those dwelling in the south, report to have experienced divine healings of physical problems. Johnson et al. (1986) surveyed a random sample of 586 adults (37% over 50 years of age) in Richmond, VA, asking them the following question: "Have you ever experienced a healing of a serious disease or physical condition that you believed resulted from prayer or considered to be a divine healing?" Fourteen percent of the sample answered yes to this question. Participants age fifty and over were significantly more likely than those under fifty to report a healing (19% vs. 11%), particularly those who were physically ill.

PRAYER AND HEALING

Where positive effects of prayer on the course of physical and mental illness have been observed, scientists have generally explained these effects to be mediated by psychological mechanisms. For instance, such activity might enhance adjustment and coping with stress that could reduce anxiety and emotional strain adversely impacting on health. A few bold investigators, however, have examined the possibility that prayer might have a direct effect—presumably supernaturally mediated—on physical illness. In 1883, Francis Galton stated the following:

It is asserted by some, that men possess the faculty of obtaining results over which they have little or no direct personal control, by means of devout and earnest prayer, while others doubt the truth of this assertion. The question regards a matter of fact, that has to be determined by observation and not by authority; and it is one that appears to be a very suitable topic for statistical inquiry . . . Are prayers answered or are they not . . . Do sick persons who pray or are prayed for, recover on the average more rapidly than others? (P. 277)

Most of the investigations thus far reported have methodological problems that are difficult if not impossible to overcome in studying such phenomena. Although we are aware of no such study that has conclusively demonstrated a direct effect of prayer on physical health in younger or older medically ill patients, we will review the studies that have attempted to examine this issue.

Joyce and Welldon (1965) examined the efficacy of prayer in 38 patients suffering from chronic stable or progressive, psychological or rheumatic disease in two outpatient clinics in the London Hospital (twenty patients over age 50). Patients were matched in pairs by day of initial clinic visit, sex, age, and primary clinical diagnosis. Half of these nineteen pairs of patients were also matched by marital status and religious faith. One of each pair of patients was assigned to the "treatment" or "placebo" group by means of a coin toss (random assignment). Neither patient nor examining physician was aware of who was being prayed for (double-blind). Information about each patient receiving "treatment" (patient identity concealed) was sent to the leader of a prayer group. These groups were each composed of one to five members. Every two weeks, for up to an hour each time, these groups prayed for the patients. At the end of six months, patients were reexamined by their treating physician for any change in their condition. The power of the study was such that a change in patient condition by 13 to 56 percent could have been detected. Of the thirty-two patients (16 pairs) who completed the trial, the condition of twenty-six remained unchanged. Six persons showed improvement, of whom five were in the treatment group and one in the control. Though suggestive, this result was not statistically significant.

The next scientific examination of the efficacy of prayer in a clinical trial was that of Collipp (1969), who studied this phenomenon among children with terminal cancer and their families. Although his study deals with pediatric patients and does not belong in a book on religion, health, and aging, it is one of the few objective studies of the consequences of prayer. The names of ten of eighteen patients with leukemia were selected "randomly" (method not described) and sent to prayer groups who prayed for them daily. Of ten children with leukemia in the prayer group, seven were still alive after fifteen months of prayer; of the eight children in the control group, only two were alive. Again, these results were not statistically significant, though suggestive. The rigor of the design of this clinical trial is highly debatable. Furthermore, the power of this study, given the sample size, to detect a difference was probably inadequate.

The final and last study of this nature (that we are aware of) is that of Dr. Byrd. Byrd (1986) conducted a double-blind, randomized trial of 393 coronary care unit patients at San Francisco General Hospital examining the efficacy of prayer. Prayer groups (5 to 7 persons each) were arranged for the 192 patients randomized to the "treatment" group. The study was conducted over a ten month period while Byrd was assistant professor of medicine at the University of California at San Francisco and a staff cardiologist at San Francisco General Hospital. Few other details are available in this brief report. At the time of this writing, the study had not yet been published in a peer-review scientific journal. The results, however, were nothing short of remarkable. Only three of the "treated" compared with eighteen of the "control" patients required antibiotics. Only six of the treated and eighteen of the control suffered from pulmonary edema. None of the treated and twelve of the control group had to be intubated (a breathing tube placed into the lungs to provide artificial respiration).

These three studies have been included to underscore the importance and possible effects on health of the religious beliefs and experience of a significant number of older adults, particularly those of the more conservative and evangelical traditions. Although scientific investigations have yet to "prove" that prayer works, it would be hard to convince many religious older adults otherwise. Conventional wisdom would suggest that the strength of these beliefs (often undergirded by religious experience), and the tenacity to which such beliefs are held, might have a considerable impact on health and healthcare behaviors, in one way or another.

8

RELIGION AND A SOCIAL STRESS MODEL

In order to make sense of the diverse research concerning religion, mental health, and physical illness in old age, we have modified the social stress model of House (1974) to include the influence of religion and other factors. The reader will recall Figure 1 from the introductory chapter of this book. With this model, we hypothesize how religious beliefs, activities, and experience might confer to older people a greater adaptive capacity when facing the stressful changes associated with aging. This assumes a direction of causation with regard to religiosity and successful coping, which has only weak empirical support. We hypothesize that religion acts directly at a variety of points in this schema to cushion the impact of social, psychological, and biological stressors. The evidence upon which this hypothesis is based comes from results of cross-sectional studies that are for the most part supported by longitudinal work as well. We recognize that other intervening variables may exist in the various pathways and would have the reader consider this only as a crude working model requiring refinement by future research.

Heredity, personality, and life experience are three vital internal personal resources (or liabilities) that the older person must carry with him or her into every stressful experience. All people are born with certain innate characteristics that are determined primarily by their genetic makeup. This may include the level of sensitivity and reactivity to internal and external changes. For example, persons who become depressed easily may have a biological makeup that causes them to be hypersensitive and easily disturbed by stress (an exaggerated "affective responsiveness") (Gallemore, Wilson, and Rhoads, 1969). There is much debate on whether this increased sensitivity is strictly due to hereditary factors or is also influenced by environmental factors such as early childhood experience. Personality influences, which arise from a mixture of heredity factors and rearing practices, are also important in determining how a person will react to a given stressful event. The hard-driving, volatile person may experience greater stress from an event that disrupts their goals or directions than a more relaxed personality that takes things a day at a time. Life experience is another important factor in determining the effectiveness and rate of adaptation to stressors. The older person today has likely lived through the Great Depression, at least one World War, and has had to deal with numerous disappointments and losses throughout life. The degree of exposure to difficulties in their earlier years and the types of and success of adaptive strategies mobilized to deal with these experiences may determine to a great extent how well these persons cope in the later years.

External personal resources are also vital in determining how the older person will react to stressors in old age (George, 1980). Health, financial comfort, and social support have been shown to be major determinants of well-being in the later years (Larson, 1978). Health and financial security are important factors in enabling older persons to be in control of their environment and to maximize their autonomy. Health provides the vital physical energy and capacity to act on and change their external environment and direct their course in the way they themselves choose to go. Ill health and disability leave the older person at the mercy of their environment and dependent on others upon whom they must rely to fill their needs. Financial security represents power over external circumstances and conveys the ability to control others so that one's needs are met in the way one desires. Social support provides meaningful contact with others who may share the burdens and trials of life. Relatives and friends help to prevent loneliness, provide love, and give the older person a chance to love others. Besides emotional support, the complexity of one's social network also determines the availability of practical assistance during times of physical illness or financial strain.

Therefore, as one or the other of these three resources diminishes (illness, poverty, desertion), the other resources take up the slack to enable a person to successfully adapt to and remain in control of circumstances.

Finally, people employ coping behaviors to deal with stressful events or unpleasant circumstances. As discussed in the introductory chapter, coping may be defined as "strategies to deal with a threat" (Lazarus, 1966), and these behaviors may be either instrumental or palliative in nature. Instrumental strategies are aimed at changing the external circumstances, while palliative strategies focus on controlling emotional reactions to stressful events. Both instrumental and palliative strategies may be external and action oriented *or* intrapsychic and cognitive in nature. For example, if someone is fired from their job, they may employ the instrumental, action-oriented strategy of searching for another job. On the other hand, they may attempt to control the disappointment and emotional pain by palliative, intrapsychic strategies, such as focusing their attention on the more positive aspects of their life or comparing themselves to others who are worse off. Note that coping behaviors are closely related to both internal resources (personality, life experience) and external resources (health, financial comfort, and social support), and often may be chosen on the basis of what has worked in the past.

Coping strategies, personal resources, hereditary factors, and life experience, then, interact to determine how well an older person will adapt to stressful life changes. External and internal resources, however, may be difficult to control in later life. While health can be optomized by healthy lifestyles at earlier ages, financial security sought by careful planning, and friendships and social networks developed and maintained throughout life, major life events often strip a person of these resources and leave them at the mercy of their environment. Internal resources such as personality and life experience are even less easily controlled or planned for. Of all factors influencing successful adaptation in later life, the ability to choose and successfully implement coping strategies may be very powerful and, most importantly, under the control of the individual. Intrapsychic coping behaviors that alter the preception of stressful events may be particularly free of the restraining influences of health, wealth, and social support, and may either support or counteract personality factors and prior life experiences. Intrapsychic or palliative coping strategies may be especially relevant for the older person, particularly the individual with health problems who may have little other means of achieving control over his or her situation.

How does religion fit into all this? Religious beliefs, activities, and experience (RBAE) may have their impact at several different points in the model, acting as both internal and external resources and as a distinct intrapsychic, cognitively oriented coping strategy. First, RBAE may act as "conditioning variables."

House (1974) defined conditioning variables as those individual and situational factors that specify the relationships among the four major variables in his original social stress model:

1. The *objective* social [and physical, psychological, or spiritual] conditions conducive to stress

2. The individual's *perceptions* of the stressor
3. Individual *responses* [intrapsychic and behavioral] to the stress [coping strategies]
4. *Outcomes* of perceived stress and responses to that stress [personal well-being, health]

George (1980) includes among conditioning variables the following items: external personal resources (health, finances, education, social support), social status variables (sex, age, race, social class, cultural factors), and internal personal resources such as personality traits relevant to coping, and socializing experiences (including anticipatory socialization). With regard to their role as conditioning variables, RBAE may: (1) serve as external resources enhancing social support, health, and financial security, and (2) act on and with internal personal resources by providing for socializing experiences in preparation for stressful life changes, and by influencing personality traits relevant to coping.

Other than as a conditioning variables, RBAE may also serve as specific coping strategies acting through intrapsychic mechanisms directly on the preception and meaning of the stressor. Religion's role as a conditioning variable and its action as a coping strategy will now be discussed.

RELIGION AS AN EXTERNAL RESOURCE

Social Support

By providing the older person with a source of social interaction among age-matched peers, religious organizations might serve as a readily available means of both social and material support, especially for those older adults without family members. Interaction with other people sharing a similar perspective on the purpose and meaning of life may further serve to strenghten religious belief and faith, and consequently enhance the comfort and reassurance derived from them. In turn, religious beliefs might encourage a greater degree of social participation and voluntary activity that would serve to enhance the local community, provide the older person with feelings of usefulness, and heighten their self-esteem. Religious beliefs further provide structural guidelines for dealing with life transitions (i.e. death, bereavement, illness), and religious organizations uniformly provide rituals for cushioning the stressful effects of such changes.

Financial Security

RBAE may impact on both actual and perceived financial security. A guiding principle undergirding the Judeo-Christian religious tradition is the need to be concerned about the physical needs of others less fortunate. In some religious communities this may in effect lead to moderation of financial extremes as the wealthy help provide for the poor. Although still a generally unrealized ideal, this principle has found practical application in Shepherds Centers, where physically and financially advantaged older persons assist their more needy elderly peers in the community (Koenig, 1986; Koenig 1987c). A second impact for religion in this area may be on the perception of financial security. Although no data exist on this subject at present, one might speculate that a religion that teaches its members to place their security in a God who promises to provide for both spiritual and physical needs, might breed in its members feelings of greater contentment and less worry concerning financial matters. Hence, regardless of actual financial assets, the older person with a strong religious faith may be more likely to perceive their situation as secure.

Health

RBAE may also have direct and indirect benefits on physical and mental health. We have seen that smoking, alcohol consumption, and drug use are much less common among religiously-oriented individuals. Many of the physical illnesses of later life are self-inflicted. Medical researchers are finding fewer and fewer diseases that can be exclusively attributed to aging. People themselves play a vital role in maintaining the condition of their bodies in the later years. Religious attitudes that regard the body as the "temple of the soul" motivate persons not to abuse their body, but rather to maintain their health and seek medical attention when appropriate. The close social networks associated with religious organizations may often prompt its members to seek medical attention and/or refer such individuals to appropriate resources in the community. The isolated older person with little social interaction may have limited feedback from concerned others regarding the meaning of physical symptoms and what is best to do about them.

Finally, religion, through its impact as a coping strategy, may allow for greater well-being and emotional adjustment, which could protect against stress-related diseases that have a devastating impact on health in later life (athersclerotic cardiovascular disease, suppression of immunity, gastrointestinal diseases, etc.). Hence, religion as an external resource may impact through multiple avenues on health.

RELIGION AS AN INTERNAL RESOURCE

Socializing Experiences

Religious organizations, guided by their belief systems, supply a common world view for members that may prepare them for major life changes when they occur. In this sense, religion emphasizes anticipatory socialization. For instance, an older person may have spent the greater part of their life as a member of a religious congregation that teaches certain attitudes and ways of coping with stressful situations. This person may also have utilized these religious behaviors successfully to cope with problems in the past. Furthermore, they may have observed close friends in their congregation who successfully use these behaviors during stress. Additional encouragement and support may come from respected leaders of their religious community. Religious literature may provide persons to model appropriate responses after in different stressful settings, as well as provide time-tested advice and encouragement during these trials. Hence, when stressful life changes occur, the religiously-oriented older person has a readily available and well-rehearsed set of behaviors that have the support of their culture and social group.

Personality Traits

Religious beliefs and involvement in religious activities may also serve to encourage or discourage personality traits relevant to coping. Religion may reinforce more extroverted personality traits directed towards interacting with and assisting others in need, and may discourage self-centeredness and a tendency toward isolation. Religious beliefs may foster attitudes of care and concern that have high value in social interactions. The religious community, acting as a social reinforcer, may further assist in molding personality traits and establishing acceptable and unacceptable coping behaviors that minimize self-destructive tendencies such as suicide or alcohol abuse, and maximize problem solving behaviors through reflection (prayer) and counseling (with clergy).

RELIGION AS A SPECIFIC COPING STRATEGY

The second point at which RBAE may act in the stress model is as a specific coping strategy in response to the perceived stressor. As noted earlier, people may respond to a stressor by either altering their perception of stress through cognitive processes such as appraisal, or through active behavioral efforts aimed at altering the stressful situation or the emotional response to it. As noted earlier, Lazarus and colleagues (1966, 1974) have written extensively on the importance of intrapsychic processes as integral to the stress experience.

Religious beliefs, and attitudes toward life that proceed from these beliefs, are *intrapsychic processes* that have the potential to alter the impact of a stressful event. Such cognitions could change the meaning of the event to the individual, and thereby make it less threatening and stress producing. For instance, if an independent older woman with arthritis falls and fractures her hip, the meaning of this event could be devastating: severe pain, the risks of surgery, hospital bills, prolonged recovery and bedrest, loss of independence, possible nursing home placement, and becoming a burden on family. In situations where finances are tight, other health problems intervene, or there are few family or friends to turn to for support, the meaning of an event like a hip fracture could bode a turbulent course ending in death or prolonged suffering and loss of control. With nothing else to sustain this person, hope in the future and desire for living might quickly disintegrate, providing fertile soil for the development of depression and lack of motivation towards recovery. The meaning of this event might be entirely different for the person with a strong religious faith. Because of their belief and trust in a God who knows about and is concerned with their situation, is in full control of what happens, and is responsive to their prayers, such a person might perceive the consequences of the event as less threatening. This person might also perceive himself or herself to be in greater control of the situation because of the relationship with God, whom that person believes is in control.

The senior author (HGK) has had frequent experiences with older patients, who in just such circumstances, conveyed to him that they had placed themselves entirely in the hands of God and had given over to Him control of their situation (see Chapter 9, Case Studies). This action reportedly resulted in a considerable lessening of worry and an enhanced feeling that the situation was under control. In Chapter 3, recall the review of studies examining the coping behaviors of older persons with medical illness; intrapsychic processes such as faith and trust in God and prayer were the most common religious coping strategies reported. This research supports the powerful effect that religious faith can have on maintaining older adults through stressful life experiences.

At the level of *behavioral responses* to stress, the religious older person may seek guidance from their clergy, fellow church members, or religious literature, or intuitively through prayer, as a means of problem solving. Religious literature, such as the Bible, may provide practical, culturally-based solutions for a number of stressful life situations. Prayer, though an intrapsychic phenomenon, may represent a behavior that can be practiced with others in a supportive social setting or may be performed in private. For those with strong religious faith, prayer may counteract a sense of loneliness and helplessness during times of severe emotional stress. The strength of religious belief is almost certain to have an impact on the degree of comfort and reassurance received from such activity. In addition to providing the comfort noted above, prayer may serve to interrupt a destructive preoccupation with a problem. It may provide distance from a situation and thus allow problem solving to take place that otherwise would have been prevented by the overwhelming stress of the moment.

With regard to religious community activity, the older person may cope with stress by increasing their level of involvement in volunteer work at church or in church-sponsored activities in the community. In this way, he or she may avoid preoccupation with his or her own problems, and thereby prevent an exaggerated stress response that might result in a loss of perspective. Hence, energies may be redirected in a constructive rather than destructive fashion. Involvement in the religious community might also provide a social setting in which the older person could come into contact with others who have undergone similar stressful experiences and successfully survived. There may be a sharing of effective coping strategies. Bereavement is an example of a stressful situation in which religious belief, activity, and experience may have a particularly salient effect through the mechanisms noted above (see previously cited research in Chapter 5).

Hence, religious belief, activity, and experience may moderate the effects of stressors by functioning as conditioning variables, and may directly impact on coping through intrapsychic and behavioral responses that alter the perception of the stressor. By their buffering influence on the stress experience, RBAE could serve to enhance personal well-being through facilitating social and psychological adjustment to stress, and as a consequence, possibly decrease the occurrence of psychophysiologically-mediated illness. As noted earlier, empirical data supporting this hypothesis is scant, and verification will depend on well-designed longitudinal studies. The above model interrelates the concepts of stressful life change, the perception of and response to stress, and individual outcomes (personal well-being and health), with a possible function of religion in the lives of older adults.

FINAL COMMENT

The older person is often subject to a large number of life changes. These changes are likely to involve losses associated with stress and anxiety. This excess stress may have an adverse impact on their physical and emotional health. Although some investigators have claimed that the impact of a given stressor on the health of the older person is less intense than that on the health of a younger person (Marsh and Thompson, 1977; R. Wilson and Maddox, 1974; Rosenman and Friedman, 1974), others have found the opposite to be true (Marsh and Thompson, 1977). Riley and Foner found that such events as sudden health changes, financial insolvency, and local neighborhood transition are more precarious in later life than at any other time (Riley and Foner, 1968). Blazer supports this notion in observing that the elderly may be more susceptible to the deleterious effects of the psychosocial environment because of a diminution of perceptual and other adaptive capacities; hence, smaller environmental changes would be required to produce a change in health status (Blazer, 1982b). The impact of religion, even if this confers only a small advantage in adaptive capacity, might yield a significant effect on the older person's mental and physical health.

9

CASE STUDIES

In my (HGK) clinical and research experience in geriatric medicine, I have come into contact with large numbers of older persons, both in the hospital and the office setting, who struggle to cope with a heavy burden of chronic illness and disability. This work has taken me into the nursing home, the acute care hospital, rehabilitation settings, and into the homes of many patients.

In the following section, I will describe cases where I perceived, and patients reported, religion to have an impact on physical or emotional health. Patients' names have been changed to fictitious ones. Where enough information is included so that true identity might be revealed, written consent from the patient was obtained. The impact of religion on health and well-being has taken a variety of forms and includes influences on the perception of illness, on the course and outcome of disease, on the ability to cope with ill-health and disability, on attitudes toward death, on the healing of estranged family relations, and on the doctor-patient relationship itself. Accompanying each case will be a short discussion of its implications.

CASE #1

Mrs. Jones is an eighty-one year old woman who was admitted to the hospital with terminal cancer. She had been living independently in the community, with the help of a home-health nurse. Recently, her illness had taken a turn for the worse, and she was told by doctors that it was only a matter of time before death would ensue. Mrs. Jones had a daughter and a son whom she had neither seen nor spoken to for nearly fifteen years (the result of an unresolvable disagreement). They both came to see her in the hospital, but Mrs. Jones refused to see them. She angrily stated that she wanted to die in peace, and that she had nothing to say to her family. Over the weeks of her hospitalization, Mrs. Jones was noted to become progressively more depressed, but remained adamant about not seeing her children. There were problems between the daughter and the son as well. Their relationship was a distant one with little communication taking place since the original family breakup fifteen years before. They made every effort to avoid one another when visiting their mother at the hospital. Both children desired very much to talk with her in order to resolve the bitterness between them before her death.

A minister was called upon by the nursing staff to have a talk with Mrs. Jones. He came regularly to the hospital to pray with her, and over a several week period, established a relationship with her. In addition to praying with her, he read the scriptures from John I concerning God's love for her. The minister had also begun to communicate with her children, and knew of their desire to make amends with their mother. He began to pray with Mrs. Jones for forgiveness, forgiveness for herself and for her children. Finally, she broke down and cried, admitting how much she really loved her family. She agreed to see her children and they were brought up to her room. Their meeting at first was an awkward one, with everyone standing around stiffly, avoiding eye contact with one another. The minister led everyone in a prayer, and then encouraged each person to pray aloud to God whatever was on their mind. After each had prayed, the children asked forgiveness from their mother and then from each other. Crying and hugging soon ensued and the family was reconciled. After that event, the children made regular visits to see their mother, and amazingly enough, Mrs. Jones became stronger and stronger both physically and mentally. She was eventually discharged from the hospital to live at home for her remaining days.

This is one of several cases where religion has assisted in family reconciliations near the time of death. It is, however, the only case that I have come into contact with where the patient actually improved physically after the reunion. Pent up anger, bitterness, and lack of forgiveness can result in a state of hypercortisolism that might suppress the immune system sufficiently to allow an immunologically-controlled disease to flare. The relationship between depression and immunosuppression has been well-established (Editorial, 1987), and psychosocial approaches have been shown to enhance immunocompetence in several studies (Kiecolt-Glasser et al., 1985; Dillon et al., 1985).

CASE #2

Mrs. Smith was a ninety-two year old Caucasian woman who lived with her fifty-six year old daughter. She came to see me because of weight loss, dizziness, and complaints of constipation. We admitted her to the hospital to determine the cause of her symptoms. While in the hospital, I frequently found her straining to read her large print Bible through the haze of her cataracts. She often talked quite openly about her faith in the Lord to protect her and care for her.

During our medical evaluation, a large mass in her rectum was identified by the CAT scan. The radiologist felt sure that this mass represented a malignant tumor and recommended that we examine the mass directly with a proctoscope and obtain a biopsy. Mrs. Smith, with her advanced age, weight loss, and constipation, was an ideal candidate for colon cancer, and we were not at all surprised at the radiologist's suspicions. Prior to the proctoscopy, I talked with her about the probable diagnosis. She took the news very calmly, asked appropriate questions, and said something about God's will. When I came to see her the next morning, her pastor and assistant pastor were at her bedside, praying for her healing. She again displayed remarkable calmness and poise as we prepared her for the exam.

The proctoscopic examination was performed uneventfully. Despite a well-prepped colon and excellent visualization, we could not locate the lesion seen on CT scan. The radiologist, sure of his prior findings, suggested a repeat CT scan. Consequently, this was done and the mass that had been seen previously was no longer present. I asked the radiologist whether the mass he had identified earlier might have been stool in her colon. He reported that there was very little chance of that, given the characteristics of the lesion and multiple cuts that were taken by the scanner. On returning to her room, I reported the news. She was understandably elated and sincerely believed that the Lord had healed her in response to prayer.

I cared for her for another six months before leaving the area to take a position in another city. She had no further problems (of this nature) during that time. Her weight stabilized, the dizziness resolved, and the constipation improved with bowel softeners. During our monthly housecalls, I would invariably find her sitting by the window reading her Bible.

Regardless of whether or not this represented a case of a "miracle" cure, Mrs. Smith was grateful and happy over what *she* believed was the response of her ever-present Lord to prayer. This further reinforced her faith and infused her life with meaning and significance. Her strong faith at the time of the initial diagnosis enabled her to accept the possibly fatal condition with only minimal distress. This faith was strengthened by her pastors being at her bedside in a timely fashion.

CASE #3

Mr. Thomas was a fifty-seven year old black man with pancreatic cancer. I cared for him during his stay on the hospice unit of our rehabilitation center. He was fully alert, but in constant severe pain. His personal physician had told him that it was unlikely that he would survive more than one or two months. Mr. Thomas had also recently lost a sister and one of his children in an auto accident and was currently separated from his wife. He had been a drinking man for many years in the past, prior to his religious conversion several years before his diagnosis.

There was not much going for Mr. Jones. His terminal condition, his constant pain, and his experience of recent losses in his family might have driven him to become a bitter man. Nevertheless, he seemed surprisingly optimistic and full of hope concerning the future. He revealed to me one day that he was praying to God to heal his cancer. A man of strong faith, he often listened to Bible tapes to help him endure the pains that reminded him constantly of the cancer that was consuming his body. Day by day he lost more and more of his appetite and his weight and physical strength decreased steadily. The morphine and other narcotics became less and less effective in relieving his pain. Despite this evidence of his progressive decline, he prayed constantly that God would heal his cancer and make him well again. When awake, he expressed a determined hopefulness of eventual recovery. I prayed with him, and our relationship grew stronger day by day. At the end of one month in my care, he died.

The depression, fear, anger, and hopelessness that I often see on the wards with patients experiencing similar circumstances, were seldom expressed by Mr. Thomas. He died with dignity, and I believe with the assurance that God would heal him of his illness. It appeared to me that part of his illness *was* healed—even though it was not the cancer.

CASE #4

Mr. Hubert is a Caucasian gentleman in his eighties who presented himself to my clinic with severe depression. On hearing his history, I was not surprised that this man was depressed. His wife had recently been diagnosed with cancer, and she had been admitted to the hospital for treatment of this disease. Because of his fragile health, Mr. Hubert could not live alone, so he moved to a more supervised living situation.

His new living situation was hardly better than a nursing home, in that his medication was administered by nurses and his life was very structured. He was not happy there and wanted to be home with his wife. Mr. Hubert, an active man most of his life, was now quite disabled. He had vision in only one eye, and this eye had a cataract, obscuring vision to a considerable degree. A man of few hobbies, Mr. Hubert's greatest pleasure was reading. Because of the cataract, his ability to read was diminishing. Another concern was instability when walking. He had suffered a stroke a year or so ago, which had left him partially paralyzed, though able to walk with the help of a cane. Recently, he had fallen several times. The concern over his falling made me reluctant to prescribe antidepressant medication, for these drugs would likely increase the risk of his falling and hurting himself. Consequently, I relied primarily on counseling as the method of treatment for his depression. Mr. Hubert clearly expressed to me that he greatly feared losing his sight or being confined to a wheelchair; he was also frightened of losing his wife and having to remain in the nursing home. All of these fears were firmly based in reality, and I could not simply reassure him that everything was going to be alright. In the week prior to one of our visits, his wife attempted suicide by taking an overdose after hearing of the sudden death of a close family member. Mr. Hubert was very distraught, both over his wife's suicide attempt and their relative's death.

During our counseling session, I asked Mr. Hubert if there was anything he really enjoyed doing. He said very little, except for reading his Bible. This, he claimed, helped give him comfort and a sense of hope. King David's Psalms were of particular help to him, in that David himself was indeed depressed on numerous occasions, but was able to endure these times with God's strength. By praising God in the midst of his depression, David was able to regain his mental health. Mr. Hubert would also read the books of first, second, and third John, which talk about God's love for his people. Reading of God's love for him apparently helped his loneliness and eased his feelings of worthlessness. Over the ensuing weeks Mr. Hubert's depression lessened, but was not cured. A factor in his maintaining hope and not giving up during the depression was his strong religious faith.

The religious person has hope in the promises that his God makes to him. These promises are often independent of circumstances. The reality of Mr. Hubert's situation was that there was not much hope for a better future and there was very little reason to live based on his current and likely future circumstances. He had to live by faith, not sight—for what he saw would likely only depress him more. Here is an instance where faith was a vital element driving the will to live. Mr. Hubert's problems continue and his religion has not cured him of his depression; nevertheless, one wonders where this man would be without his beliefs.

CASE #5

Mr. Jergins is a seventy-five year old Caucasian man who was admitted to the hospital to determine the cause of blood in his stool, pain in his rectum, increasing constipation, low back pain, and increased leg weakness. He had just six months prior undergone a major colon operation to remove a cancer in his lower colon. The operative report noted that the cancer had spread beyond the lymph nodes (Duke's Stage C). At that time he was offered chemotherapy or radiation therapy as palliative treatment, but refused to undergo these treatments. Mr. Jergins had recently experienced ten days of bleeding from his rectum, passing about two or three cupfuls of dark maroon stool and had noticed blood on the toilet tissue on three occasions in the past week. With his recent history of metastatic colon cancer, these symptoms were quite grim.

When I interviewed him, he told me that God had directed him to come to this particular hospital for evaluation. His trip by car to our tertiary care center had gone smoothly. What otherwise is usually a very difficult process—the admission procedure—also had been completed without waiting or other complication, confirming to Mr. Jergins that the Lord's will was in this decision of his. In coming to our medical center, he believed that God would miraculously heal him of whatever was causing the bleeding and that the doctors would find nothing. A bit more of his background and life experience might help to explain this man's actions and thinking.

Up until the age of forty, Mr. Jergins had lived a whirlwind of a life. Despite growing up in a very religious home where his parents frequently read the Bible and attended church, he began to live a bit recklessly as he entered his teens. His large size and physical strength enabled him to enter a professional boxing and then wrestling career in his twenties. At the age of twenty-two, he fought the light heavyweight champion of Germany with all the German military officials, including Adolf Hitler, at the ringside. After a knockout victory over the German champion, his self-confidence ballooned and he began drinking heavily, overeating, and was nightly with different women. Despite these activities, he was able to fight over 170 professional fights, losing only seven. He also took up professional wrestling and was involved in circus performances and vaudeville acts for many years.

One night when he was driving in a car with six other wrestlers, an episode occurred that changed him. One of the men with him was reading aloud from his Bible. This offended another fellow, who reached over to snatch the Bible and tear it up. In a second, recalling how much his parents had revered the Bible, he reached over and subdued his angry teammate. More details follow, but the end result was that he felt motivated to rekindle his relationship with God. He began attending church, stopped wrestling, stopped drinking, retired from the entertainment business, and began preaching—an activity he has continued to the present. When troubles arise with his health or other matters, Mr. Jergins says that he "throws all his troubles on the Lord." With regard to his colon cancer, he says "I'm not a bit frightened of this cancer—even if Jesus takes me, its been well-worth living the Christian life. He gives me strength, power, and peace of mind; it's the peace of mind, though, that is so important to me."

Mr. Jergins underwent a comprehensive psychiatric and medical examination on his admission to the hospital. He was found to have no evidence of depression or other psychiatric illness; in fact, several of his evaluators commented "what a delightful man" this person was. On physical examination, he was found to have no masses in his rectum and no blood was found in his stool. His chest x-ray, back x-rays, and bone scan—performed to detect spread of his colon cancer—were normal except for some changes from arthritis. His blood tests, often reflective of metastatic disease (spread of cancer), were likewise unremarkable. Finally, a decision was made to perform a colonoscopy in order to directly visualize the rectum and entire colon. No evidence of cancer was found; the anastomosis site of the previous surgery appeared clean.

Mr. Jergins was discharged without a diagnosis and no evidence for a recurrence of his cancer. He believes that the Lord healed him. Based on the information available at the time of his discharge, we could not refute or substantiate his claim. His original symptoms had been highly suggestive of recurrent cancer in a man with recent proven metastatic disease. In light of these symptoms, our failure to find any organic pathology is not easily explained. An episode of divine healing? Regardless of the etiology of his symptoms or cause of his healing, Mr. Jergin's religious faith brought him a peace, security, and hope that are infrequently seen in the setting of serious, life-threatening illness.

CASE #6

Mr. Tom is a 102 year old black gentleman who was admitted to the hospital after fainting. Up until this episode, he lived by himself in a congregate housing facility (not a nursing home or rest home) and cared for all of his needs. Mr. Tom had a long history of bleeding from his stomach and intestine. Over time, his blood volume gradually dropped to only about one-quarter the usual amount. After receiving blood, he became much more alert and was able to talk a bit about his life. I asked him how he managed to cope with problems over the years, particularly his declining physical vigor and health problems. Immediately he responded that about the only thing that kept his spirits up and himself going was his faith in God. Mr. Tom had experienced ups and downs in his mood in response to his fluctuating physical disability. He admitted to often watching other people do things that he wanted to do but couldn't. In such low times, he would raise his spirits by singing religious songs, quoting verses out of the Bible, and praying to God. In his younger days, he noted habitual periods of depression that were often serious enough that he contemplated suicide. Currently, however, he did enjoy life—despite his disabilities—and wanted to continue living. He attributed the origins of his strong religious faith to the devout faith and teachings of his parents who had instilled these principles in him at an early age.

CASE #7

Mr. Timber was a Caucasian man in his seventies who was admitted to the acute care hospital in which I was working. He was undergoing testing for a rather serious medical problem concerning his kidneys and heart. Over the past three months he had been restricted in his physical activity and was consequently unable to care for the financial needs of his family. He began to feel progressively more fatigued, developed increasing worry and concern, irritability, and low spirits over his medical and financial problems. He began to blame himself over not having previously planned for his retirement and security of his family in these later years.

Mr. Timber was also a very religious man. He belonged to a fundamentalist Protestant denomination and had been previously active in his church. His family and church friends were dear to him and were at the center of his social life; in general, however, he was a private sort of person. He often read the Bible and prayed to God, and such activity was observed while he was in the hospital. In evaluating Mr. Timber for depression, I noticed that he was very reluctant to say that he was worrying about his situation, yet clearly expressed his distress over recent events that had occurred. He seemed to be upset over the fact that he was experiencing worry and some despondency over these problems. A truly Christian person with enough faith should not be experiencing such worry or depression, he reasoned. He communicated to me that he felt angry at himself for not trusting enough in God to handle his current situation. Many times in the past he had prayed and laid his problems at the feet of his Lord, and each time he had received an answer and peace within himself. He recalled his experience with open heart surgery just the year before, and how he had gone through it with a peace that was even difficult for him to understand. This time, however, he did not have such peace, and he was concerned and maybe even a bit guilty that his faith was not strong enough.

The point brought out by this case is the following. Mr. Timber had the attitude that, because of his Christian faith, he should not be experiencing worry or depression over his circumstances. When he did feel that way, he became angry at himself for not having a strong enough faith in God to prevent this. Thus, feeling that his faith was weak, he was experiencing an added guilt and self-blame that may have added to his emotional turmoil. Ressurance that even "good" and faithful Christians experience anxiety and depression, may have combatted some of his anger against himself and feelings of failure. In order to understand this man's problem, it was essential to explore his religious beliefs and expectations.

CASE #8

Mr. Wilaby is a seventy-two year old white man who lost his wife about ten years ago. He was admitted to the hospital for a diagnostic procedure, and had a history of moderately severe lung problems, arthritis, and ulcers. He did not have any acute symptoms on this admission. He used alcohol daily in an unknown quantity, consuming a minimum of three drinks per day; he also regularly took minor tranquilizers for his "nerves." For nearly all of his life, he had depended on his wife for support and comfort; they had been married almost fifty years. When she died, life became very difficult. This, in addition to the chronic health problems that limited his activity, left him with few resources and coping alternatives. He had been living alone since her death. How did he deal with his problems now? Partly by drinking. What really kept him going? His response was:

I pray a lot. It settles me down when I get agitated and picks me up when I'm down. I can talk to the Lord about anything. Since my wife passed away, I pray every night and during the day when I can. Since I can't depend on her anymore, I now depend on the Lord.

Mr. Wilaby was almost sixty-five years old when, during the time surrounding his wife's death, he turned to religion for help. He had been raised in a religious home, and his father was a preacher. Religion, however, had not played much of a role in his life until his wife died. At that time and as he grew older, Mr. Wilaby noted that religion had become increasingly important in his life, particularly as his own death approached.

Here is an interesting situation. Both religion and alcohol were used as coping behaviors. Despite his drinking behavior, his relationship with his Lord still apparently had a sustaining quality about it that did a great deal to help him in coping. Not long ago, a seventy-eight year old Black-Indian man presented in kidney failure to the hospital with almost the same story as Mr. Wilaby. This particular man reported that he almost always had high spirits, and a good appetite and energy level, except when he drank excessively; unfortunately, he had drunk excessively for nearly sixty years, and had multiple medical problems resulting from this habit. Nevertheless, his spontaneous response to the question of how he coped with problems in life and kept himself going was that the Lord helped him. He appeared completely sincere in his answer and gave several examples of how his beliefs assisted him in dealing with troubles.

In my practice and research, I have also observed other older patients who, despite being immersed in religiously incongruent behaviors (excessive use of alcohol or drugs), find strength in their personal religious faith. In general, however, both drug and alcohol use are less frequent among the religiously active and religiously oriented elderly than among the nonreligious (see earlier reviews).

CASE #9

Mr. Goss was an 82 year old white man with extensively metastasized lung cancer who was admitted with a collapsed lung and extreme shortness of breath. He had been very depressed since an accident happened to a family member about 6 months before. He had only recently been diagnosed with lung cancer. When asked how he coped with his illness and problems in life, he quickly raised his finger upward indicating that God was his source of strength. Over the past months, he had frequently contemplated suicide—but was held back only because of his belief in God and that such an act would be an unpardonable sin. He noted that he was not a church goer and never had been, claiming no religious denomination. Neither of his parents were religious, but his grandmother was very much so and taught him to first love God, then his family, then his country, and then books. He related this information in a tearful manner. Despite being deeply distraught over his condition and recent experiences, this man's religious faith remained strong and continued to help sustain him (by self-report).

CASE #10

Mr. Cody is a seventy-four year old black man who was admitted to the hospital for a colonoscopy (visual examination of his large intestine) as part of routine screening he had undergone every six months since surgery five years ago for cancer of the colon. In addition, he had a past medical history significant for poorly controlled diabetes mellitus, with the associated complications of vision problems (retinopathy), kidney involvement (nephropathy), and numbness of his extremities (peripheral neuropathy). Other problems included high blood pressure, glaucoma, chronic lung disease, degenerative arthritis, and prostate problems. I came in contact with Mr. Cody while screening patients for depressive symptoms in a mental health study at our institution. When asked how his spirits had been recently, he said they were good and that he very seldom ever worried. He still enjoyed his activities at home and loved to go fishing and work outdoors, though his physical condition had restricted this activity for some time now. He enjoyed being with people very much, had a very positive self-image, and was very satisfied with his life.

Mr. Cody, however, had not always felt this way. He volunteered that his combat experience in World War II had really upset him. Being on the front line, he had seen many of his friends killed, and with great effort he had struggled to remain alive himself. For many months, he had slept underneath the large field artillery guns, which would fire periodically throughout the night. After the war, he began to develop a nervous condition (post-traumatic stress disorder). He saw a physician who prescribed some nerve medicine, advised him to stay away from alcohol, and suggested he focus his mind completely on his work (in a tobacco factory). Things got worse, however, and between 1951 and 1955 he developed a deep depression. At that time, he began to pray— and pray hard and persistently. For six months he remained deeply depressed, yet he persisted in prayer. Finally in 1955, it broke. Since then, he has prayed to God daily, and claimed that he had not been depressed since.

Through this experience, he had "learned how to pray" to keep himself from getting depressed. Mr. Cody noted that he'd "learned how to be happy and not to carry unworthy things on my mind, but rather let God handle them." Today, he claimed to almost never feel depressed. "I do a lot of praying now and God always lightens up my problems, no matter how serious they might be."

Church is also very important to Mr. Cody, and he claimed not to have missed a single weekly church service since 1955, except for sickness or illness. "You can't worship God alone; you've got to worship Him in a temple with your brothers and sisters." Even at age seventy-four, with his long list of medical problems, he continued to be an active man in his church, and was presently chairman of his church's deacon board.

When asked how he coped with his physical condition, increasing disability, and other problems, he said he: (1) read the scriptures, (2) simply gave up to God to handle things that he had no control over, and (3) made an effort to try to live peacefully with everybody, treat

them right, and do things for them; and if he was ever offended, to try
to overlook it. Religion for him, he claimed, was the most important
thing that kept him going.

Here is an example of an older person who in middle age had experienced prolonged mental disability and depression following a trau-
matic war experience. He apparently used religion to help overcome his
mental condition and consequently learned how to continue to use it to
maintain his psychological health. A sudden resolution of depressive
symptoms in the severely depressed through religious conversion has
been reported by others and is discussed more fully in Chapter 7. For
Mr. Cody, however, it was a long process (6 months of persevering in
prayer). Today, a combination of private religious devotion (prayer),
intrapsychic religious behaviors (giving the problems up to God), and
community religious activity provided Mr. Cody with a firm base of
religious support to assist him in coping with his multiple medical problems and progressive physical disability.

CASE #11

Mr. Jackson is a white man in his seventies who was admitted to the
hospital for treatment of pneumonia. He was a retired mechanical engineer who had been all over the world during his lifetime working on
projects for the federal government. Over the past couple of months,
however, problems with his lungs had seriously compromised his
health. Research screening for depressive symptoms surprisingly uncovered no symptoms of depression, worry, or anxiety. He seemed to
be coping quite well by staying busy and being as active as his physical
condition would permit. He repeatedly emphasized that he never worried about anything, and that when difficulties arose, he simply did
whatever had to be done to resolve the problem. Aside from his health,
his life at this time was going pretty well. He was relatively free of
financial problems and lived with his wife in a nice home in the country.

When I asked him about his religious denomination—a demographic
characteristic collected on all patients in our study—he hesitated. He
then volunteered the information that he had been struggling and had
many questions that he was seeking answers to regarding religion. He
remarked that he was not the sort of person who would fall to his knees
and pray in front of others unless he really felt something inside; in
other words, he didn't want to be a hypocrite. He was uncertain about
his belief in God, and so would not pray to someone he didn't believe
in. Yet, he truly wanted to believe. Too many unanswered questions
seemed to stand in his way. For instance, who had created God? And
what about the conflicts between the Bible story of creation and the
scientifically based theory of evolution? Being a mechanical engineer,

he had always heavily relied on his sense of reasoning, and therefore refused to believe something unless he could find evidence to back it up. Mr. Jackson was in the midst of an existential dilemma, and was intensely seeking help in this matter.

What was my response as a physician? Sensing the earnestness of this man's struggle, I asked him if he would feel comfortable sharing with me some of the questions he had been wrestling with. I listened intently, interjecting questions to help clarify the issues he was addressing. I validated the importance of these questions, shared with him some of the answers that I had personally found helpful, and encouraged his continued earnest search for answers. At the end of the interview, Mr. Jackson expressed sincere gratitude to me for allowing him to express these deep thoughts and asked me if I would be interested in visiting him and his wife someday.

In retrospect, referral to a clergyperson (from a religious tradition acceptable to Mr. Jackson) may have been a more optimal course to take. Certainly, that would have been the best action had I not felt comfortable discussing such issues. However, my *taking the time* to listen, allow him to express his concerns, and validate the importance of the questions that were troubling him, was deeply appreciated by this man who simply needed to share his struggles with another person who would not condemn or judge. As noted earlier (Chapter 11), the roles of the physician include those of confidante and counselor. The assistance rendered a patient with existential or spiritual struggles may go a long way to help relieve anxiety and unrest, as this case demonstrates.

Although few patients may be as verbal about these issues as Mr. Jackson, religious and spiritual concerns are likely to be prevalent among a significant proportion of older persons when serious physical illness strikes or death approaches. If the physician does not feel competent in this area, or his or her beliefs conflict with those of the patient, referral should be made to a sensitive and sensible clergyperson who may discuss such issues in an open and nonjudgmental manner with the patient.

CASE #12

Mr. Gilley is a seventy-two year old black gentleman who was admitted to the hospital with a severely swollen abdomen due to the obstruction of his bile ducts and liver by a cancer in his pancreas. He had lost over thirty pounds in the past couple of months. On interviewing this man about how his spirits were doing in the midst of this physical sickness, he said they were doing good, and that whenever he began feeling down he would read the Bible. He then spontaneously offered that he was a faithful and diligent believer in Jesus Christ, and that he had worked faithfully in his church for a number of years, being a deacon and member of the choir. He had also, until just recently, spent six to eight hours a day as a volunteer for the VA hospital, driving disabled veterans back and forth from their homes to clinic visits.

How long had Mr. Gilley been so involved in his church and active in his community? Only about ten years, was his answer. Prior to the age of sixty-two, despite coming from a very religious family, he had lived a rough life and was caught in the grips of alcoholism; he had made alcohol, sold it, and consumed large quantities himself. He had been shot twice during this time and jailed innumerable times. Finally, he just got tired of cheating and drinking, and said to himself, "I'm going to put it all down and live for the Lord." At that time, he gave up drinking and began to involve himself in his church and other community activity.

Getting back to his physical condition and current circumstances, I asked him how he managed to cope with his disease and the inevitable feelings of discouragement and fear that all persons experience during such troubling times. Again, his response was religious in nature:

I get on my knees and pray to the Lord and read my Bible—it's the *only* way I can get relief. After I read Psalms 23 and 121, I begin to feel better. When I can't sleep at night, I read my Bible, say a prayer, and this usually helps me to return to sleep. But don't get me wrong, the doctors here help a lot as well.

Pursuing this a bit further, I persisted: "But how does your religion really help you to deal better with your problems?" He responded with the following:

If you take your problems to the Lord, He will solve them for you; you have to do your part too, though. When a big problem faces me, I'll call a friend and call my pastor, and then the three of us will meet somewhere and pray together. We'll pray over the problem and then give it up to the Lord; I can then go about my business, relieved that things will be taken care of.

Note that religion was for this man the *only* source of relief from feelings of depression and discouragement that he encountered in life. Now, when his very existence was being threatened by cancer, he was prepared to deal with it, having a belief system that gave him a sense of continuity between this life and the next, and a close support system provided by friends in his church. This case also exemplifies the impact that religion can have in changing a person's life around, even in later life.

CASE #13

Mr. Lincoln is a seventy-two year old white gentleman who was admitted to the hospital with pneumonia and a mass in his chest (probably lung cancer). On admission his blood count was low and he had signs of an active lung infection. Included in his past medical history was a stroke eight years prior that had left him completely paralyzed on his left side and interfered with his speech somewhat. A year later, he developed a seizure disorder. For many years, Mr. Lincoln had been a farmer and was active in the outdoors. He currently lived at home with his wife, but required much assistance with his daily care and toileting. Mr. Lincoln was very alert, cooperative, and did his best to answer our questions. When asked about how his spirits had been over the past few months, he said that he only occasionally felt down, but always built his spirits back up with help from God.

When asked how he coped with his illness and physical disability, he said that what really kept him going was that people would come to see him and ask him to pray for them. This gave him a sense of feeling useful and that he was playing his part in helping others. He also noted that, "the Lord helps me—it pays to believe in God" and that, "my family also helps me—I couldn't manage without them." Religion had been of assistance to Mr. Lincoln since his World War II experience in his mid twenties. Being in war scared him; one of his company at that time gave him a small Bible, which he began to read. Since then, religion had been very important to him in coping with problems. Interestingly, neither of his parents were very religious, and he had little religious training in his early years. It was not until his wartime experience that religion had become meaningful to him.

Of particular note in this case is the fact that Mr. Lincoln was made to feel worthy and useful because people came to him to ask for prayer. Being virtually helpless in every way, with little control over his environment, he was set up for the development of feelings of uselessness, worthlessness, and of being a burden to his family—emotional and cognitive patterns that frequently arouse deep feelings of depression in the post-stroke patient. Nevertheless, Mr. Lincoln's sense of self-esteem was maintained by his usefulness to others by praying for them, making him feel that he could still be of help to someone in a very important way. Through his religious beliefs, he was able to transform a situation over which he had no control into one in which he believed his actions (prayer) might have powerful and helpful consequences.

SUMMARY

Many of these cases arose in a study of coping and depression among a consecutive series of hospitalized, medically ill, older veterans (Durham, N.C.). When asked how they coped with difficult life situations, physical illness, and increasing disability, a significant proportion of participants noted that their religious beliefs and activities were the most important thing that kept them going. The cases presented here represent only a fraction of the patients claiming religion to be their source of strength. Of note here is the common report by patients that prayer or faith in God calmed them down when upset or picked up their spirits when they were feeling down or depressed. Many reported that religion had increased in importance for them as they had grown older.

In many of these cases, social support from church attendance is not mentioned as the primary religious factor involved in coping. Direct communication with God, often through prayer, in a relationship akin almost to friendship seems to be a common element in many of these cases. These anecdotal reports, and data from research mentioned previously (Koenig et al., 1988c), suggest a role for religion in coping that goes beyond the social support benefits of church attendance.

These personal testimonies suggest that religion (based in the Judeo-Christian tradition) is an important coping behavior for a significant proportion of older adults. Although the study mentioned above concerns only male veterans, it is likely that among older women, religion is even more frequently used to cope. In fact, an earlier study of participants in the Second Duke Longitudinal Study of Aging revealed that religious coping behaviors were employed almost twice as often by women as by men (Koenig et al., 1988c). Recall that in both of these studies (the VA and Duke), coping behaviors were illicited by an open-ended question in order to decrease the likelihood of obtaining socially desirable responses and to increase the validity of responses.

It is notable, however, that in over half of the patients interviewed in both the VA and Duke studies, religion was not mentioned spontaneously as being of help in coping. Many of those persons seemed to cope quite well utilizing other behaviors like keeping busy, talking with friends, or focusing their mind on other things.

Thus far, very little is known about that significant proportion of older adults who use religion as their primary coping method. What differentiates this group from those who use nonreligious behaviors to deal with illness and other life problems? Preliminary data from our work suggest that these people are more likely to be from the working or middle class, to be women, and to have experienced more stressful life events in their past. It is likely that personality type and early childhood experience are also vital factors in determining whether or not a person will use religious behaviors to cope in later life. Studies addressing these issues are presently being undertaken by our group.

10

THE SOCIAL GERONTOLOGIST'S PERSPECTIVE

Barbara Payne

The role of the social gerontologist as a professional concerned with issues of religion, health, and aging is not as immediately recognizable as the role of the physician, the clergy, and the nurse. Therefore, this chapter begins with a description of what a social gerontologist is, followed by the social gerontologist's perspectives and views on the interaction of religion, health, and aging. This includes the emerging interest in the meaning and effects of religion on the health of older adults and the role of religious institutions in the health and well-being of an aging population. Finally, but central to the chapter, are a social gerontologist's impressions and experiences regarding the impact of religious attitudes, faith practices, and church membership on physical and mental health of older persons. Since Koenig has incorporated the social gerontological research literature in Chapter 1 through 8, this chapter will generalize from these in order to describe the social gerontologist's perspective.

GERONTOLOGY AND THE SOCIAL GERONTOLOGIST

Gerontology is the multidisciplinary study of the processes of aging and the factors that affect these processes. It includes the disciplines of biology, sociology, psychology, economics, anthropology, the humanities, and health disciplines, including medicine. The university survey

Dr. Payne is director of The Gerontology Center, Georgia State University, Atlanta, Georgia.

by social gerontologists Peterson and Bolton (1980), identified more than twenty departments with faculty teaching courses with gerontological content. Most social gerontologists usually have a sociology, social psychology, economics, or political science degree. In this chapter, the social gerontologist's perspective is primarily sociological. Social gerontologists focus on the social aspects of aging (i.e., the aging of individuals in the social context of family, friends, work/retirement, politics, economics), and the effects of significant numbers of older persons on the social context and the major institutions of society (Ward, 1984).

Social gerontologists have studied: health and aging; healthcare systems for the elderly; the social roles and attitudes of physicians, nurses, and clergy as they relate to older persons; health; and longevity. They have systematically excluded, however, the relationship that religious activities have to the health and well-being of older persons.

For that matter, they have systematically excluded the study of religion, associational and nonassociational, to the aging process (Payne, 1988a). Few gerontological textbooks include any reference to religion. When they do, some are limited to a few pages or paragraphs related to death and dying (Payne, 1975; 1988b). Since 1975, several textbooks have included a chapter on religion.

This omission or limited treatment seems strange since early sociologists, such as Durkheim (1951) and Sorokin (1954), placed a major emphasis on religion as a factor in mental and physical health. Durkheim argued that "the fundamental categories of thought, and consequently of science, are of religious origin"; "that religion has given birth to all that is essential in society." Since religious forces are human forces, moral forces, and an expression of the collective life, religion would be expected to affect health and the aging process.

In his work on suicide, Durkheim (1965) was the first sociologist to identify the social structure of the church (or organized religion) as social intervention and prevention of mental health conditions leading to suicide. He maintained that the ritual and social structure of churches provided identity and cohesiveness, which reduced the state of alienation leading to suicide.

Sorokin's (1954) research focused on the power of love as it is experienced in various forms, and especially in the Judeo-Christian faith. He found religious altruistic love to be one of the most important factors contributing to longevity and good health, both mental and physical. In additional studies he found substantial evidence of the curative power of love for certain physical and mental disorders. Sorokin's research supports the earlier findings of Durkheim on suicide:

We know now that the main choice of suicide is psychosocial isolation of the individual, his state of being lonely in the human universe, not loving or caring for anybody and not being loved by anybody . . . when the love ties . . . are break-ing down, especially abruptly . . . chances of suicide are increasing. (Sorokin, 1954, pp. 62–66)

Sorokin concluded that to love and be loved are necessary conditions for mental and physical health and as a curative agent when illnesses attack at any age.

Another classical sociologist, Max Weber (1946, 1963) focused on the meaning religion had for individuals and society. He argued that there are certain basic issues or "why" questions (e.g., why is there suffering and injustice?). Responses to these questions have been based primarily on religious belief systems. Although religion has lost some of its ca-pacity to answer the why questions or give meaning to life events, traditional religious beliefs continue to be very important in the personal life of the majority of Americans (55%), but more important to those over sixty-five years of age (65%). Furthermore, older Americans believe that religion can answer (solve or make sense of) all or most of today's problems (Briggs, 1987). It must be noted that slightly more than one-third of older Americans, however, do not rely on religion in their per-sonal lives.

Weber's focus on meaning and religion provides the theoretical tra-dition for social gerontologists to relate the meaning of religion to health issues of aging and longevity. See Chapter 8 for Koenig's discussion of the meaning of religion in stressful situations. These three classical so-ciologists provide a theoretical framework for the social gerontologist's perspective presented in the following sections.

Before turning to these perspectives, it is important to define religion as it is used in this chapter. Religion is an institutional system of symbols, beliefs, values, and practices that focus on supernatural beings and forces (Wilson, 1978). Sociologists and social gerontologists rarely use such a broad definition; they observe and seek to explain the particular beliefs and practices of a particular people. In this chapter, the particular people are the elderly. The particular practices include associational (church-related) and nonassociational practices.

SOCIAL GERONTOLOGISTS' PERSPECTIVES ON RELIGION, HEALTH, AND AGING

In the first eight chapters, Koenig has reviewed and utilized the re-search findings of social gerontologists as they apply to the areas of mental and physical health. Most of the views and research of social gerontologists represent one-time research projects rather than a profes-sional interest in religion as it relates to health and aging. Most social gerontologists either have no perspective on religion and health in later life or they hold a limited view of the importance of religion, except as a coping mechanism in death, dying, and bereavement (Marshall, 1980).

Efforts to organize the scattered social gerontological literature relevant to religion and health suggest the following contributions to a perspective.

Retirement and the Effects on Health

Studies that focus on adaptation to retirement and the aging process frequently include the effects on health. A recurring and much disputed issue has been that retirement results in an immediate decline in health or results in death. Recent social gerontologists' analyses show that the health of retirees is much improved and that the current generation of sixty-five to seventy-four year olds are healthier than the same age group in past decades. Also, the myth of death at retirement has (hopefully) been put to rest (Atchley, 1985).

Death, Dying, and Bereavement

The most consistent perspective of the impact of religion on mental and physical health in later life is at the time of the older person's dying, or in bereavement over the loss of a significant person in their lives. The impact of religion at this time varies. For some, it is a positive means of coping; for others, it is negative.

Religious Institutions and the Community Service System

Social gerontologists Tobin, Ellor, and Anderson-Ray (1986) have introduced a focus on the religious institution's role in providing programs to promote health and wellness, and a caring community for emotional problems. They recommend the expansion of the churches'/synagogues' outreach programs that provide psychological and basic services to the homebound and to nursing home residents, and support and counseling for the dying. The most innovative part of their study is their model for increasing interaction between churches/synagogues and social service agencies that will expand and increase mental and physical health services for the elderly.

Demographic Description

The analysis of demographic data or secondary data from national surveys (e.g., NORC), include health status, religious affiliation, church attendance, and religious practice. Social gerontologists seldom, however, relate health status and religion. Religion or religiosity is most frequently a dependent or descriptive variable, which limits the understanding of the impact of religion on mental and physical health.

Religion and Social Roles

Religious activities and involvement in church programs are viewed as replacement of social roles, activities, and voluntary association memberships lost with retirement. The social structure of associational religious involvement is perceived as reducing isolation and increasing life satisfaction and happiness. Consequently, those retirees who are "religious" are expected to have better mental and physical health.

In conclusion, there is no systematic social gerontologists' perspective on the impact of religion on mental and physical health in late life. For the most part they have relied on surveys, utilized crude measures of religiosity, and have avoided the religious meaning questions.

A SOCIAL GERONTOLOGIST'S IMPRESSIONS AND EXPERIENCES ON THE IMPACT OF RELIGION ON MENTAL AND PHYSICAL HEALTH IN LATER LIFE

The research effort of one social gerontologist on the impact of religion on mental and physical health in late life does not general perspective make. The perspective presented in this section is based on the research, impressions, and experiences of one social gerontologist on mental and physical health in late life, and should be suggestive for researchers, but not used for generalizations.

My earliest impressions are based on nine years of experience as a state executive director of young adult and older adult work for a major Protestant denomination in the 1950s. The first experience was with ageism. Youth and young adults received much attention in the local congregation, the state, and the national level of the denomination as the "future" of the church, whereas older adults were viewed as anchored in the past, too conservative, and obsolete in their leadership skills. Despite these attitudes, the older adults drew on their lifetime of faith and church experience in dealing with age-related physical changes and chronic illnesses. The church provided them with continuity in the midst of the changes accompanying aging and reinforced their faith.

Their strong desire to remain visible and contributing church members, expressing faith in their daily lives, kept them involved in groups and church activities. At this period in time, I became aware of the church's benign exclusion and "tolerance" of older members and the widely held view of older members as a burden rather than a resource. Most of the older adults ignored these negatives and continued their commitment to the church. In groups we discussed their beliefs, practices, and church life in relation to their present situations.

At this time a Christian adult educator, Ruel Howe (1953), published his book, *Man's Needs and God's Action*. He maintained that man's need is to love and be loved, but human love can never completely meet this human need. It takes God's action to love the unlovely—to meet the deepest human needs. This was a popular version of Sorokin's theory of the power of love to cure and contribute to a long life. My nine years of experience with these older adults demonstrated that when given a little love, they responded with an outpouring of love. They were most verbal about their need for God's love, a love that was "different" from the love of family and friends. These experiences influenced the research for my doctoral dissertation on the meaning and measurement of commitment to the church (Payne-Pittard, 1966).

Interest in and focus on the religious meaning question in both quantitative and qualitative research has remained the theoretical and methodological focus of my research. For ten years I studied older volunteers in three ecumenical programs called Shepherd's Centers. These volunteers reported better health and knowledge about prevention of illness and coping with illness and death. At the same time they reported that the meaning of the church and their faith practices increased (Payne and Bull, 1979). The major reason older volunteers dropped out was a change in their health—theirs or that of a close family member. Over the ten year period of the study, the active volunteers reported no change in their "good" health.

IMPRESSIONS OF AND EXPERIENCES WITH SELECTED OLDER ADULTS

Another source of views and impressions about the meaning of religion in mental and physical health in later life comes from older adults themselves. I have selected only three of the many persons as examples.

The first is a well-known historical person, John Wesley. As a Church of England minister and founder of the Methodist church, Wesley held strong beliefs about the impact of religion on health, health habits, and longevity. In 1755 he published a tract of rules "for the sake of those who desire, through the blessing of God, to retain the health they have recovered." These rules sound like the U.S. Surgeon General's recommendations for 1988. Wesley's few plain rules included:

1. The air we breathe is of great consequence to our health. Those who have been long abroad in easterly or northerly winds should drink some thin and warm liquor going to bed or a draught of toast and water;

2. Tender people should have those who lie with them, or are much about them, sound, sweet, and healthy;

3. Everyone that would preserve health should be as clean and sweet as possible in their houses, clothes, and furniture;

4. The great rule of eating and drinking is, to suit the quality and quantity of the food to the strength of our digestion; to take always such a sort and such a measure of food as sits light and easy to the stomach.

5. Walking is the best exercise for those who are able to bear it; riding for those who are not. The open air, when the weather is fair, contributes much to the benefit of exercise.

6. They should frequently shave, and frequently wash their feet.

7. All violent and sudden passions dispose to, or actually throw people into, acute diseases.

8. The slow and lasting passions, such as grief and hopeless love, bring on chronical diseases. (Jackson, 1984, p. 212)

Wesley believed that:

The love of God, as it is the sovereign remedy of all miseries, so in particular it effectually prevents all the bodily disorders the passions introduce, by keeping the passions themselves within due bounds. And by the unspeakable joy, and perfect calm, serenity, and tranquility it gives the mind, it becomes the most powerful of all the means of health and long life. (Jackson, 1984, p. 316)

Wesley followed his many health rules and he enjoyed good health. He lived to be eighty-nine at a time when the average life expectancy was thirty to forty years. Although this is a personal impression of how religious beliefs impact mental and physical health, it is also the teaching of a popular evangelist who founded a major denomination and incorporated these religion, health, and aging views into the belief system of a new denomination (Jackson, 1984).

The second older person is Paul B. Maves. I have known Paul for over thirty years and have followed his professional activities in the field of aging and benefited from his early research and writings on the aging experience and the role of the church. He has been my friend and colleague. I have observed the quiet expression of his deep faith, gentleness, and caring for people. Now in his seventies he is still writing books and articles on faith, the church, and religion while also working as the Director of Otterbein Gerontology Center. He tells us "I have seen the shadow of death passing down the hall just outside my door and know that it will not be too many years before we walk together" (Maves, 1986). He has shared with all of us his faith for the older years—a faith of hope and love—even as he battled cancer and enjoyed remission. Now, the cancer may be active again, and he has accepted this uncertainty with faith and hope. He writes, "hope allows me to make plans and take on projects that stretch several years ahead. Hope lets me rejoice in each day as it comes. It lets me anticipate the days to come." His hope is based on his Christian faith. He is mentally healthy, professionally productive, and as physically active as his strength will permit.

The third older person we will call Beth Adams. She was the daughter of a minister, and was married forty years to the son of a minister. Personal faith and commitment to the church were the foundations of her life. She was a homemaker and was not involved in voluntary associations or other civic organizations. She was reserved about the meaning of religion to her, and she assumed everybody knew she was religious, a "church person," and did not need to talk about it. It was not until her mid-seventies that disease—cancer—attacked her "good health." Those who watched and shared in her struggle to "beat" it and to be cured, knew without verbal expression that she drew heavily on her faith and church for coping, hoping, and fighting the disease. We did not really know the meaning, however, until she told us with the music she loved, played, and sang daily, and until we witnessed some clippings carefully arranged with scotch tape in a Bible.

On her piano she arranged—for herself, her family, and friends—the pieces of music that told us the meaning of her religion: "This Time Lord You Have Sent Me a Mountain;" "Take My Hand Precious Lord;" "One Day at a Time Sweet Jesus;" "How Great Thou Art;" and the Methodist Hymnal. She played and sang these as long as she could get to the piano. After her death her daughter found the clippings. Excerpts of these tell us more: God stabilizes those who maintain faith in Him amid life's changes.

Prayer: Grant me, O God, the grace of gratitude for your forgiveness of my faults. Use me to reflect the light of your forgiving love on all who do me wrong for Jesus's sake. Amen.

Thought for the Day: Oh, to be as aware of offenses others overlook in me as I am of irritations I receive from them! What a price to pay for one's false pride! Many of us suffer a lifetime of regret for refusing to say—and mean it—"I'm sorry." There can be no repentance without humility.

A Song: "The King's Highway"
I know not where the road will lead I follow day by day, or where it ends: I only know I walk the King's Highway. I know not if the way is long, and no one else can say; but roughly or smooth, up hill or down, I walk the King's Highway.

And some I love have reached the end, but some with me may stay. Their faith and hope still guiding me, I walk the King's Highway. The way is truth, the way is love; for light and strength I pray, And through the years of life, to God, I walk the King's Highway. The countless hosts lead on before, I must not fear nor stray; With them the pilgrims of all creeds, I walk the King's Highway. Through light and dark the road leads on, till dawns the endless day, When I shall know why in this life I walk the King's Highway. (Cummings, 1940, p. 432)

Quotes were found in her handwriting: "You cannot walk diligently with God without finding true vitality and meaning in your existence," and "many people close the windows of heaven with self pity." Finally, there was one, "Where to Look in the Bible," to lead her to specific passages for support in a range of feelings—discouragement, depression, death, need for faith, support, etcetera.

These clippings show us how Beth, living alone, maintained her positive attitude and hopefulness despite her very discouraging physical condition. These things supported her determination to live until after Christmas and other important family holidays had passed. In fact, she lived five weeks longer than her physician had expected.

For the social gerontologist the cases presented here provide indepth and specific statements suggestive for qualitative research and generate items for quantitative research. They reinforce the need to ask older adults the "why" questions and the meaning question. These observations make a major contribution by not overlooking the meaning of religion in mental and physical health in later life. Such an omission would impede our efforts to understand and explain the social-psychological factors influencing the aging process.

IMPRESSIONS AND EXPERIENCES WITH INSTITUTIONAL RELIGION

As early as the mid-thirties the churches (Protestant, Catholic, and Jewish), were responding to the needs of older persons for homes and institutional care. Long before the Older American's Act of 1965, the first major research on churches' responses to older members' needs (Maves & Cedarleaf, 1949), and denominational programming needs were addressed and staff support provided (Payne, 1984).

Like the social gerontologists, the churches' interest waned, and support for the elderly declined during the sixties until the mid-seventies. In the mid-seventies the churches (Protestant, Catholic, and Jewish) became aware of the graying of their congregations and of society, and began to develop policy statements on aging (Payne and Brewer, 1982). In the 1980s, the seminaries are aware of the need for gerontology in the training of the clergy. Congregational members have begun to seek continuing education on how to minister with, for, and to older members, (Clingan, 1975). This renewed interest includes concern about wellness, support services for the homebound, and counseling for families and older members to assist with the physical and mental stress of the negative effects of aging. There is strong evidence that older persons and their families prefer those services from their congregation as a part of their religion, rather than from public agencies.

Experiences with the traditional faith groups add another dimension to my social gerontological perspective. As the associational form of religion in our society, they have the greatest opportunity of any social institution outside of the family to promote, intervene, and serve as a curative power in the mental and physical health of persons in late life—and to prepare their members from infancy for a healthier, longer life. I view this as an appropriate and traditional role of organized religion that has been overlooked by the social gerontologists and overshadowed by other social concerns of the churches. The day of a new or, for many, a first-time perspective on the practical integration of religion, health, and aging is dawning.

CONCLUSION

The sociological perspective in this chapter paints a negative and discouraging picture. There are some bright spots, however, indicating that a change is beginning to occur. Koenig's literature review and those works cited in this chapter contain many articles published by the *Journal of Gerontology* and *The Gerontologist*, as well as other social science journals, since 1980. There is a slight increase in textbook treatment of religion and aging.

There have been more sessions on religion in the social and behavioral sections of the Gerontological Society of America and the American Society on Aging. If social gerontologists begin to focus on religion (associational and nonassociational), we can expect the interaction with mental and physical health to be included, especially since health/wellness, and mental health and aging are currently receiving top priority by gerontologists.

Research methodology can be expected to include more qualitative or meaning research to supplement quantitative analysis and account for the heterogeneity of the aging cohort.

11

THE PHYSICIAN'S
PERSPECTIVE

Harold George Koenig

In this chapter, the role of the physician will be described and examined to see whether or not religious issues of older patients should be of any concern to the physician. The views and opinions of a number of physicians will be presented on the topic of religion and how it relates to healthcare. Finally, the results will be presented of a survey of family physicians and general practitioners on their experiences and attitudes towards addressing religious issues with their elderly patients (Koenig et al. 1988e). The objective of this section is to explore what it means to be a physician and how religion might impact on this role in the care of older patients.

THE ROLE OF THE PHYSICIAN

What is the role of the physician in the healthcare system? Edmund Pelligrino, president of the Catholic University of America, a well-known ethicist and practicing physician, has written extensively on what it means to be a physician (Pelligrino, 1978, 1979a, 1979b). His model is purely secular and humanistic, in that it is constructed without referral to religious or philosophical ideals. Pelligrino's model is based on four words: profession, patient, compassion, and consent. This model rests on many principles underlying the major codes of physician ethics that have arisen over the past centuries. Briefly, *profession* includes: (1) the promise and obligation to be competent and skillful in one's area of expertise, (2) the need to place the well-being of those served above self-interest or personal gain, and (3) a voluntary, freely undertaken task in which the physician offers his or her skills to the patient who needs them. *Patient* means that the person seeking medical care is suffering and in a vulnerable position, whereas the physician has the power to strongly influence the patient's life and at times affects whether or not he or she will live. *Compassion* indicates that the physician is called to "suffer with" the patient in a way that Pelligrino interprets as meaning to share in the existential situation with the patient. Finally, *consent* implies that the physician-patient relationship is based on a mutual informed consent by both parties involved. The emphasis on consent is that it is a shared experience that both the physician and the patient feel and understand to be their own decision, in the absence of pressure or force by one party over the other. Sevensky (1982) goes on to draw a parallel between these four guiding principles and the Judeo-Christian values of vocation, neighbor, love, and covenant. He demonstrates that religious values are closely related to many of the ethical principles upon which medicine is practiced today and has been practiced in the past.

Another view of the role of the physician is given by Butler (1968) as he presents an updated version of the Hippocratic Oath in the *New England Journal of Medicine*, describing the principles by which physicians should practice medicine.

We physicians shall re-emphasize as basic to our profession the rational ethical principle of minimizing suffering. In the course of our training and practice, let us not be so intrigued with the intellectual satisfaction of understanding disease that we forget the priority of this humanitarian principle and consideration of patients as people. In our role as specialists, let us have empathy with our patients. May we seek the potentialities of physical, mental and *spiritual* health of each person and family and of society. (p. 48, emphasis added)

Thomas Percival (1740–1804), a physician and founder of the Manchester Literary and Philosophical Society, authored a code of medical ethics entitled: "Of Professional Conduct in Private or General Practice" (Etziony, 1973).

For the physician should be the minister of hope and comfort to the sick; that by such cordials to the drooping spirit, he may smooth the bed of death, revive expiring life, and counteract the depressing influence of those maladies which rob the philosopher of fortitude, and the Christian of consolation. (p. 59)

Barsky (1981) has written an article entitle "Hidden Reasons Some Patients Visit Doctors," in which he emphasizes that although patients obviously visit physicians to seek medical diagnosis and treatment, they often also seek consultation because of upsetting events, social isolation, psychiatric disorder, and need of advice concerning their health. He underscores that when symptoms are mild, *chronic*, or common, non-biomedical factors influence the decision of whether or not to seek medical advice. Barsky notes the following: "Thus many patients come seeking something other than palliation or cure of physical disease. Other factors motivate them, and the clinical encounter becomes more intelligible if the physician can diagnose these additional reasons for coming."

Blum (Director of Research, Medical Review and Advisory Board, California Medical Association, and Associate Scientist, Stanford Research Institute) writes of the important role of the physician as counselor and confidante to his or her patients:

As a result of the apostolic mission of doctors to teach patients what doctors do, patients have come to expect their physician to be a combination father confessor, advisor, comforter, confidant, and counselor. These activities may or may not have any demonstrable relationship to the diagnosis and treatment of somatic pathology. Nevertheless, they have come to be part of the business of being a physician, as defined by the expectations of doctors and patients alike. . . . The difficulties stem from differing definitions of the doctor's job by doctor and patient." (Blum, 1980, p. 282)

Given that 50 percent of visits to physicians are for complaints without physiologic origins, Kleinman et al. (1978) have emphasized the need for physicians to consider social and cultural factors in the diagnosis and treatment of their patients. They make a distinction between disease (what physicians diagnose) and illness (what the patient experiences). Disease is a malfunctioning or maladaptation of biologic and psycho-physiologic processes, whereas illness represents personal, interpersonal, and cultural reactions to disease. Illness, then, is strongly influenced by culture and may be culturally constructed. The manner in which patients perceive, experience, and deal with changes in their health is based on their explanatory models of sickness, which are inexorably linked with their systems of meaning in life or world view. For chronic medical illness, the patient's improvement in their illness may be more substantial after seeing "folk" practitioners (faith healers, etc.) than medical physicians, because of the greater concordance between the cultural and explanatory systems of the folk practitioners and the patient. Kleinman et al. conclude that: "The incorporation of 'clinical social science' is then essential if physicians are to understand, respond to, and help patients deal with the concerns they bring to the doctor."

The role of the physician, then, is to provide for the physical, emotional, and spiritual well-being of their patients. Cultural factors, such as religion, may have an important influence on how persons perceive their health, whether or not they seek medical attention for symptoms, and how they cope with the consequences of illness. This may be especially true among the elderly, for whom religion is particularly salient, and in whom chronic illness often presents special adaptive challenges for which religion might be helpful.

RELIGION, HEALTH, AND PATIENT CARE

A number of physicians, both psychiatrists and medical specialists, have written on the relationship between religion, health, and patient care. Unfortunately, patient age has seldom been focused on in such discussions. Whereas mental health experts such as Freud (Spinks, 1963) and Ellis (1980) considered religion as a psychopathological influence that should clearly be separated from the psychotherapeutic relationship, others have strongly defended its inclusion and integration into the therapist-client relationship (Nelson and Wilson, 1984; Bergin, 1980 (psychologist); Jung, 1933). Duke University psychiatrists Nelson and Wilson (1984) refuted the classical psychoanalytic perspective that labeled Christianity as a delusion, and defended sharing the Christian faith with a patient when that patient's ethical belief system is the same as the therapist's, and when the patient has indicated a willingness to explore this area of life. They emphasized the ethical nature and benefits of including spiritual interventions in psychotherapy, but advised that a clearly defined contract should be made with the patient beforehand that includes such interventions.

Foster (1982), Professor of Medicine at Texas Southwestern Medical School in Dallas, examined the interaction between religion, the physician, and the sick patient. He gave four reasons why the physician must deal with religion in the routine care of his or her patients: (1) religion influences the feelings and actions of many people, (2) patients often place the doctor in the role of secular priest, (3) illness is frequently accompanied by serious religious questions, and (4) the physician's own beliefs may impinge on and influence the care rendered to patients.

With regard to the influence of religion on people's feelings and actions, Foster noted that religious beliefs are often intensely held. If these beliefs are not taken seriously by medical personnel, but rather seen as irrational or as a needless obstruction to patient care, the consequence may be a serious disruption of the doctor-patient relationship. Several examples were cited by the author.

In the role as secular priest, the physician responds to nonbiomedical responsibilities to their patients. The three areas that were discussed include the patient's emotional response to stress, the problem of social isolation, and the need for health-related information. The physician must deal with the fear and worry that accompany illness since these may cause more discomfort than the disease itself. He must often fill the role of a person who cares and listens to the lonely, socially isolated patient. Finally, in fulfilling the informational-confessional needs of patients, the physician must inform the patient about the diagnosis, or provide reassurance that nothing serious is wrong. The confessional component of the above responsibility includes the hearing of troubling secrets that the patient is too embarrassed or ashamed about to tell others, but which need to be released to a trusted person. Foster emphasized the importance of fulfilling these priestly roles and the consequences of their neglect.

Illness is associated with existential questions about death and dying and the meaning of life. Foster discussed three phases that seriously ill patients go through: an informational phase, a behavioral phase, and a religious phase. In the first two phases, the patient asks what their medical diagnosis is and questions whether or not they have the courage to make it through the ordeal. In the religious phase, patients must deal with questions about meaning and destiny, such as, why did this happen, what can be learned about life from this experience, and what can be hoped for. The answers to these questions are dependent on what one believes. Foster discussed the physician's responsibility in helping the patient address such issues and provided guidelines for doing this.

Finally, Foster touched on the impact that the physician's own religious beliefs might have on patient care, particularly when those beliefs are at odds with those of the patient. He noted the controversial nature of the role of religion and the appropriateness of allowing religious dialogue between patient and physician, referring to Bergin's (1980) and Ellis' (1980) heated debates on this subject. He emphasized that because of the patient's dependence on the doctor and their position of vulnerability in the relationship, it is unethical to *force* personal beliefs on patients, particularly since even theological doctrines expound the freedom of choice necessary in religious matters. The sharing by the physician of his or her religious beliefs with the patient is appropriate when presented as being personally valuable and helpful to the physician, while not insisting that these beliefs represent the ultimate truth. He emphasized that the purpose of such discussions should always be burden sharing or burden lifting, not burden or guilt provoking.

A SURVEY OF ILLINOIS PHYSICIANS

Although it is very enlightening to hear the opinions of individual physicians on this subject, what assurance do we have that these opinions are shared by even a minority of physicians out in practice? Epidemiological data on the experience and attitudes of practicing physicians on religious issues among their patients is virtually non-existent. This is particularly true for these issues among older patients.

The only study that we are aware of that addressed these questions is that of Koenig et al. (1988e). In that study, 160 physicians in the state of Illinois were surveyed concerning their experience in and attitudes toward religious issues in their elderly patients. This study is reviewed below.

In 1987, Illinois physicians were surveyed on: (1) beliefs regarding the importance of religion among older medical patients, (2) attitudes concerning the circumstances under which it would be appropriate to address religious issues with patients, and (3) experience with and responses to religious issues arising in older patients. Questionnaires were mailed or distributed on site to 210 Illinois family physicians (FPs) and general practitioners (GPs). Participants were recruited in two ways. First, a random sample of 5 percent of all FPs and GPs in the state were selected from the roles of the American Academy of Family Physicians' membership directory; questionnaires were sent to this group by mail; 72 percent (N = 73) completed the questionnaires and returned them. Second, eighty-seven physicians were approached during a series of statewide geriatric medicine teaching conferences held by the senior author (HGK) (90% response rate). The mean age of the combined sample was forty-eight years; almost half of physicians (49%) noted that more that 10 percent of their practice consisted of patients sixty years of age or older; 89 percent of participants were men.

The questionnaire contained twenty-three items, of which seventeen focused on the beliefs and practices of physicians concerning religion in the lives of their older patients and its role in the medical encounter. Over two-thirds (69%) strongly agreed that religion had a positive effect on the mental health of their older patients, whereas 42 percent agreed to its positive effect on physical health. Two-thirds of the sample felt that the statement, "Religion is the most important influence in the life of an older adult," was true, although only 17 percent felt strongly about this (i.e. rated this item an eight or higher on a ten-point scale). The majority (63%) reported that they did not believe that older patients would want their physicians to pray with them during severe medical illness or near death; however, only 8 percent of physicians felt it was rarely or never appropriate to address religious issues in the context of a medical encounter.

Concerning the conditions under which it was appropriate to address religious issues, nearly all physicians (88%) felt it was appropriate to do so if directly approached by the patient; eighty-two percent acknowledged the appropriateness of addressing religious issues when the patient only *indirectly* communicated a need to do so; and sixty-six percent believed it appropriate to address religious issues even if the patient gave no indication of religion's salience to them yet the extremity of the circumstances (i.e. bereavement, impending death) suggested religious issues to be pertinent. Less than a third (31%) felt that the religious needs of the older patient during times of stressful and severe illness should be left entirely for the clergy to deal with.

What actions are considered by physicians to be appropriate during the above circumstances? Physicians were asked to note the appropriateness or inappropriateness of: (1) encouragement and support of the patient's religious beliefs, (2) prayer with patients, and (3) the physician's sharing of his or her own beliefs with the patient. Most agreed (77%) that encouragement and support of the patient's religious beliefs were appropriate activities for the physician. The majority (66%) also felt that praying with patients was not inappropriate physician behavior. Finally, sixty-three percent of the physicians agreed that sharing their beliefs with patients was appropriate during times of severe emotional crisis.

With regard to experience, only six percent of physicians reported that their older patients often or always mentioned religious issues in the context of a medical visit, and over half (51%) stated that they never, or only rarely encountered such issues. More than a third (37%) of physicians reported having prayed with older patients during times of great emotional distress or proximity to death. Of those who did, the vast majority (89%) felt that it had helped the patient somewhat or a great deal. Of concern is that less than half (45%) of the physicians admitted to regularly referring older patients for spiritual support to the clergy during times of major stress or near death.

The relationship between physicians' responses to different items was revealing. First, which physician responses significantly correlated with the feeling that it was appropriate to address religious issues during the medical visit? Physicians more likely to agree that religion is the most important influence in the life of an older person were also more likely to feel that addressing religious issues in the medical encounter is appropriate ($r = .45$). Those believing that religion enhances physical health or mental health were more likely to feel that religion could be discussed between physician and patient ($r = .30$ and $r = .23$, respectively). Also, physicians who felt that patients would desire their doctor to pray with them were more likely to affirm the appropriateness of addressing religious issues in the medical setting. Regression analysis revealed that physician demographic characteristics were poorly correlated with the feeling that religion is an appropriate topic for discussion during the medical encounter. Only physician attitudes, (i.e. the belief that patients desired their doctor to pray with them and the recognition of religion's important influence in older people's lives) were significant predictors of appropriateness.

Second, which physician attitudes were significantly correlated with the frequency of patients mentioning religious issues in the medical visit? Strong correlations ($r = .23$ to $.39$) arose between favorable physician

attitudes toward religion and the likelihood of patients mentioning religion. In other words, where physicians were receptive to such discussions, patients more commonly mentioned religious concerns that
troubled them. Those physicians who had actually prayed with patients
were also much more likely to report that they had discussed religious
issues with them (mean score 4.7 vs. 3.6, p < .001).

Conclusions drawn from this study are the following. Whether or not
physicians feel it is appropriate to address religious issues depends to
a great extent on the influence that they believe religion plays in the
lives of older people, and on whether they believe that patients desire
their doctor's involvement in religious activities with them. Also, the
likelihood of patients mentioning religious issues in the context of the
medical visit appears to depend on the attitudes and receptiveness of
physicians in this regard. Hence, if the physician does not think that
religion is important or influential in their patients' lives and that patients
do not want their doctors involved in such issues, then they are unlikely
to be receptive to religious issues and patients will probably not mention
them. Further research on this topic, preferably longitudinal work, is
vital to either confirm or refute this hypothesis.

The next question, of course, is do the opinions offered by physicians
on this subject accurately reflect the real situation? In other words, does
religion have a strong influence in the lives of older persons? Do older
persons desire their doctors to address religious issues or become involved in religious activities, such as prayer, with them? As we have
seen in prior sections (Chapter 1), both national surveys and more local
investigations consistently report that religion plays a major role and
influence in the lives of older persons—at least by their self-report. Next,
we will examine how patients feel about praying with their doctors. The
data presented in the following study conducted by the senior author
(HGK) is unpublished and until now has not appeared elsewhere.

DO OLDER PATIENTS WANT THEIR PHYSICIANS TO
PRAY WITH THEM?

Methods

A questionnaire was distributed to: (1) elderly participants in a seniors'
lunch program, and (2) patients of a state-affiliated university-based
outpatient geriatric clinic. Neither site had an affiliation with a religious
institution. Questionnaires were distributed at the nutrition sites during
lunch time by the local program coordinators. These nutrition sites were
located in two moderately sized midwestern urban areas ranging in
population size from 65,000 to 100,000. In the second phase of the survey,
consecutive new patients attending a geriatric outpatient clinic between

February and May 1986, were asked to complete the same questionnaires. Due to small numbers in each group (N = 38 in senior center group (41% response) and N = 34 in geriatric clinic group (70% response), they were combined for analysis purposes. Of the 135 persons receiving questionnaires, seventy-two responded for an overall response rate of fifty-three percent.

Elderly Person Questionnaire

The forty-nine-item questionnaire distributed to the senior lunch program and geriatric clinic sample was designed to answer several research questions in addition to those posed in this study. For our purposes, two questions were of interest and corresponded to similar questions asked in the previously mentioned physician survey. First, participants were asked to indicate the degree to which the following statement applied to them: "My religious faith is the most important influence in my life." Response categories included the following: "Completely untrue," "Mostly untrue," "Mostly true," "Completely true." The second question of relevance was the following: "If you were experiencing great emotional distress, were very sick, or near death, would you like your personal physician to pray with you?" The four possible response categories included: "No, definitely not," "No, probably not," "Yes, somewhat," "Yes, very much."

RESULTS

Demographic Characteristics of Elderly Sample

The sample consisted predominantly of Caucasian (>90%)[91%], Protestant (69%)[66%], women (76%)[59%], with a mean age of 75.5 years [73.7]. Figures in brackets [] indicate values for the general U.S. population age sixty-five years and over, and may be used for comparison (Princeton Religion Research Center, 1982; U.S. Bureau of the Census). The reader should take note of the differences between our sample and the general population and consider the small sample size (N = 72) and nonrandom sources from which the sample was drawn; these factors may have introduced important selection biases that must be considered when attempting to generalize results. Unfortunately little data is known on nonrespondents except for those nonrespondents (N = 16) from the geriatric's clinic sample, who differed from respondents in being all Caucasian (100%), women (100%), and of more advanced age (78.9 years).

Responses

The responses of older persons to questions about religion's influence in their lives, and feelings toward their physician's praying with them are presented in Table 3. Note that 85 percent reported "mostly" or "completely" true to the statement: "My religious faith is the most important influence in my life." This figure may be inflated somewhat by selection bias; however, it compares favorably to Gallup's figure of 82 percent obtained in the national surveys. With regard to feelings on prayer with physicians, 51 percent reported that they would like this very much, and another 27 percent noted that they would probably be in favor of such activity. Only 23 percent showed little or no interest in prayer with their physicians. When responses to the above questions were dichotomized and crosstabulated, persons in favor of physician prayer were considerably more inclined to report religion to be a significant influence in their lives (94%; $x^2 = 10.4$, DF = 2, p = .001).

CONCLUSIONS

It appears that older persons, particularly those who are religious, would indeed like their doctors to pray with them under stressful circumstances that include severe illness, emotional distress, or proximity to death. Several respondents also noted that their answer to the physician prayer question depended a lot on *who* their doctor was and what his religious beliefs were. These findings suggest that when physicians' beliefs are consonant with those of their older patients, the likelihood of these patients being receptive to religious behaviors such as prayer with their physicians is quite high.

If religion is important in the lives of older people, and under certain circumstances these persons do indeed desire their doctor to address religious issues with them, then this information is important for physicians to know. Recall in the physician survey that the feelings of physicians regarding the appropriateness of addressing religious issues in the medical context depended greatly on these two pieces of information. Recall also that the likelihood of patients mentioning religious issues was strongly correlated with their physician's attitudes on the appropriateness of this subject for the medical encounter. These findings suggest that increasing physicians' awareness of the importance of religion to older persons and of the desire of the religious elderly to have their physician involved in this area (under certain circumstances), might enhance medical professionals' receptivity to such issues and facilitate communication on this subject with their patients.

As discussed earlier, at no time is it ethical for a physician to force their beliefs on a patient who is dependent on that physician in a ther-

Table 3
Reports from older persons concerning (1) the influence of religion in their lives, and (2) the desire to have their physicians pray with them during times of extreme physical or emotional distress.

	Geriatric Clinic %(N)	Senior Centers %(N)	Combined %(N)	1982 Gallup Poll %(N)
Religious faith most important influence in life				
1. Completely untrue	14 (5)	0 (0)	8 (5)	4 (11)
2. Mostly untrue	9 (3)	7 (2)	8 (5)	11 (29)
3. Mostly true	17 (6)	52 (16)	33 (22)	40 (106)
4. Completely true	60 (21)	42 (13)	52 (34)	42 (111)
TOTALS	100 (35)	101+ (31)	101 (66)	97++ (257)
Would like personal physicians to pray with them				
1. No, definitely not	3 (1)	9 (3)	5 (4)	
2. No, probably not	26 (10)	9 (3)	18 (13)	
3. Yes, somewhat	24 (9)	29 (10)	27 (19)	
4. Yes, very much	47 (18)	53 (18)	51 (36)	
TOTALS	100 (38)	100 (34)	101 (72)	

+ Totals not 100 due to rounding
++ 3% (9) no opinion

apeutic relationship. Maintaining an open and sensitive attitude towards religious issues in older patients, however, may have a positive effect on the patient-physician relationship and may enhance communication and understanding so vital to the healing process.

12

A MINISTERIAL PERSPECTIVE

Mona Smiley

The preceding chapters have examined in-depth the relationship between religion, health, and aging. The purpose of this chapter is threefold: first, to review the relationship between religion and aging; second, to examine a role of the minister to elders focusing on a hitherto underemphasized role; third, to review data from a survey on retired women religious.

The title was deliberately chosen to avoid even the appearance of a complete discussion of the many dimensions of ministry relating to religion and aging. The words "church" and "minister" will be used in their generic sense to include all denominations in the Judeo-Christian tradition.

The term ministry comes from the Latin word for service. Thus, minister is defined as servant—one who waits upon or ministers to the needs of another (Knight, 1982). The term "ministry" will be applied to those who represent their church in some formal way and who act formally in the name of the church community (Mahoney, 1987). A goal of ministry is,

to help . . . discover in a changing and absurd world a sense of meaning and purpose. The minister whether ordained, vowed, or lay, proclaims the kingdom of God through preaching, counseling, teaching, organizing, serving, and reconciling. . . . the minister consistently witnesses to the truth that human history and our individual histories are filled with meaning.

Thus, the minister's role in an age of introspection and narcissism, an age of isolation and alienation, is to offer deliverance from the estrangement of narcissism, through the experience of community, and the recovery of meaning through commitment and faith. (Cozzens, 1983, p. 37)

Commenting on Western Christianity, Knapp reports that the theme of respect for age in scripture is seen almost exclusively in terms of respect for parents (Knapp, 1981). The commandment tells us to "Honor your father and your mother so that you may have a long life in the land that Yahweh your God has given to you" (Genesis, 20:12). As children we assume that the primary focus of this precept is young children's attitudes toward their parents. It is important to realize that this commandment, as with all the commandments, was originally addressed to adults. This was aimed not only at the adult son and daughter's attitudes toward their parents, but it was also protection for the elderly (Pilli, 1984). This commandment is one that pervades the teachings of all major Western churches.

According to Katz, aging is an arbitrary nomenclature, a variable, subject to the widest interpretation. It is therefore important to consider the inputs of both religion and science in trying to expand our grasp of the phenomenon of aging in our culture, and in reaching for a system of values or attitudes that will be intelligent, realistic, and spiritually valid (Katz, 1975). Nouwen and Gaffney (1974) remind us that "The elderly are our prophets, they remind us that what we see so clearly in them is a process in which we all share". A decade after the publication of Nouwen and Gaffney's *Aging: The Fulfillment of Life*, Charles Fahey, director of the Third Age Center at Fordham University, said during a national teleconference on the elderly, that the elderly need a "distinct spirituality" to help their "growth in the Lord" (Fahey, 1985).

Robert Butler pointed out in 1973 that:

Old people are led to see themselves as "beginning to fail" as they age, a phrase that refers as much to self-worth as it does to physical strength. Religion has been the traditional solace by promising another world wherein the aging self springs to life, never to be further threatened by loss of its own integrity. Thus the consummate dream of immortality for Western man is fulfilled by religion while the integration of the aging experience into his life process remains incomplete. (p. 17)

Until the 1960s most of the empirical research on the aged was done on institutionalized elders. Is it any wonder then, that the prejudice of ageism began its subliminally seductive task and that gerontophobia, with its many myths of aging, became the norm in our society?

It is only since the sixties that the human sciences began to deal in a systematic way with aging. Researchers of the fifties and sixties, notably Moberg (1953a, 1958, 1965, 1968), O'Reilly (1957), Orbach (1961), Stark

(1968), Fichter (1969), and Shanas (1962), were ahead of the churches in their interest in religion, health, and aging.

Heenan (1972), in a comprehensive survey of the literature on religion and aging examined 140 social science journals. Eighty journals were reviewed in their entirety and sixty were surveyed from the period 1945–1971. Of the fifty-five empirical studies found, twenty-two were published before 1961 and thirty-three after that date. Heenan praised Moberg as "The only sociologist of religion who has consistently explored the relationship between religion and the aged." Heenan categorized the extant research studies on religion and aging into four groups: (1) organizational participation, (2) the meaning of religion to the aged, (3) religion and personal adjustment for the aged, and (4) religion and death. Heenan criticized the design and methodology of many of these studies, but of major interest for the purpose of this chapter is his criticism of the researchers for their "neglect of the possibility that religiosity takes new forms among the elderly as they approach death" (Heenan, 1972).

Since the majority of older persons in the United States belong to local congregations, churches and their ministers are in ideal positions to serve their aged members. As was reported in Chapter one of this text, the church is "the single most pervasive" resource available to the elderly (Palmore, 1980). Although it is true that the major religions have long been in the forefront in providing social welfare services and in sponsoring institutions that care for the elderly, "it was 1972 before these bodies came together to deal with the concern for the spiritual well-being of the aging—an area of responsibility no other agency has the capability of fulfilling" (Letzig, 1986).

After the 1971 White House Conference on Aging (WHCoA), the Administration on Aging invited and indeed urged religious bodies to respond to the recommendation from the section on spiritual well-being. Thus the National Interfaith Coalition on Aging (NICA) was formed in 1972. The implementation of NICA's objectives included the development of the definition of "spiritual well-being." NICA defines spiritual well-being as "the affirmation of life in a relationship with God, self, community and environment that nurtures and celebrates wholeness" (Letzig, 1986).

Of the fifteen recommendations concerning what the government should do to help religions meet the religious needs of the aged, one is worthy of note: "that the government cooperate with religious organizations in helping the aged meet their spiritual needs." Indeed, as far back as 1959 Wolff reported that religious beliefs, prayer, and faith in God all helped the aged to overcome many of the common problems in old age such as loneliness, grief, and unhappiness.

It has been estimated that from one-third to one-half of ministers' counseling and pastoral calling time is devoted to the aged (Hammond, 1981; Moberg, 1975). Among Baptist ministers, attitudes toward spending time with elders was not the minister's "most enjoyable" activity, neither was it the "least enjoyable" (Longino and Kitson, 1976). It was also found that ministers tended to be somewhat ageist in their attitudes and responses toward the aged. There is no evidence to show that Baptist ministers were any more or less ageist than ministers of other major denominations. Ten years after the Longino and Kitson study, Becker wrote,

It is highly probable that in pastoral ministry with older persons we are guilty of a subtle form of ageism that we are not even aware; i.e., the tendency to assume that the spiritual or theological problems of those over sixty-five are out of the same cloth. (Becker, 1986, p. 14)

During the late seventies the relationship between religion and aging became important to churches and to their ministries (Wingrove and Alston, 1971; Mindel and Vaughan, 1978; Moberg, 1970, 1974, 1975). In 1977, Maggie Kuhn, the founder of the Gray Panthers, wrote that "churches are acculturated like other institutions in Western society and still remain youth-oriented." Kuhn believed that this was a great detriment to their ministry to elders. Being youth-oriented may be one reason that churches and their ministers have come so recently to see the important relationship of religion to health and aging. Another reason could be that phenomenon in modern higher education that to a great extent still prevents the wholistic view of humankind from being shared, even with the educated. Henri Nouwen commented in his trailblazing 1974 book, which is now a classic:

In these new halls of learning . . . numerous students spend most of their four years of college education almost exclusively with their peers, unable to play with a child, work with a teenager, talk with any adult or have any human contact with the elderly. . . . when there is no world around you as a reminder of where you came from and where you will go . . . that is a real tragedy. (p. 120)

Those in ministry are subject to the same stereotypes as the society in which they live. A glance back at a ministerial view of aging in American history shows Cotton Mather, who preached in the late seventeenth and early eighteenth centuries, writing in his diary the following:

There are several aged People, that I have a strong disposition to Visit, upon the Intention of bringing their Preparations for Death into its perfect work. There is a very old man, whom I would bring into the Church before he dies; and I would make it an Occasion of Speaking very pungent things to the old People in the Assembly.

The scandalous Profaneness of those who even to Old Age, neglect preparing for and approaching the Table of the Lord, is to have yet more pungent Rebukes bestowed upon it. (Taylor, 1984, pp. 116–117)

Despite its ominous tone, it shows that Mather's primary ministerial concern was for the *spirituality* of the aged in his congregation.

To understand what it means to grow old today in America, Cole reviewed approximately one thousand Protestant sermons given by twenty representative ministers between 1800 and 1900. He found that "nineteenth-century Protestantism's approach to aging and old age grew out of its view of life as a spiritual journey from this world to the next" (Cole, 1984). Since life was viewed as a pilgrimage, old age became the important time to prepare for "the Judgment of God." Cole goes on to state that:

Throughout the seventeenth, eighteenth, and nineteenth centuries, the vision of life as a spiritual voyage, with its emphasis on introspection, on receiving experience as well as actively modeling it, on reconciling past and future in the present, on yielding one's life up to its maker, had provided an inwardly viable sense of continuity and meaning in old age. During the twentieth century, the accelerating pace of scientific discovery and of capitalist productivity badly weakened this vision and with it the incentives to grow old at all. (p. 332)

Early in the twentieth century, then, with the popularity of the scientific world view, it is no surprise that hostility to "all forms of decline or decay—especially old age and death became the norm," Cole commented.

As has been cited in an earlier chapter of this text, "patterns of belief, religious orientation, activity and the importance of religion remain fairly stable over time" (Blazer and Palmore, 1976). Moberg refrained from drawing any causal inferences in his study on religion, although he does conclude that there apparently is a positive connection between adjustment, religious interest, and activities, though it may in turn reflect the presence of other factors (Moberg, 1975). In general there does not seem to be any widespread tendency toward greater religiosity with age. It is important to point out, however, that with the dearth of longitudinal studies, the research jury is still out on that question.

Webster defines "religiosity" as "relating to or manifesting faithful devotion to an acknowledged ultimate reality or deity." Levin and Schiller (1987) make the distinction between institutionalized and interiorized religiosity. They define interiorized religiosity as "an individually experienced and subjectively interpreted phenomenon, that can be characterized by cognitive and affective traits, such as . . . 'faith' or the particular salient beliefs held by an individual" (p. 11). It would seem then, that a primary focus of ministry should be aimed at interiorized religiosity. If, then, sociologists of religion and gerontologists have not shown too much interest in the past in interiorized religiosity, it is certainly time to do so. Do ministers of religion have to await the ultimate, strictly controlled, empirical study on religion and aging before they move forward in a ministry to elders that Fahey calls a "distinct spirituality" to help their growth in the Lord? Ministers across all major religions usually have a role with a long history and tradition and one that is familiar to their parishioners. The development of a "distinct spirituality" then, is certainly a task for men and women of deep faith.

In 1984 Cole asked, "How does a culture meet the existential needs of its old people?" He answers his own question by saying that essentially culture draws from its core values and beliefs. He goes on to quote David Gutmann, who draws on cross-cultural research and argues that traditional folk societies integrate the aged into their sacred belief systems. Thus the aged graduate from control over production, to control over ritual; the aged in many preliterate societies serve as "bridgeheads to the sacred."

The Princeton Religion Research Center did a survey before the 1981 White House Conference on Aging. It was found that only 3 percent of persons in the sixty-five-plus age category reported having no religious preference (Letzig, 1986). Koenig, the principal researcher for this text, reports a 73 percent disagreement on a negatively worded question, "I rely very little on religious beliefs when dealing with stress and difficulties" (Koenig et al., 1988a). Two years before Koenig's study, Conway (1985–86) reported that of the most action-oriented coping behaviors of elders, prayer ranked first—in the top five. This seems to fulfill the description of interiorized religiosity described above by Levin and Schiller.

Among the hundreds of recommendations adopted by the 1981 WHCoA, fifty are relevant to the religious sector and therefore to the ministerial role. Recommendation number 219 should be of particular importance to those in ministry. It states that a blue ribbon panel "be appointed by the Secretary of Health and Human Services to originate and disseminate, consistent with the First Amendment provision of the Constitution . . . the concept of spiritual well-being, as a valid part of human wholeness" (Letzig, 1986). Since the federal government recognizes "spiritual well-being as a valid part of human wholeness," the question can be asked, how can this continue to be largely ignored even by those whose vocation in life is to minister?

David Belgum, in an address to community ministers in Elkhart, Indiana, in 1984 reminded them that some ministers feel intimidated by the special expertise of those, in this techno-scientific age, who can delve deeply into the sea of knowledge and come up with the pearl of great price, a clear answer to a specific question. He went on to say that those in ministry defer and refer to a variety of expert specialists, and he then posed the question: "Is there a place for our kind of generalist as practitioners of pastoral care?"

Moberg reported that few modern clergy have received pastoral training appropriate for dealing with elderly parishioners. One small study in the midwestern United States revealed that less than 30 percent of the ministers had been given specific advice on meeting the needs of older people, and that still fewer felt their training was adequate—this is in spite of the fact that one-third to one-half of their work is directly tied to older people (Moberg, 1975).

When researching barriers to assimilation of the elderly into parishes, Fountain posits that sometimes there are physical barriers and that there may even be emotional barriers. When speaking of ministry to elders he wrote in 1986:

Finally, the clergy also have to share the blame. Too often the pastor has the tragic idea that the senior adult is not too important to his ministry. Or worse, he may see the elderly as a hindrance to ministry. It goes like this; "Older members can't help me in ministry. They can't contribute financially to the congregation. . . . Because of their health problems I'm going to be tied down with hospital calls and shut-ins. Why bother?"

This type of thinking reflects societal attitudes and standards. . . . In earlier days . . . Our society regarded the senior as someone to look to for wisdom, knowledge, and leadership. But times have changed. Now when someone reaches age 65, we are ready to discard them as useless. On the part of society, that attitude is irresponsible. On the part of the church, it is inexcusable. (p. 51)

Studies of aging tell us that not only are all old people not alike, but also that they are unique. Becker, writing in the same vein and in the same year as Fountain, says that, "Examined pastoral experience, clinical evidence, and what little empirical research has been done in this field suggests that this uniqueness of the elderly is also present in the spiritual domain" (p. 14). Why, then, is there such a gap between what is known about elders and aging, and the failure on the part of many in ministry to address the essential element of spirituality? The youth-orientation and ageist attitude of society, including ministers, has been mentioned. College and university campuses and courses of study, which not only do not include human lifespan development courses in their curricula, but may still for the most part be described as "youth ghettos," may be a contributing factor. The inappropriate and incomplete education of future ministers may also be a part of the reason.

In 1982, a study was conducted that involved young ministers who had graduated in 1977, 1978, and 1980. The participants were drawn from two seminaries, one was interdenominational and the other was Roman Catholic. Two of the research questions concerned role adjustment and role discrepancy. The researcher asked the questions: "Does seminary performance predict performance in the role of full-time ministry?" A second question asked: "Does discrepancy between performance and congregational expectations in the seminary predict that similar differences will occur when the full-time role is assumed?" Connors reported in 1985 that:

The study revealed that role discrepancy in training is a reliable prediction of role discrepancy in the full-time practice of ministry. . . . The strongest correlation between role discrepancy in the seminary and role discrepancy experienced later in the parish was in the area of development of fellowship and worship. (p. 39)

The research goes on to point out that to expect no difference because of the highly personal nature of worship is somewhat unrealistic. Changes in seminary education during the late seventies and the early eighties seem to have helped seminarians in their transition from seminary to full-time ministry. Nevertheless, when ministers' role expectations differ from those of their church members, this is bound to have a great impact on ministerial performance. Connors recommends more continuing education, assessment programs, and supervision for young ministers. More research is certainly needed to ascertain if role discrepancy in the seminary predicts future discrepancy in the later ministerial role.

This study of seminarians is important in the context of this book because it highlights an area of ministry closely related to spiritual well-being. Also if there is perceived role discrepancy in the area of fellowship and worship in general, this suggests that the discrepancy is further compounded for older church members. This reveals another expansive area open for future research.

Do today's ministers have a concern for the spiritual well-being of the elderly? Both in the present and the past, churches have been involved with nutrition, housing, clinics, and even legal guardianship for the elderly (Keyser, 1986). In almost every aspect of the lives of elders these corporal works of mercy have been and will continue to be necessary. As Becker reminded his readers in 1986, however, those in ministry would do well to remember that the spiritual well-being of the elderly should be their primary concern.

McFadden's study is another case in point. McFadden presented her research at the annual meeting of the American Society on Aging in 1986. She reported that although ministers "were specifically asked about elders who wanted to discuss spiritual matters with them," very few ministers interviewed "had much to say about this." The ministers in the study represented twelve different Christian denominations in Wisconsin. Some of them avoided the issue of spiritual well-being en-

tirely; one noted how his church emphasized spiritual growth throughout life; one Catholic sister noted that,

the only time spiritual matters came up in her contacts with elders were when
they were coupled with talk of death. She commented that she found elders'
concerns about whether God is merciful to be troubling and she does not always
know how best to handle this situation. (McFadden, 1986, p. 20)

In that same study another Catholic sister whose duties were "wholly
pastoral" had much more to say about spiritual well-being. This sister
found the elders "to be very prayerful people, concerned about their
spiritual lives." She added that she urged the pastor to initiate a "Ministry of Praise," where those elders who are homebound pray for members of the parish. The pastor perceived that this would only create an
"administrative burden" for him.

Of the 150 questionnaires sent out to ministers by McFadden, only
twenty-nine (18%) were returned, hence no conclusive results, only
observations based on response frequencies, were offered. The failure,
however, of 123 ministers to respond may shout a great deal louder
than any rigidly controlled study.

In 1985, Thomas Robb, the Director of the Presbyterian Office of Aging, Atlanta, Georgia, in launching "The Gift of a Lifetime" project,
wrote about the lack of ministries involving older adults and remarked
that this lack constituted a crisis within the Presbyterian Church (U.S.).
He then went on to specify ministries that respond to older adults' life
experiences and spiritual needs. As in the case of the Baptist ministers,
the Presbyterian Church has no monopoly on the crisis described by
Reverend Robb.

From the extant studies mentioned before in this text, more recently
those of Conway, (1985), Koenig et al. (1988a), and Folkman and Lazarus
(1980), can there be any doubt about the central place the spiritual holds
in the lives of the majority of today's elders? Cozzens made the point
in 1983 that, "Ministry is therapeutic when it points to the central place
of the spiritual in the drama of human life." Becker points to the "central
theme" of ministry to elders as their spiritual well-being, and says that
ministers must not confuse the spiritual with other "undifferentiated
counseling" offered by social workers and other professionals. Cozzens
reiterated in 1983 that ministry must flow from "a life of faith, prayer
and commitment because when the minister is a person of prayer and
trust, his or her ministry calls forth the power of the Spirit."

What then, should ministers do about the need for a "distinct spirituality" for the elderly? First, they must listen. To whom must they
listen? Missinne wrote it very clearly in 1983. He said that the elderly
themselves can teach best about their spiritual needs and how to minister

to them. He went on to qualify, however, that this listening must be "compassionate listening . . . in order to assist the elderly in this search for meaning in their lives." Where does compassion come from? Le-Veque tells us that it comes from an inner strength "that is secure enough to admit that the minister shares the same human nature as the sufferer and as a member of the human race is subject to the same fate." What LeVeque said in 1987 about compassion, in general, can be very well applied to the kind of "compassionate listening" Missinne recommends. When one begins to listen with a compassionate ear and heart, it immediately becomes apparent that the religion and the religiosity of each elder is unique and not "cut from the same cloth."

Missinne goes on in his gadfly role to declare:

Human beings are spiritual; they cannot live by bread alone. Churches need to respond to the spiritual needs of the elderly, for a person would not grow to be 70, 80 or 90 years old if this longevity had no meaning.

Religion and worship are not separate aspects of being human. Our minds, bodies, and souls make us human. To neglect any one of the three is to ignore a very important part of our humanity. Each of us has an inner drive to seek order, purpose, and meaning in life. (Missinne, 1983, p. 25)

At the beginning of this chapter a goal of ministry included "the recovery of meaning through commitment and faith." If elders are aided to find meaning in their lives, their integrity is affirmed.

If compassionate listening is the first requirement in ministry to the elderly, the next requirement is relationship. Missinne says that this relationship must be one of friendship in which the minister becomes vulnerable so that "deep trust and sharing, may result." Elders need someone that they can trust, someone who has a loving and a compassionate heart, someone who will never stoop to condescension.

A recent follow-up survey (Smiley, 1987b) was done of a qualitative study on a convenience sample of retired women religious. In the original study the sample size was fifty-six and in the 1987 followup, it was forty. The attrition rate between studies was 28.6 percent, 19.6 percent by death and 8.9 percent by illness. The mean age of the subjects was eighty-two years at followup. The age range in the 1987 survey was seventy-two to ninety-six years. An open-ended question was asked to ascertain what these women judged to be the three most important qualities of those who were in ministry to them. The question read: "In a person who ministers to me, what three qualities do I judge to be the most important for the effectiveness of their ministry?" The subjects were asked to prioritize their three top responses from a list of qualities that had emerged in a previous free-association exercise. The qualities that emerged were first, "compassion" (47.5%); second, "caring"

(32.5%); and third, "trust" (27.5%). Stratifying the sample by age yielded the following responses: ages seventy-two to seventy-nine (N = 13): compassion (46.2%), caring (30.8%), and trust (15.4%); ages eighty to eighty-nine (N = 23): compassion (43.4%), caring (30.8%), and trust (15.4%); and ages ninety to ninety-six (N = 4): caring (100%), compassion (75%), and trust (50%).

The composition of the sample was as follows: 25 percent born in the U.S., 8 percent in Mexico, 18 percent in Germany, and 50 percent in Ireland. The priorities remained stable across age and country of origin. The ninety-plus subject category showed more unanimity than those in their seventies and eighties, although the N for this group was small. The quality around which there was most agreement was compassion. Seventy-five percent of the ninety-plus subjects marked compassion as their second choice while 43.4 percent of those eighty-plus years, and 46 percent of those in the seventy-two-plus years marked compassion as number two. The data from these two studies are as yet unpublished. Since this was a convenience sample it does not admit for generalization. These, however, are articulate women, 85 percent of whom achieved college degrees and held professional and responsible jobs both in education and in healthcare during their active years. Their report on priorities for qualities in those who minister to them yields a collective wisdom that represents 3,284 years and should say something to those who would be ministers, to those who select or appoint ministers, and most of all, to those who educate others for ministry to elders.

This is a challenge for ministers who must be persons of prayer and trust before they can face their own vulnerability. How frequently this researcher has heard middle-aged ministers exclaim: "I cannot visit that nursing home or retirement center, it is too sad, it makes me feel very uncomfortable." Nouwen states that we carry within us a deep-seated resistance against care. Caring means we have to come in touch with our own sufferings, pains, and anxieties. Ministers must begin with themselves for they cannot help elders to grow if they themselves are not also striving to find meaning in their own lives. McFadden writes that ministries might be greatly enriched by ministers,

taking the time and the risk of opening themselves to the whole being of the elder—the sorrows as well as the joys, the dissatisfactions as well as the contentedness—. . . not to do so is to assume implicitly that elders have finished in their growing. (McFadden, 1986, p. 23)

Perhaps this is an added reason for the popularity of the electronic TV church, particularly with elders. The hunger for a "distinct spirituality" is there. Maybe the hunger is not being satisfied by the local churches or their ministries.

Because the needs of elders are myriad and complex, what Haring advised in 1985 in the case of terminally ill persons can be appropriately applied to elders. Time and aging, a wholistic approach, including the spiritual dimension as well as the others, leads to astonishing results. In this faith journey there are no easy solutions; however, there is a new awareness, of the need for a pastoral team approach based on a wholistic vision that requires great trust, compassion, and caring. This pastoral team must help elders to find the meaning in their individual life histories. As Haring points out in his book *In Pursuit of Wholeness*,

As scientists and doctors begin to see more clearly that health and sickness cannot really be understood if the dimensions of salvation and wholeness are ignored, so too, theologians have begun to realize that their striving for a wholistic vision is not adequate unless they integrate the insights of the various disciplines that study the human person and human life conditions. (pp. 21–22)

Just as churches and their ministers in the past have been very aware of the material needs of elders and have developed programs and projects to meet these needs, so too, there is a great opportunity for ministers in the future. Pilli had this challenge in mind when he wrote in 1984 that "Elders are called to a depth of faith and feeling where they see that death is not the end, that God is truly with them." Pilli then invited ministers to go on this "inner journey" with the elderly where they can together mutually "discover that God loves them unconditionally, freely, and indeed passionately."

The psalmist's cry echoes into the twenty-first century. "You have taught me since I was young and I still tell of your wonderful acts. Now that I am old and my hair is gray, do not abandon me, God" (Psalms 71:17–18). The development of a "distinct spirituality" for elders has only just begun.

13

IMPLICATIONS FOR CLINICIANS AND AVENUES FOR FUTURE RESEARCH

As we have seen in earlier chapters, national surveys and gerontological studies have confirmed the conventional wisdom that older Americans, on the average, are highly religious and involved in church and private religious activities. We have also presented studies suggesting that, for many older persons, religion has a positive impact on various dimensions of well-being: life satisfaction, social adjustment, and mental health. A growing body of research points to the prospect that religion may have at least an indirect effect on older people's physical health in that it affects how they view and respond to states of health and illness. The present chapter is intended to help healthcare professionals, educators, and policy makers recognize and understand religiosity in older persons and use that knowledge to improve the quality of healthcare. The following ten sections will review religion's role as a coping resource, point to the ways in which religious beliefs affect health behaviors and the doctor-patient relationship, describe how religious affiliations enhance social support and how some churches facilitate access to care, and discuss religious issues in terminal care.

1. *Maximizing Coping and Adjustment to Stressful Changes in Later Life.* Patients frequently seek advice from their physicians on nonmedical matters (Barsky, 1981). There may be a need for information concerning strategies to assist them in dealing with changes in their own health or the health of their spouse. Coping with chronic illness and issues surrounding death and dying may result in considerable anxiety or depression that could interfere with motivation necessary to comply with longterm, sometimes unpleasant treatment regimens. The adjust-

ment of patients to their illness is an important concern for physicians who seek increased knowledge about helpful coping strategies, and resources available to older patients, to assist them in adjusting to stressful health transitions.

As other less durable coping resources such as health, wealth, and social support decline with age, many older adults are left to rely on intrapsychic coping behaviors. Religious cognitions may be particularly common and effective in this regard (by their self-report). National and regional surveys of older adults have repeatedly shown that when asked whether religious beliefs or behaviors assist them in coping with major life changes, responses are affirmative in 85 to 90 percent of cases (Princeton Religion Research Center, 1982; Americana Healthcare Corporation 1980–81, survey). Recent studies examining spontaneously reported coping behaviors of older adults during stressful life experiences indicate that 45 percent of these persons used religious beliefs or activities to help them to regulate their emotional responses (Koenig et al., 1988c). This study and others have shown that among older adults, particularly the black elderly, religious coping behaviors are more prevalent than any other emotion-regulating strategy (Conway, 1985–86; Manfredi and Pickett, 1987). Supporting these cross-sectional observations are the results reported from the First Duke Longitudinal Study of Aging, in which correlations between adjustment and religion were found to increase with aging during an eighteen year followup period (Blazer and Palmore, 1976). A recent cross-sectional study employing a community sample of older adults (N = 836) with widely varying types and levels of religiosity, likewise found the strongest correlations between religion and subjective well-being among adults age seventy-five years and over (Koenig et al., 1988b). More intrinsically oriented religious individuals are also more likely to have an internal locus of control and a positive ideal self-concept; both of the latter psychological indices associate with mental health (Kivett, 1979). See Chapters 3, 5, and 7 for a more comprehensive literature review on this subject.

2. *A Potential Mental Healthcare Resource.* Ministers with special training in pastoral counseling may be in an important position to provide personal counseling to religiously oriented older adults with complex psychosocial needs and concerns (Cluff and Cluff, 1983; Rosen, 1974). In an age where the increasing mental health needs of the burgeoning over age sixty-five population threatens to overwhelm the formal mental healthcare system, other resources need to be identified. Reynolds (1982) has described the many ways by which religious institutions may assist in community efforts at prevention of mental illness. The busy primary care physician often does not have the time or expertise to deal with ethical, social, and psychological needs of older patients, particularly those patients whose complex medical problems consume most of the

medical encounter. The ready availability, low cost, and often greater acceptability of the church, as a mental health resource, must be emphasized, particularly for a population that often subsists on a fixed income and that in the past has shown substantial resistance to psychiatric referral, due to the stigma often associated with such treatment. Whether or not churches and synagogues will answer this call by developing ministries to the aged, is another question (see Chapter 12).

3. *Effect on Perception of Illness and Healthcare Behavior.* Cultural factors have been shown to impact on patients' views of "illness", and the perception of those symptoms that constitute medical illness may be affected by beliefs and attitudes (Kleinman et al., 1978). Religious factors may affect responses to early signs of medical illness, in that explanations and interpretations of symptoms are often culturally based. For some cultural groups, spiritual beliefs may actually form the basis for their health belief system, particularly with regard to ideas about the meaning of health, health promotion, prevention of illness, locus of control, causality of illness, and methods to pursue in the restoration of health problems (Robertson, 1985; Levin and Schiller, 1986). For instance, early signs and symptoms of illness may be accepted more readily, as the fear of death and dying are lessened because of a religious outlook and belief in an afterlife. Belief in an afterlife was one of the few religious beliefs that Stark (1968) found to increase with age during his study of religious attitudes among over three thousand San Francisco Bay area church members. In other cases, symptoms and signs of illness may be identified as requiring healing through religious avenues such as faith healing, rather than through medical consultation. Failure to seek conventional medical evaluation may thus result. On the other hand, the close integration found in the social network of many religious bodies may provide greater surveillance for illness symptoms and reinforce appropriate healthcare-seeking behavior.

4. *Religious Doctrines and Social Milieu Supporting Healthy Lifestyles and Favorable Attitudes Towards Preventive Medicine.* Religious groups often promote a social environment that is conducive to healthy lifestyles. Smoking, excessive alcohol consumption, and illicit drug use are usually discouraged, and such behaviors may be viewed as contrary to doctrinal teachings. The lower frequency of these adverse health behaviors among religiously active persons has been demonstrated in numerous epidemiologic surveys among Mormons (Gardner and Lyons, 1982a, 1982b) and Seventh Day Adventists (Armstrong et al., 1977), as well as among older medical patients of other Christian traditions (Koenig et al., 1988a). Support from church members may play a significant role in both instituting and maintaining lifestyle changes such as smoking cessation, discontinuation or moderation of drinking habits, and appetite control. Another study has shown that women who were active church members

were more likely to participate in cervical cancer screening, thus indicating a greater concern over health maintenance (Naguib et al., 1968). (See Chapters 4 and 6.)

5. *Maximizing Compliance*. Compliance with medical treatment recommendations may be influenced by religious factors, particularly when medical prescriptions run consistent with or counter to strongly held religious beliefs and practices. For instance, a rigidly fundamentalist believer may feel that taking medication to treat an illness is a sign of weakness in their faith, believing that God possesses the power (and willingness) to heal them without assistance from the medical profession. A considerable amount of guilt and frustration might arise from such a situation, particularly if the person does not verbalize his or her concerns or seek counseling. Certain religious groups have dietary restrictions that might also interfere with compliance for certain treatment regimens. On the other hand, compliance may be enhanced through the common religious belief in a need to care for one's body, in that it is created in the image of God and is the dwelling place of the soul. Most traditions currently accept that doctors and medicines do indeed represent resources given to man by God, to help him or her in caring for and maintaining the physical body. Hence, taking one's medicines and complying with lifestyle changes may be viewed as a sign of faithfulness in the stewardship of one's body. Unfortunately, very little data are presently available to support or reject such speculations.

6. *Relevance to the Doctor-Patient Relationship*. The physician's understanding and respect for deeply ingrained religious beliefs of older patients may enhance trust and create an atmosphere that is conducive to greater cooperation by the patient in terms of both compliance and timely reporting of symptoms. A knowledge of religious beliefs and attitudes may also assist the physician in moderating such beliefs where extremes in such behaviors result in a negative impact on health. A serious breakdown in communication along with feelings of bitterness and anger can result from lack of understanding and acceptance of the cultural or religious systems of the patient or their family, which at times may be widely disparate from that of the physician or other healthcare providers (Redlener and Scott, 1979).

7. *An Important Source of Social Support*. Religious organizations have been shown to represent a major source of social support for older adults and have often met practical, in addition to spiritual, needs (see Chapter 5). Cluff and Cluff (1983) have noted that a fragmentation of traditional informal support systems (the church, family, etc.) in recent years has played a major role in the increasing need for government sponsorship of formal programs to now supply these needs. They emphasized the duty of religious communities to reassume some of this responsibility,

and thus help to relieve the pressure on governmental agencies. In addition to supplying practical needs, however, a recent study has shown that churches and synagogues continue to represent a major source of human support for many older adults. In that study, patients attending a geriatric medicine clinic were asked how many of their five closest friends came from their church congregation; over half stated that four or five of their five closest friends came from this source (Koenig et al., 1988a). Social support has been shown to be closely related to indicators of both mental and physical health in both old and young populations. Social concerns are often the most complex and difficult ones that physicians are faced with in their care of geriatric patients, and consequently, they should welcome assistance from religious bodies.

8. *Religious Organizations' Increasing Involvement in Geriatric Healthcare.* Religious groups have begun to take a more active role in providing care to their elderly members. Many religiously sponsored long-term care facilities are arising and some of these institutions represent model efforts in this regard. For example, the Hebrew Home for the Aged in Boston and the Philadelphia Geriatric Center, are among the premier long-term care facilities in this country. Methodists and other Christian denominations have taken leading roles in developing both long-term care facilities and acting as sponsoring organizations to supply practical needs of the community-dwelling elderly. An example of the latter effort are Shepherd Centers, which utilize older persons themselves as a resource to serve the needs of their less fortunate neighbors (Koenig, 1986; Koenig, 1987c). Tobin, Ellor, and Anderson-Ray (1986), in a recent important publication, thoroughly examine the role of religious institutions within the community service system, with a focus on enabling the elderly to help themselves and each other. With this increasingly active role played by churches and synagogues in the care of the elderly, it behooves healthcare practitioners to begin to establish alliances with such organizations and move towards additional joint efforts in supplying healthcare to a population whose demands are becoming greater and more urgent.

9. *Potential Impact on Healthcare Utilization.* The inverse relationship between religious practices/attitudes and mental ill-health, such as anxiety and depression among older populations, should be of significant interest to healthcare providers and policy-makers from both mental health and cost-containment perspectives. Symptoms of mental illness in the elderly, among which anxiety and depression are most common, also frequently present as somatic complaints, thereby cleverly masking their true identity. Consequently, utilization of healthcare resources may be increased and physician time expended in evaluating such compliants for physical causes. Although no studies have examined this issue di-

rectly, the prospect that the more religiously active older adults consume less mental and physical healthcare resources seems to warrant more critical analysis.

10. *Relevance to Death and Dying Issues.* Many intensely religious issues arise in the course of caring for the chronically ill or dying patient. Religious beliefs and activities are in general inversely related to anxiety and fear in this setting (see Chapters 4 and 6). Patients and/or their families may have religious needs that are unmet at this time, particularly during emergencies when there is insufficient time to mobilize their own religious resources (minister or other religious advisor). In the tertiary care setting, patients and their families may be hundreds of miles away from their home congregations and therefore relatively isolated in the sterile environment of the modern day medical center. Physicians and other healthcare professionals, by virtue of their managerial position in the healthcare system, may facilitate access to religious personnel equipped to deal with existential and spiritual needs of these patients and their families. Understanding the importance and pervasiveness of religion among older adults may help to overcome resistance among clinicians in making such arrangements.

In summary, then, religion may impact on health though various social, psychological, and cognitive mechanisms. Healthcare practitioners should benefit from a greater awareness of the role that religion plays in the lives of older adults. This awareness may help to achieve the goal of delivering comprehensive, cost-effective medical care that is sensitive and in harmony with the physical, mental, and spiritual needs of older patients.

RELIGION AND MEDICINE: COOPERATIVE EFFORTS

The goals of religion and medicine are similar. Each seeks to deal with the mysteries and struggles of human existence from birth to death. Both are concerned with the health and well-being of individuals. Religion was the first to address these issues. The understanding of diseases, both physical and mental, in terms of possession by demons or evil spirits is probably the most ancient of all models of causation and healing in human history. Plato wrote the following in his Charmides: "If the head and body are to be well, you must begin by curing the soul, that is the first thing . . . The great error of our day is that physicians separate the soul and the body, when they treat the body" (Merrill, 1981, p. 45).

Merrill (1981) notes that in the twelfth century,

physicians were forbidden to treat a sick person or do more than call the priest, since all sickness was considered by the Church to be the result of sin and so could only be treated by confession and absolution. As recently as 200 years ago in Catholic countries, a physician was forbidden by law to have anything to do with a patient who had not confessed his sins to his priest. (p. 47)

Clearly, religion has been closely linked with health throughout history, and it is only recently that a separation of the two has developed.

The undaunted exclusive reliance on religious cures and the neglect of modern medical intervention, however, may adversely affect health in the same way as does the treatment of illness strictly by the biomedical model with its neglect of emotional and spiritual needs of patients. Vanderpool (1977) has emphasized that health is maximized when religion and medicine are juxtaposed, not counterposed. He emphasizes that both sides need and have much to learn from the other.

Certain questions in life have not been adequately addressed by traditional medicine. Levin and Idler (1981) note that "medicine completely lacks the answers to the question of the meaning of living and dying that religion or even a set of ideological beliefs about history would provide" (p. 35). The amazing "cures" that have occurred in religious settings such as Lourdes can hardly be denied; in fact, medicine might learn much from the study of such cases. Also undeniable, on the other hand, are the fraud and fake healings that may occur in this setting (Nolan, 1974); careful scrutiny by medical professionals serve to ferret out the real from the false cures and thus validate the truth of healings that occur. The power of medicine to affect healing might also be improved when it occurs in a setting where the patient's religious beliefs and world view are supported and strengthened (Vanderpool, 1977). Moberg (1965) comments on this point with particular emphasis on the care of the aged patient:

Above all, the geriatrician must be discerning. Each patient is a distinct person with his own unique background of religious practices, knowledge, beliefs, and feelings which colors his reactions to illness and medical treatment. The broader one's knowledge and the deeper one's understanding, the more effective one will be. (p. 982)

There have been several organized attempts to include spiritual or religious concerns in the medical or psychiatric care of patients, although little attention has been given to the elderly in particular. Holistic health groups, which incorporate both psychological and spiritual dimensions into healthcare, have arisen in several parts of the country (Yahn, 1979). Some medical associations have likewise formed with this concept in mind: American Holistic Medical Association, the Association for Holistic Health, the American Foundation for the Science of Creative Intelligence, and the Institute of Holistic Potential. Both American and British journals exist (*Journal of Holistic Health* (USA) and *British Journal of Holistic Health*). Holistic health groups have interested governmental agencies because of the low cost of the healthcare which they render, particularly in the case of the chronically ill. More research needs to be directed at the influence of holistic type medicine on quality, satisfaction with, and cost of care in older populations. A valid concern, however, is that the latter groups—which may often emphasize Eastern or Hindu religious methods—may not be as oriented to serving the spiritual needs of elderly Americans coming from a predominantly Judeo-Christian perspective.

For years (since 1963) there was a special American Medical Association committee, the AMA Committee on Medicine and Religion, whose purpose was to work towards treating the whole person and promoting closer understanding between physicians, the clergy, and rabbis (Editorial, 1979). The AMA offerred to supply material for the genesis of programs in local communities and major medical institutions (Editorial, 1979). Hoffman (1970), chairman of the Pennsylvania Committee on Medicine and Religion, writes the following in an article entitled "Medicine and Religion: A Natural Alliance": "The question has often been raised as to what areas medicine works in partnership with religion. It is obvious that common goals are shared by clergy and physicians, for both are deeply concerned with the well-being of man" (p. 71). With regard to the outcomes of their meetings, Hoffman further notes that,

Many physicians were surprised to learn of the wide range of problems which the clergy were called upon to handle, many of which had clear medical implications. In turn, it was clear to many clergymen that physicians routinely became involved in the personal problems of their patients, many of these problems touching on issues of morality. (p. 72)

Rosen (1974), a physician and the director of Education at the Cleveland Psychiatric Institute, notes seven health-related functions of the clergyman in the community and hospital:

1. *Consultant-Religious Expert.* Examines the influence of religious beliefs and practices on health, the meaning of sickness to the patient, patient's attitudes toward the body and sex, toward emotional outlets like crying, toward self-pampering behaviors like resting and recreating; can separate out religious phenomena like conversion from symptoms of mental illness.

2. *Consultant-Ethicist.* Contributes on ethical aspects of new medical and surgical technology.

3. *Ombudsman.* Counteracts the impersonality of the hospital or of treatment; can visit the transient, the lonely, the presurgical, and all those who are extremely anxious for any reason.

4. *Preventive Function.* Provides various kinds of education for family living;

intervenes in life's stages and crises; provides a base of security or community root; gives the person a chance to function in a role in a small cohesive community that gives him status.

5. *Physician advocate.* Helps patient accept treatment; schizophrenics not admitting they are ill, ulcer patients not willing to comply with therapy concerning rest and diet, and cardiac patients who refuse to slow down; enhances compliance with therapeutic regimen.

6. *Consumer advocate.* Monitors medical system from his value perspective; questions long-term effects of physician's short-term, crisis-oriented, often simply organic treatment; questions the effect of premature hospital release on family.

7. *Spiritual advisor to physicians.* Doctors need help too; if they didn't, they wouldn't rank so high in suicide and addiction.

Weikart (1986), pastoral counselor and ethicist in the department of Family Practice at the University of Michigan, also points to the value of the potential alliance between the primary care physician and the clergy:

Family practice physicians often refer people to counselors of varied interests for assistance in resolving their psychosocial issues. Traditional referral sources have included psychiatrists, psychologists and social workers. Members of the clergy have been infrequently considered as a referral source. One reason is that many physicians are not familiar with the competence of the clergy . . . Clergy would be members of the healing community for several reasons. First, communities often are small and do not have psychologists, psychiatrists and social workers available locally. However, almost every community has at least one member of the clergy available and in residence. Second, clergy have very minimal fees if any charges are rendered. This allows more people to utilize the available counseling services than if only higher charging resources (psychiatrists, psychologists, social workers) were used. (p. 151)

Such considerations are particularly relevant to older persons who live in rural areas and to those on fixed incomes.

In conclusion, then, the comprehensive healthcare of the older adult depends on the close cooperation between healthcare professionals, religious institutions, and the clergy. The reason for this lies in the importance of religion in the lives of many older persons and its consequent impact on mental and physical health. Our ignorance about the manner in which religion affects health, however, is a major stumbling block in the efforts of both religious communities and healthcare professionals.

FUTURE RESEARCH NEEDS

The field of religion, health, and aging represents virgin territory that has been virtually untouched by clinical investigators. So many questions remain unanswered. Researchers now possess the capability of developing comprehensive survey instruments that can collect vast amounts of data on older people, and the statistical sophistication to analyze relationships at one point in time and longitudinally at many points, while controlling for confounding variables. New models are being developed (Figure 1) which need testing. The time is indeed ripe for researchers to forge ahead in attempts to unravel the complex relationship between religion and health variables throughout life and at the end of life.

Vanderpool (1980) has examined the interaction between religion and medicine and sets important theoretical groundwork for future research. Although his comments are not particularly directed towards older adults, they are probably applicable to any age group. He notes that in research examining the relationship between religion and health, the assumption that religion should somehow always have a positive relationship with health acts only to sabotage efforts at critical and unbiased investigation necessary to attract funding sources for such efforts. Vanderpool underscores that the influence of religion on health and well-being can be either positive or negative depending on how religion is expressed: "religion per se is not positive but, like other aspects of life, can become a blessing or a curse, a destructive or constructive influence" (p. 8).

The following are just a few of the research questions that need to be answered:

1. What is the direction of causation in relationships between religion, and mental and physical health? There is a dire need for longitudinal studies that follow middle-aged persons (with a wide spectrum of religious commitment and activity) over time into late old age. Dropouts from such studies need to be carefully accounted for and characterized, adjusting the final analysis accordingly. Highly sensitive and validated instruments capable of detecting small changes over time are needed to measure both psychological well-being and religiosity. Personality characteristics should be established on all participants at baseline; life events should be documented and characterized during the followup period. Due to funding considerations, it is unlikely that such prospective studies will be designed specifically to examine religion-health issues; instead, such projects must be piggybacked onto longitudinal studies examining other psychosocial and health questions. Answers to questions 2 and 3 below may be vital in structuring such research endeavors.

2. What particular religious beliefs, degree of religious commitment, types of religious expression (personal-intrapsychic vs. social-religious community involvement), and varieties of religious experience are related to psychological well-being and physical health? What major social, cultural, and racial influences affect these relationships?

3. What aspects of psychological and physical health are related to which of the many different religious characteristics of older persons?

4. Are there specific physical illnesses, stress-related or not, that are more influenced by religious beliefs, attitudes, and practices than are other illnesses? For example, are coronary artery disease, colon cancer, or pneumonia more strongly related to religiosity than kidney failure, arthritis, or diabetes? Larger samples and more specific religious information on participants, besides religious denomination, should be collected.

5. What is the relationship between religion and the severity, chronicity, and disability of physical illness? Do older persons who are sicker or more disabled actually turn to religion in an attempt to cope? Upon what factors is this dependent—previous life experience, childhood rearing, underlying personality, social or health characteristics? Is the relationship between church attendance and health due *only* to church activity serving as a proxy for functional ability (i.e. having the physical capacity to get to church)?

6. What life history factors (family rearing practices, life experiences, etc.) are relevant in determining those persons on whom religion has a very positive impact, no discernable impact, or a negative one?

7. Are the benefits of religion in old age solely restricted to its "social aspects" or are "religious factors" present that confer additional psychological and physical health?

8. To what extent do religious beliefs and attitudes really affect healthcare behavior, and for which religious groups may this be particularly true? Which specific beliefs and attitudes affect healthcare behavior? Do these enhance or harm timely health-seeking actions and compliance with medical treatments?

9. What effect does religious belief, commitment, and level of community participation have on healthcare utilization? Are hypocondriacal complaints more or less frequent among religious persons? Is there an association with any particular religious characteristics?

10. What particular mental disorders in old age are particularly responsive to pastoral counseling? Which mental illnesses should be referred to mental health professionals for management?

11. How does a "conversion" or "born again" experience cause spontaneous resolution of major depressive illness, or alcoholism, or addiction? How long does this remission last? What role does the church and support from its members have on maintaining remissions? What are the long-term effects of religious conversion on mental health?

12. What is the relationship between specific psychiatric disorders (major depression, schizophrenia, anxiety disorders, panic attacks) and various religious groups and ideologies? How does age affect this relationship?

13. How might a clinician best approach the religious older person to learn about the religious factors that might be influencing their beliefs about health and compliance with treatment?

14. How can religious teachings be best used to help counsel the older person with psychological distress, in order to allay excessive guilt or feelings of failure, to build up self-esteem, and to allow forgiveness to occur?

15. Further research on ministerial skills is necessary to ascertain if future ministers are being educated to serve the needs of elders in the spiritual domain. Samples could be drawn not only from seminaries, but also from clinical pastoral education programs and from post-secondary religious education courses/programs. In this way, the ordained, the vowed, and the lay ministries could be represented.

16. Additional interdisciplinary studies on aging should be encouraged so that all professionals who serve elders have a more integrated wholistic vision of those being served.

17. What is the impact of geographic location on the prevalence of religious attitudes and beliefs among older adults? Would surveys of older persons in New York and California find equally high prevalence rates for religious coping, as those have shown in the Midwest and South? How about different locations in North and South America, Europe, and other predominantly Christian areas?

18. Virtually all the research on religion, health, and aging has focused on participants of Christian or Jewish religious traditions. What about similar questions for Moslems, Hindus, Buddhists, and other religious traditions? Cross-cultural studies on the relationship between religion and psychological well-being in later life are virtually nonexistent. Good data exist only for a positive relationship between the Judeo-Christian religious tradition and well-being and coping. Do other religions serve a similar purpose? Are particular religious traditions more effective in this regard than others (for persons in later life)?

19. What are the opinions of healthcare professionals with regard to the appropriateness of addressing religious issues in the context of medical encounters? Under what circumstances is this appropriate and what types of behaviors are permissible? Opinions of physicians from a variety of medical and surgical specialties, as well as those from nurses, social workers, and other healthcare professionals are needed. Studies are needed to address these issues in different locations of the country, such as the West and the Northeast, because of the influence of geographic location on religious beliefs and practices. Finally, how do the personal religious beliefs and the activities of clinicians influence their opinions about, and receptiveness to, discussions of religious issues with patients?

20. Prospective studies need to examine whether or not holistic models of healthcare provide better care to older adults in a cost-effective

manner. Outcome variables should include recovery rates from illness, patient and family satisfaction with care, level of adjustment to chronic illness, compliance with therapy, healthcare utilization, and clinician satisfaction, as well as healthcare costs.

21. Methods used to measure religious attitudes, commitment, and behaviors need to be validated among older populations. Short simple, nonthreatening questions need to be developed that are sensitive in differentiating the sincerely religious from the religious by name or social tradition only. Although there is much room for improvement in developing methods that capture the specific dimensions of religion and the older adult, many good measures are currently available (Robinson and Shaver, 1973). Gorsuch (1984) emphasizes that the problem may not be so much that of developing new instruments, but rather of using those already available for investigative efforts focused at answering specific questions. A more uniform use of these measures will allow more meaningful comparisons between studies and assist in detecting geographical factors influencing results. For measuring religious orientation, the Hoge Intrinisic Religiosity Scale is a short, easily understood measure for which validity and reliability have been demonstrated in studies of older populations (see Appendix I). As a brief measure of religious attitudes and orientation (i.e. subjective religiosity), it is the one we currently recommend for use in studies involving older persons coming from a Judeo-Christian religious tradition.

In conclusion, these are but a few of the many possible avenues of research that need to be pursued. The major impact of religion in the lives of many older people makes this topic an important one for scientific study. The potentially powerful influence of religion on mental and physical health demands that medical researchers and social scientists include this variable in any investigation attempting to better understand human behavior and health in later life.

14

CONCLUSION

Religion is a common and potent force in the lives of the majority of older persons in America today. Data to support this statement are abundant. Religion's positive association with mental and physical health in later life is also supported by the majority of studies, but this effect is difficult to demonstrate conclusively. For one, the complexity of such research is enormous. Major problems involve determining: (1) what exactly encompasses the term "religious;" (2) how its components should be measured; (3) what the validity is of the information thus acquired; (4) what types of mental and physical health perameters should be examined and how they should be measured; and (5) what confounding variables need to be controlled in comparative analyses.

In the present cohort of older Americans it is possible, at least for research purposes, to arrive at a consensus on the type of religion to consider. Because over 90 percent of this population comes from a Judeo-Christian tradition, belief in a single Creator who has an interest in man as His creation, can form the basis for studying persons with this belief system and variations upon it. In fact, a number of multi-dimensional measures based on this belief system are available for researchers to utilize, (Robinson and Shaver, 1973) and at least some have been validated for use in older populations (see Appendix I). Other religious traditions will require different measures for assessment based upon their particular beliefs and religious rituals.

Religion, regardless of tradition, may be divided into personal or private religion (beliefs and attitudes) and social or group-oriented religion (church attendance). These are distinct dimensions of religion whose importance may either run parallel within the individual or may diverge markedly. The more common situation is that participation in religious group activity reinforces personal belief and private activity, and vice-versa. This, however, may not always be the case. Church attendance and religious social activities may be of great salience to a person thriving on social contact, yet this does not guarantee that personal belief and attitudes play a similarly important role. On the other hand, many older individuals may derive much comfort and strength from their personal religious beliefs and private activities, yet attend religious services or group gatherings only infrequently, either because of physical disability that prevents them from doing so, or because of other reasons such as disagreements with the local pastor. Consequently, each of these two religious expressions may have differential effects on health, and therefore should be distinguished in research efforts.

Even when agreement has been reached on what religion is, what elements compose it, and what questions to ask in order to capture those elements, the actual acquisition of accurate data presents a formidable barrier to such research. Although many elderly persons delight in the discussion of religion and how it has affected their lives, religion can be for many older adults a very personal topic, and some may have difficulty in discussing this subject for the sake of scientific scrutiny. Some persons may be very verbal about their religion, yet incorporate little of it into daily life. Some persons may be very active in the religious community, yet do so mostly for social reasons in the same way that others join social clubs. The religious connection of such activity, then, may have little meaning. Likewise, religion is a dynamic process whose importance and relevance to the individual is constantly changing in response to life experiences. Such problems make the accurate assessment of religiosity in older persons a difficult assignment when questionnaire or interview methods are the only techniques available to the researcher. The problem is compounded when investigations are cross-sectional rather than longitudinal in design. Lack of interest by the scientific community and the absence of financial support, however, have often resulted in less than adequate consideration of religious factors in longitudinal studies.

Mental health is also a very complex phenomenon. Psychological dynamics considered healthy for younger adults with abundant coping resources and control over their environment, may be maladaptive for older adults in more restrictive settings. Happiness and life-satisfaction, as measured by questionnaire or structured interview, may also be difficult to assess, due to the transient nature of such mood states and the powerful interactions that may occur with life events, personality style, previous adult or early childhood experiences, and social, health, and financial resources.

Although physical health is a more objective phenomenon, its measurement can also be frought with difficulty, particularly when its evaluation is performed by self-assessment rather than direct examination by a trained professional. Self-assessment always includes the person's *perception* of their health, which may be influenced by many psychological factors. Consequently, subjective health may differ from health assessed by careful observation. This problem may be further compounded by the presence of multiple medical illnesses managed with an assortment of powerful drugs with their own attendant side effects. The wide variability of health in older adults is another factor that must be contended with. This variability is dependent on genetic, developmental, and health behaviors that are difficult to predict.

The nature of such investigations is exceedingly complex due to the confounding influences of many social and psychological factors, the difficulties in measurement of many strategic variables, and the relative absence of control by the investigator of the research setting. Consequently, there is little wonder that correlations between religion and health variables have not been as impressive as one would expect after hearing the often dramatic personal testimonies of many older adults concerning the impact that religion has played in their lives (see Chapter 9). Persistent, careful, well-designed research, building on work that has preceded it, should provide a better understanding of this potentially powerful resource in later life.

The evidence is mounting to support a positive impact of Judeo-Christian-based religion on both mental and physical health in later life. While this positive effect is more obvious for mental health, benefits on physical health have also been observed. Because of the few longitudinal studies on this topic, it is difficult to infer causation from the positive associations that have been reported. There are also a number of studies that have shown only marginal associations, if any at all, between religious and health variables. The wide diversity of populations studied and research methods employed is almost certain to account for a large proportion of the variability among these reports. There is considerable evidence to suggest that there are subgroups of the population, based on age, sex, race, personality, life experience, socioeconomic status, even geographical location, for whom religious attitudes and activities may be particularly salient in maintaining physical and mental health in later life.

Religion and health in later life is a topic that has been enshrouded by controversy and personal bias. An objective, critical, and focused research approach is needed to provide solid answers to these important but difficult questions. Because of the many social, psychological, and medical factors involved in such investigations, communication and collaboration between professionals in this effort is vital for progress. The lack of success in previous efforts can be largely attributed to the ignorance of one discipline of the research findings from parallel efforts in other disciplines (for instance, medicine, psychiatry, or psychology's lack of awareness of findings by social gerontologists and sociologists of religion). Religion needs to be studied utilizing the tools of the social sciences, since excellent multi-dimensional tools have been developed for this purpose; however, sociologists may not have access to patient populations to study and acquire data. On the other hand, medical researchers and clinicians have access to populations of psychologically and medically ill older persons who can provide data needed for the testing of many of the hypotheses considered in this text. Collaboration among different professionals and the pooling of their strengths, then, is vital for future progress. The complexity of religion and diversity of its expression, along with its wide prevalence and potentially powerful impact on health in later life, makes such research exciting and challenging for the scientist, regardless of discipline.

APPENDIX I:
CONSTRUCTION AND VALIDATION OF THE SPRINGFIELD RELIGIOSITY SCHEDULE (SRS)

In the design phase of our studies to examine the religious characteristics of geriatric patients (Koenig et al., 1988a) and community-dwelling older adults (Koenig et al., 1988b), we were frustrated in attempts to find in the literature a suitably detailed instrument to measure these characteristics. A review of the literature uncovered a potpourri of instruments, all proporting to measure various aspects of religiosity. None, however, were designed with the intention of surveying elderly populations. Hence, we decided to construct an instrument that would be relevant to the religious beliefs and activities of older Americans (Springfield Religiosity Schedule [SRS]). The contents of this instrument were decided upon after careful review of elderly Americans' responses to questions on religion asked by the Gallup polls over the past fifty years (Princeton Religion Research Center, 1976, 1982, 1985). In addition, David Moberg, one of American's foremost sociologists of religion, who has written and lectured extensively on religion in later life, provided expert guidance and assistance.

Items comprising the resulting instrument came from a variety of religiosity scales already in existence. In some instances we incorporated large sections of established scales and, on one occasion, the entire scale was used. The aim was to capture as many dimensions as possible of the religiosity that characterizes the older adult. As our first step, due to the great variety of religious traditions in this country, we needed to choose a religious perspective upon which to base the contents of our instrument. Without deciding upon a specific religious tradition, we could not have explored religious characteristics in the detail that was desired. We chose the Judeo-Christian religious tradition, based on the fact that 90 percent of Americans age sixty-five and over claim a Protestant or Catholic religious tradition, 3 percent a Jewish preference, 2 percent other traditions, and 5 percent no religious preference (Princeton Religion Research Center, 1985). Hence, Christianity accounts for nearly 95 percent of all older adults reporting a religious preference, with the next largest group being Jewish, at a little over 3 percent. Given this pattern among older Americans, we felt that the use of an instrument that reflects beliefs and activities of these traditions would be quite appropriate.

The resulting instrument, then, consisted of items based predominantly on the Christian tradition, though several of its subscales seemed equally relevant to the Jewish faith. The emphasis was on belief in a single, supreme God, which both traditions share. A description of the components of the schedule and reasons for their inclusion now follows.

First, the four major dimensions of religiosity proposed by Glock and Stark (1965) were selected (their questionnaire and a discussion of methods employed in its use in a large population study can be found in Glock and Stark, 1966). These four dimensions were belief, ritual, experience, and knowledge, and represent the most important of their original five dimensions. Their fifth dimension, "consequences," was not included here because Glock and Stark later dropped it from their instrument on the grounds that "it is not entirely clear the extent to which religious consequences are a part of religious commitment or simply follow from it" (J. Wilson, 1978). Another dimension, the communal aspect of religion, was also chosen to be included in our measure. Finally, spiritual well-being and intrinsic religiosity were incorporated to complete the instrument.

Belief was measured here using Glock and Stark's "Orthodoxy Index" (Glock and Stark, 1966, p. 11). It is based upon orthodox Judeo-Christian tenets and measures the degree of acceptance of the prescribed doctrines of this religious tradition. The portion of our instrument reflecting the belief dimension consisted of items one to four.

Ritual, the next dimension considered, consisted of religious activities of both an organizational and nonorganizational nature. Organizational activities, reflecting in part the social aspects of religion, include church attendance and participation in Bible study or prayer groups (items 5 and 6). Nonorganizational activities included private prayer, reading devotional literature, and watching or listening to religious programs on television or radio (items 8, 9, and 10). We felt that the latter activities might be particularly germane for many elderly individuals, who, because of illness or disability, were not capable of more formal group-related activities (Mindel and Vaughan, 1978). None of the items used in our instrument to measure ritual activities came from an established scale. We did, however, include Glock and Stark's "Devotional Index" to measure both the frequency and importance of private prayer (items 8 and 17). Stark found high scores for this index among older persons (Stark, 1968, p. 8).

The third dimension, *Experience*, was measured following Glock and Stark's (1966) original definition of the term (Stark and Glock, 1970, p. 127). They postulated four general types of religious experience: (1) the *confirming* type, where the human actor simply senses the existence or presence of God; (2) the *responsive* type, where God responds to the presence of the human actor, i.e. answers prayer, punishes or chastises, provides assistance or help in times of need; (3) the *ecstatic* type, described as the experience of an affectionate relationship akin to love or friendship (including "salvational" experiences); and (4) the *revelational* type, where the human actor perceives himself to be a confidant of or participant in God's plans and actions. For our instrument, questions were composed reflecting each of these types of experience (items 23, 18, 12, and 19, respectively).

The fourth and last of Glock and Stark's dimensions used here was *Religious Knowledge*, which reflects knowledge about beliefs, writings, and rituals that comprise one's religious tradition. As a measure for this dimension, we used Glock and Stark's (1966) original item evaluating the ability to recognize prophets of the Old Testament (item 11).

The *Communal* dimension is another aspect of religiosity that has been noted by others (Lenski, 1963), and though not formally recognized by Glock and Stark, was included among the items in their original study. This dimension comprises the extent to which an individual's religion constitutes a community to them (J. Wilson, 1978), and was measured here, as elsewhere (Lenski, 1963; Glock and Stark, 1966), by the number of an individual's friendship ties within their religious congregation (item 7). Fichter (1969) also addressed the communal dimension, referring to it as "social communion", meaning the association of people with each other in religious groups.

Although not a dimension in itself, the concept of *Spiritual Well-Being* (SWB), as developed by Moberg (1974) and others, has recently received much attention. This construct is proported to infuse or cut across all the other dimensions of religiosity. The most well-known current scale measuring SWB is that of Paloutzian and Ellison (1982). Their SWB scale is comprised of ten items measuring "existential well-being" and ten items measuring "religious well-being." Since existential well-being does not measure religiosity, we chose to use only the religious well-being subscale here. Before incorporation into the present instrument, further revision of the religion subscale was undertaken because of the repetitive nature of several of the items and the inclusion of words such as "satisfying," "satisfaction," or "well-being" in some items, which might bias scores obtained on this subscale in favor of individuals with higher subjective well-being. This caution was taken because subjective well-being was the major dependent variable we had planned to examine in relationship to religiosity (Koenig, Kvale, Ferrel, 1988b). Eventually six of the original ten items of Paloutzian and Ellison's (1982) religious well-being scale were included in the present instrument (see items 12 to 16, and 21).

Intrinsic Religiosity is a construct that some investigators have considered a dimension of religiosity; however, rather than representing a dimension, intrinsic orientation may be better understood as similar to spiritual well-being, in that it cuts across all other dimensions and permeates them. Nevertheless, the domain of intrinsic religiosity lies primarily within the subjective or nonorganizational sphere, in contrast to involvement in the religious community.

The "intrinsic-extrinsic" concept of religiosity was birthed by Gordon Allport, a psychologist of religion who has written extensively on this subject since the early 1950's (Allport, 1950, 1954). In developing this concept, Allport's aim was to characterize the "truly" religious person. Such a person was seen as one who takes their religion seriously and tries to put it into practice in their daily life. In their seminal paper on the subject, Allport and Ross (1967) noted that religious persons fell on a continuum between two extremes term "extrinsic" and "intrinsic." Allport described the extrinsically oriented individual as someone possessing a relatively superficial religious faith who finds "religion useful in a variety of ways—to provide security, solace, sociability and distraction, status and self-justification" (Allport and Ross, 1967, p. 434). The intrinsically oriented individual, on the other hand, is described as follows:

[The person who finds their] master motivation for living in their religion, thereby subjecting other needs and concerns to their religious beliefs and prescriptions. . . . Having embraced a creed, the individual endeavors to internalize it and follow it fully. It is in this sense that he *lives* his religion. (Allport and Ross, 1967, p. 434)

Several sociologists have proposed similar characteristics for the religiously committed person (Fichter, 1954; Lenski, 1961; Feagin, 1964). Allport and Ross (1967) originally developed a twenty-item scale to measure and distinguish extrinsically and intrinsically oriented individuals (Document no. 9268, ADI Auxiliary Publication Project, Library of Congress, Washington, D.C.).

Soon afterwards, however, Hunt and King (1971) launched an attack on Allport's intrinsic-extrinsic concept (and the scale used to measure it) as being too unstable and diffuse for research purposes. Hoge (1972), taking into consideration the criticisms of Hunt and King, proceeded to construct a ten-item scale to capture the basic characteristics of intrinsically oriented individuals. Correlations between Hoge's intrinsic religiosity scale and Allport's intrinsic subscale were reported as quite acceptable (.863). Similarly, a high correlation was found between Hoge's scale and Feagin's Factor I (intrinsic) scale (.871). Independently, Hoge then established the validity of his scale by comparison with minister's judgements (r = .585) (Hoge, 1972). Because of its underlying conceptual basis and demonstrated validity, we chose to incorporate all ten items of Hoge's scale into our instrument (items 22 to 28, and 30 to 32).

Several items are included in the SRS for other reasons. First, a single item from a recent national survey by the Gallup organization (Princeton Religion Research Center, 1982, p. 112) was included (item 29). This was done in order to compare religion's influence on older persons in Gallup's randomly selected national sample with local samples surveyed by the current instrument. This would also allow for the comparison of different populations studied by our instrument in the future. Finally, two items were included to measure religious coping (items 15 and 20), since a major objective of our studies was to examine the prevalence of this behavior.

Having developed an instrument capable of gathering data of sufficient detail to characterize religous activities and attitudes of older adults, we proceeded to establish its validity in a fashion similar to the procedure employed by Hoge. A complete list of all the ministers, priests, and rabbis in the Springfield, Illinois, area was obtained from the phone directory. The SRS (expanded) was then mailed to these religious leaders with the request that they answer the items in a manner that might reflect a "truly" religious person (by their own definition). Of the 158 churchmen to whom questionnaires were sent, eighty-five returned completed forms. Respondents represented eighteen Christian denominations and two Jewish traditions (a liberal and a conservative). There was strong agreement in the responses given by these religious leaders.

Reliability was tested by computing Cronbach's alpha for the data obtained from surveying a sample of 836 community-dwelling older adults with the SRS (shortened version). Cronbach's alpha for different parts of the schedule were .61 for the organizational religious activity index, .63 for the nonorganizational religious activity index, and .87 for the Hoge's intrinsic religiosity scale.

Test-retest reliability was also determined. Six-week test-retest determinations in eleven persons age sixty to ninety-two revealed an overall agreement of 91.7 percent (330/360) for all items of the SRS. For individual aspects of the schedule, reliability in belief measurement exceeded all others with 97.7 percent agreement (43/44). The lowest stability was in reported ritual activity, with agreement at 76.2 percent (48/63). Intermediate in reliability were religious knowledge with 88.9 percent agreement (8/9), religious well-being and experience at 96.8 percent agreement (122/126), and the Hoge scale at 91.3 percent agreement (95/104). Similarly, Dr. Lucille Bearon reported a three-week test-retest reliability of 88.0 percent (44/50) for the Hoge scale in five adults age sixty-five to seventy-four (1987, Bearon, unpublished data). Reliability was calculated by examining significant changes in response from one test time to the other. A significant change for the Hoge scale, religious well-being, and religious experience items, consisted of a change from agreement to disagreement on any of the items; for the religious ritual and belief items, a change of more than one category was defined as significant.

Finally, the mean scores obtained from three groups of community-dwelling older persons were compared with those of the pastor group (N = 87) and those of a group of retired nuns (N = 183). This comparison revealed that the scores were uniformly highest for the religious groups (Koenig, Kvale, and Ferrel, 1988b), thus providing further validity to the SRS instrument (see Figure 12). Denominational affiliation and other characteristics of the pastor sample are given, along with their responses to the individual items of the SRS.

Since the development of the SRS, it has been employed in two studies. The first investigation (Koenig, Moberg, and Kvale, 1988a) examined the religious characteristics of older patients (mean age 74) attending a geriatric assessment clinic. The "expanded" form of the SRS was used in that study. Of 139 consecutive patients, 106 agreed to participate and completed questionnaires. This high response rate (76%) indicates that the length of this instrument does not preclude its administration to an older population (even when medically ill).

Recall also that the expanded SRS was administered to eighty-seven pastors in the validation study. Although the mean age of the pastors was forty-seven years, 20 percent were over age sixty.

In a second study, a "shortened" SRS was distributed to almost a thousand community-dwelling elderly (Koenig, Kvale, and Ferrel, 1988b). In order to maximize our response rate, we chose to shorten the form by eliminating certain items from the expanded SRS: belief (items 1 to 4), experience (items 12, 18, and 19), knowledge (item 11), communal (item 7), and spiritual well-being (items 12 to 14, 16, and 21). Remaining in the shortened version were ritual activities (both organizational and nonorganizational), the private devotional index of Glock and Stark, Gallup's item concerning the influence of religion on life, a single item on religious coping, and all the items in Hoge's intrinsic religiosity scale. Only a single distribution without followup was possible because of the anonymous nature of the study. Despite this, and the fact that many individuals were of advanced age and of frail health, 836 completed

Figure 12

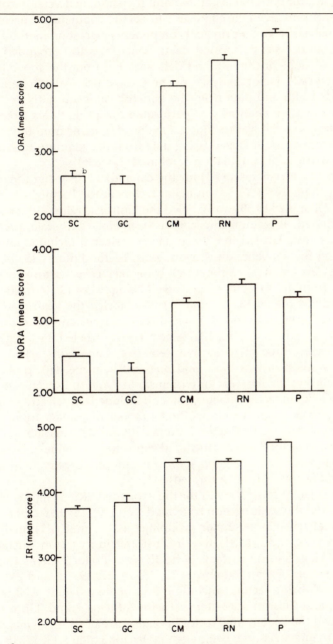

a For ORA, significant differences (p<.05) are present between all groups except GC and SC; RN and P; and CM and P. For IR, significant differences are present between all groups except GC and SC; RN and CM. GC = geriatric clinic (N=95); SC = senior centers (N=318); CM = church members (N=224); RN = retired nuns (N=183); and P = pastors (N=86).

b Standard error of the mean

questionnaires, yielding a final response rate of 74 percent. Hence, the response rates for both the expanded and the shortened versions of the SRS were excellent given the characteristics of the populations surveyed.

Factor analysis, using a principal components extraction method and varimax rotation, was performed using items from the expanded and shortened versions of the SRS and data acquired from the above three studies. First (#1), factor analysis was performed using all the items on the expanded SRS and data from the geriatric clinic study (N = 106). Next (#2), the same analysis was performed except that data from the pastor group (N = 85) was included. Finally (#3), items from the short-ened SRS were factor analyzed using data from the community sample and the geriatric clinic population combined (N = 836).

In the first factor analysis (#1) for the expanded SRS using the clinic population alone (N = 106), seven major factors arose: Factor 1 (items 8, 12, 19, 22, 23, and 25 to 30) was labeled the "intrinsic religiosity factor," since it included all seven intrinsic items from Hoge's IR scale; Factor 2 (items 1 to 4) was labeled the "belief factor," since it included all four of Glock and Stark's belief dimension items; Factor 3 (items 12, 14, 17, and 21) was labeled the "religious well-being factor," since three of four items were from the six-item religious well-being scale of Paloutzian and Ellison; Factor 4 (items 13, 24, and 31) was labeled the "extrinsic reli-giosity factor," since it included two of three extrinsic items from Hoge's IR scale; Factor 5 (items 11, 15, 18, 20, and 32) was labeled the "negative factor," because three of these five items were questions asked in a negatively worded fashion (i.e. God does *not* help me with problems and difficulties in my life); Factor 6 (items 5 to 7 and 9) was labeled the "organized religious activity factor," since it included church attendance, Bible and prayer group meetings, and number of friends from their church congregation; and Factor 7 (items 10 and 33) was labeled the "miscellaneous factor," since it included exposure to religious television and radio and religious denomination (i.e., the items remaining after the other six factors had been formed).

In the next factor analysis (#2) for the expanded SRS using the clinic population and the pastor group combined (N = 190), seven factors were extracted that fell within similar groupings as the first (#1) analysis: Factor 1 (items 22, and 25 to 31), the "intrinsic religiosity factor," included all seven of Hoge's intrinsic items of his IR scale; Factor 2 (items 1 to 4), the "belief factor;" Factor 3 (items 8, 12, 13, 16, 17, 19, 21, and 23), the "religious well-being factor," including four of six religious well-being (Paloutzian and Ellison) scale items; Factor 4 (items 7 and 33), a new factor, labeled the "communal factor" because one of its items included number of friends in church congregation; Factor 5 (items 13, 15, 18 and 20), the "negative factor," with all four items worded in a negative fashion; Factor 6 (items 5, 6, 9, 11, 24, and 32), the "organized religious activity and knowledge factor," since it included group activity items, Bible reading, and religious knowledge; and Factor 7 (item 10) called the "miscellaneous factor" completed the groupings. Note that in this analysis (#2), no extrinsic religiosity factor was extracted to correspond to Factor 4 in the first analysis (#1).

In factor analysis #3, the shortened SRS using the combined clinic and community population (without the pastors) (N = 836) displayed only three definite factors. Factor 1 (items 8 to 10, and 12 to 17), the "intrinsic religiosity factor," included all seven of Hoge's intrinsic items in his IR scale; Factor 2 (items 11 to 5), the "religious ritual factor," included all of Glock and Stark's ritual items that made up both our organized religious activity dimension (ORA) and nonorganized activity dimension (NORA); and Factor 3 (items 7, 11, 18 and 19), the "extrinsic religiosity factor" that included all three extrinsic items on Hoge's IR scale.

In summary, then, for the *expanded SRS* there appears to be *five* dominant factors: (1) an intrinsic religiosity factor, (2) an extrinsic religiosity factor (or a factor that corresponds to negatively worded items), (3) a religious ritual factor (out of which a social or group-related religious activity factor may be separated), (4) a religious well-being factor, and (5) a belief factor. For the *shortened SRS, three* major factors arise that include: (1) an intrinsic factor, (2) an extrinsic factor (and/or negatively worded factor), and (3) a ritual factor including both organizational and nonorganizational activities. These different factors are consistent with much of the theory on the multi-dimensional nature of religion that is expounded in this text.

SURVEY OF RELIGIOUS BELIEFS, PRACTICES, AND EXPERIENCES
FAMILY PRACTICE CENTER GERIATRICS CLINIC
SOUTHERN ILLINOIS UNIVERSITY SCHOOL OF MEDICINE

THE GERIATRICS CLINIC IS REQUESTING YOUR COOPERATION IN COMPLETING THE FOLLOWING QUESTION-
NAIRE. WE ARE HOPING TO LEARN ABOUT HOW THE ELDERLY FEEL ABOUT THEIR RELIGIOUS BELIEFS IN
GENERAL. THERE ARE NO RIGHT OR WRONG ANSWERS. FOR EACH OF THE ITEMS LISTED BELOW, PLEASE
CHECK THE ANSWER WHICH BEST DESCRIBES YOUR FEELINGS. ALL YOUR RESPONSES ARE CONFIDENTIAL.
COMPLETION OF THIS FORM IS ENTIRELY VOLUNTARY AND WILL IN NO WAY AFFECT YOUR CONTINUED
MEDICAL CARE.

1.   WHICH OF THE FOLLOWING STATEMENTS COMES CLOSEST TO EXPRESSING WHAT YOU BELIEVE ABOUT
      GOD?

            _____I KNOW GOD REALLY EXISTS AND I HAVE NO DOUBTS ABOUT IT

            _____WHILE I HAVE DOUBTS, I FEEL THAT I DO BELIEVE IN GOD

            _____I DON'T BELIEVE IN A PERSONAL GOD, BUT I DO BELIEVE IN A HIGHER
                 POWER OF SOME KIND

            _____I DON'T KNOW WHETHER THERE IS A GOD OR NOT AND I DON'T BELIEVE
                 THERE IS ANY WAY TO FIND OUT

            _____I DON'T BELIEVE IN GOD

2.   WHICH OF THE FOLLOWING STATEMENTS COMES CLOSEST TO EXPRESSING WHAT YOU BELIEVE
      ABOUT JESUS?

            _____JESUS IS THE DIVINE SON OF GOD AND I HAVE NO DOUBTS ABOUT IT

            _____WHILE I HAVE SOME DOUBTS, I FEEL BASICALLY THAT JESUS IS DIVINE

            _____I FEEL THAT JESUS WAS A GREAT MAN AND VERY HOLY, BUT I DON'T FEEL HIM TO
                 BE THE SON OF GOD ANY MORE THAN ALL OF US ARE CHILDREN OF GOD

            _____I THINK JESUS WAS ONLY A MAN, ALTHOUGH AN EXTRAORDINARY ONE

            _____FRANKLY, I'M NOT ENTIRELY SURE THERE REALLY WAS SUCH A PERSON AS JESUS

3.   THE BIBLE TELLS OF MANY MIRACLES, SOME CREDITED TO CHRIST AND SOME TO OTHER PROPHETS
      AND APOSTLES. GENERALLY SPEAKING, WHICH OF THE FOLLOWING STATEMENTS COMES CLOSEST TO
      WHAT YOU BELIEVE ABOUT BIBLICAL MIRACLES?

            _____I BELIEVE MIRACLES ARE STORIES AND NEVER REALLY HAPPENED

            _____I AM NOT SURE WHETHER THESE MIRACLES REALLY HAPPENED OR NOT

            _____I BELIEVE THE MIRACLES HAPPENED, BUT CAN BE EXPLAINED BY NATURAL CAUSES

            _____I BELIEVE THE MIRACLES ACTUALLY HAPPENED JUST AS THE BIBLE SAYS THEY DID

4.   THE DEVIL ACTUALLY EXISTS. DO YOU BELIEVE THIS IS. . .

                        _____COMPLETELY TRUE   _____PROBABLY NOT TRUE

                        _____PROBABLY TRUE   _____DEFINITELY NOT TRUE

5.   HOW OFTEN DO YOU ATTEND CHURCH SERVICES?

    _____SEVERAL TIMES A WEEK   _____SEVERAL TIMES A YEAR

    _____ABOUT ONCE A WEEK   _____SELDOM

    _____SEVERAL TIMES A MONTH   _____NEVER

6.   HOW OFTEN DO YOU PARTICIPATE IN OTHER RELIGIOUS GROUP ACTIVITIES (I.E. ADULT
SUNDAY SCHOOL CLASSES, BIBLE STUDY GROUPS, PRAYER GROUPS, ETC.)?

    _____SEVERAL TIMES A WEEK   _____SEVERAL TIMES A YEAR

    _____ABOUT ONCE A WEEK   _____SELDOM

    _____SEVERAL TIMES A MONTH   _____NEVER

7.   THINK OF YOUR FIVE CLOSEST FRIENDS. HOW MANY OF THEM ARE MEMBERS OF YOUR CHURCH
CONGREGATION?

  _____NONE   _____ONE   _____TWO   _____THREE   _____FOUR   _____FIVE

8.   HOW OFTEN DO YOU PRAY PRIVATELY?

    _____NOT AT ALL   _____ONCE A DAY

    _____ONLY OCCASIONALLY   _____TWICE A DAY

    _____SEVERAL TIMES A WEEK   _____THREE OR MORE TIMES A DAY

9.   HOW OFTEN DO YOU READ THE BIBLE OR OTHER RELIGIOUS LITERATURE (MAGAZINES, PAPERS,
BOOKS) AT HOME?

    _____SEVERAL TIMES A DAY   _____SEVERAL TIMES A MONTH

    _____DAILY   _____ONLY OCCASIONALLY

    _____SEVERAL TIMES A WEEK   _____NOT AT ALL

10. HOW OFTEN DO YOU LISTEN TO OR WATCH RELIGIOUS PROGRAMS ON RADIO OR TV?

    _____NOT AT ALL   _____SEVERAL TIMES A WEEK

    _____ONLY OCCASIONALLY   _____DAILY

    _____SEVERAL TIMES A MONTH   _____SEVERAL TIMES A DAY

11. WHICH OF THE FOLLOWING WERE OLD TESTAMENT PROPHETS? (FOR THIS QUESTION, PLEASE
CHECK AS MANY AS APPLY.)

  _____ELIJAH   _____DEUTERONOMY   _____JEREMIAH   _____PAUL

  _____LEVITICUS   _____EZEKIEL   _____NONE OF THESE WERE PROPHETS

THE NEXT SECTION OF THE QUESTIONNAIRE ASKS HOW MUCH YOU <u>AGREE OR DISAGREE</u> WITH EACH ITEM. PLACE A CHECK NEXT TO THE PHRASE WHICH BEST DESCRIBES YOUR FEELING FOR EACH ITEM.

12. I EXPERIENCE GOD'S LOVE AND CARE FOR ME IN MY RELATIONSHIP WITH HIM.

___STRONGLY   ___MODERATELY   ___SLIGHTLY   ___SLIGHTLY   ___MODERATELY   ___STRONGLY
   AGREE   AGREE   AGREE   DISAGREE   DISAGREE   DISAGREE

13. I BELIEVE THAT GOD IS IMPERSONAL AND NOT INTERESTED IN MY DAILY SITUATIONS.

___STRONGLY   ___MODERATELY   ___SLIGHTLY   ___SLIGHTLY   ___MODERATELY   ___STRONGLY
   AGREE   AGREE   AGREE   DISAGREE   DISAGREE   DISAGREE

14. I HAVE A PERSONALLY MEANINGFUL RELATIONSHIP WITH GOD.

___STRONGLY   ___MODERATELY   ___SLIGHTLY   ___SLIGHTLY   ___MODERATELY   ___STRONGLY
   AGREE   AGREE   AGREE   DISAGREE   DISAGREE   DISAGREE

15. WHILE DEALING WITH DIFFICULT TIMES IN MY LIFE, I <u>DON'T</u> GET MUCH PERSONAL STRENGTH AND SUPPORT FROM GOD.

___STRONGLY   ___MODERATELY   ___SLIGHTLY   ___SLIGHTLY   ___MODERATELY   ___STRONGLY
   AGREE   AGREE   AGREE   DISAGREE   DISAGREE   DISAGREE

16. MY RELATIONSHIP WITH GOD HELPS ME NOT TO FEEL LONELY.

___STRONGLY   ___MODERATELY   ___SLIGHTLY   ___SLIGHTLY   ___MODERATELY   ___STRONGLY
   AGREE   AGREE   AGREE   DISAGREE   DISAGREE   DISAGREE

17. PRIVATE PRAYER IS IMPORTANT IN MY LIFE.

___STRONGLY   ___MODERATELY   ___SLIGHTLY   ___SLIGHTLY   ___MODERATELY   ___STRONGLY
   AGREE   AGREE   AGREE   DISAGREE   DISAGREE   DISAGREE

18. I DO <u>NOT</u> EXPERIENCE GOD'S INTERVENTION IN MY LIFE IN ANY CONCRETE OR PERSONAL WAY.

___STRONGLY   ___MODERATELY   ___SLIGHTLY   ___SLIGHTLY   ___MODERATELY   ___STRONGLY
   AGREE   AGREE   AGREE   DISAGREE   DISAGREE   DISAGREE

19. GOD HAS REVEALED THINGS TO ME ABOUT MY LIFE, OTHER PEOPLE, HIMSELF, OR HIS DIVINE PLAN

___STRONGLY   ___MODERATELY   ___SLIGHTLY   ___SLIGHTLY   ___MODERATELY   ___STRONGLY
   AGREE   AGREE   AGREE   DISAGREE   DISAGREE   DISAGREE

20. PRAYER DOES <u>NOT</u> HELP ME TO COPE WITH DIFFICULTIES AND STRESS IN MY LIFE.

___STRONGLY   ___MODERATELY   ___SLIGHTLY   ___SLIGHTLY   ___MODERATELY   ___STRONGLY
   AGREE   AGREE   AGREE   DISAGREE   DISAGREE   DISAGREE

21. I FEEL MOST FULFILLED WHEN I AM IN CLOSE COMMUNION WITH GOD.

___STRONGLY   ___MODERATELY   ___SLIGHTLY   ___SLIGHTLY   ___MODERATELY   ___STRONGLY
   AGREE   AGREE   AGREE   DISAGREE   DISAGREE   DISAGREE

THE NEXT SECTION OF THE QUESTIONNAIRE ASKS HOW TRUE YOU BELIEVE EACH STATEMENT TO BE ABOUT
YOU. CHECK THE PHRASE WHICH BEST DESCRIBES YOUR FEELINGS ABOUT EACH ITEM.

22. MY FAITH INVOLVES ALL OF MY LIFE.

___DEFINITELY   ___TENDS TO   ___TENDS NOT   ___DEFINITELY NOT   ___UNSURE
   TRUE OF ME   BE TRUE   TO BE TRUE   TRUE OF ME

23. IN MY LIFE I EXPERIENCE THE PRESENCE OF THE DIVINE (THAT IS, OF GOD).

___DEFINITELY   ___TENDS TO   ___TENDS NOT   ___DEFINITELY NOT   ___UNSUPE
   TRUE OF ME   BE TRUE   TO BE TRUE   TRUE OF ME

24. ALTHOUGH I AM A RELIGIOUS PERSON, I REFUSE TO LET RELIGIOUS CONSIDERATIONS INFLUENCE
     MY EVERYDAY AFFAIRS.

___DEFINITELY   ___TENDS TO   ___TENDS NOT   ___DEFINITELY NOT   ___UNSURE
   TRUE OF ME   BE TRUE   TO BE TRUE   TRUE OF ME

25. NOTHING IS AS IMPORTANT TO ME AS SERVING GOD AS BEST AS I KNOW HOW.

___DEFINITELY   ___TENDS TO   ___TENDS NOT   ___DEFINITELY NOT   ___UNSURE
   TRUE OF ME   BE TRUE   TO BE TRUE   TRUE OF ME

26. MY FAITH SOMETIMES RESTRICTS MY ACTIONS.

___DEFINITELY   ___TENDS TO   ___TENDS NOT   ___DEFINITELY NOT   ___UNSURE
   TRUE OF ME   BE TRUE   TO BE TRUE   TRUE OF ME

27. MY RELIGIOUS BELIEFS ARE WHAT REALLY LIE BEHIND MY WHOLE APPROACH TO LIFE.

___DEFINITELY   ___TENDS TO   ___TENDS NOT   ___DEFINITELY NOT   ___UNSURE
   TRUE OF ME   BE TRUE   TO BE TRUE   TRUE OF ME

28. I TRY HARD TO CARRY MY RELIGION OVER INTO ALL MY OTHER DEALINGS IN LIFE.

___DEFINITELY   ___TENDS TO   ___TENDS NOT   ___DEFINITELY NOT   ___UNSURE
   TRUE OF ME   BE TRUE   TO BE TRUE   TRUE OF ME

29. MY RELIGIOUS FAITH IS THE MOST IMPORTANT INFLUENCE IN MY LIFE.

___COMPLETELY TRUE   ___MOSTLY TRUE   ___MOSTLY UNTRUE   ___COMPLETELY UNTRUE

THE FINAL SECTION OF THE QUESTIONNAIRE ASKS HOW MUCH YOU <u>AGREE OR DISAGREE</u> WITH EACH ITEM.
PLACE A CHECK NEXT TO THE PHRASE WHICH BEST DESCRIBES YOUR FEELING ABOUT EACH ITEM.

30. ONE SHOULD SEEK GOD'S GUIDANCE WHEN MAKING EVERY IMPORTANT DECISION.

    ___DEFINITELY   ___TEND TO   ___TEND TO   ___DEFINITELY   ___UNSURE
       AGREE   AGREE   DISAGREE   DISAGREE

31. ALTHOUGH I BELIEVE IN RELIGION, I FEEL THERE ARE MANY MORE IMPORTANT THINGS IN LIFE.

    ___DEFINITELY   ___TEND TO   ___TEND TO   ___DEFINITELY   ___UNSURE
       AGREE   AGREE   DISAGREE   DISAGREE

32. IT DOESN'T MATTER SO MUCH WHAT I BELIEVE AS LONG AS I LEAD A MORAL LIFE.

    ___DEFINITELY   ___TEND TO   ___TEND TO   ___DEFINITELY   ___UNSURE
       AGREE   AGREE   DISAGREE   DISAGREE

33. PLEASE CHECK YOUR RELIGIOUS PREFERENCE.

                _____PROTESTANT   _____CATHOLIC   _____JEWISH   _____NONE

34. IF YOU WERE EXPERIENCING GREAT EMOTIONAL DISTRESS, WERE VERY SICK
OR NEAR DEATH, WOULD YOU LIKE YOUR PERSONAL PHYSICIAN TO PRAY WITH YOU?

    _____YES,   _____YES,   _____NO,   _____NO,
       VERY MUCH   SOMEWHAT   PROBABLY NOT   DEFINITELY

THAT CONCLUDES THE QUESTIONNAIRE. THANK YOU VERY MUCH FOR YOUR COOPERATION.
ALL RESPONSES WILL BE STRICTLY CONFIDENTIAL.

1. HOW OFTEN DO YOU ATTEND CHURCH SERVICES?

_____ SEVERAL TIMES A WEEK   _____ SEVERAL TIMES A YEAR

_____ ABOUT ONCE A WEEK   _____ SELDOM

_____ SEVERAL TIMES A MONTH   _____ NEVER

2. HOW OFTEN DO YOU PRAY PRIVATELY?

_____ NOT AT ALL   _____ ONCE A DAY

_____ ONLY OCCASIONALLY   _____ TWICE A DAY

_____ SEVERAL TIMES A WEEK   _____ THREE OR MORE TIMES A DAY

3. HOW OFTEN DO YOU READ THE BIBLE OR OTHER RELIGIOUS LITERATURE (MAGAZINES, PAPERS, BOOKS) AT HOME?

_____ SEVERAL TIMES A DAY   _____ SEVERAL TIMES A MONTH

_____ DAILY   _____ ONLY OCCASIONALLY

_____ SEVERAL TIMES A WEEK   _____ NOT AT ALL

4. HOW OFTEN DO YOU LISTEN TO OR WATCH RELIGIOUS PROGRAMS ON RADIO OR TV?

_____ NOT AT ALL   _____ SEVERAL TIMES A WEEK

_____ ONLY OCCASIONALLY   _____ DAILY

_____ SEVERAL TIMES A MONTH   _____ SEVERAL TIMES A DAY

5. HOW OFTEN DO YOU PARTICIPATE IN RELIGIOUS GROUP ACTIVITIES (I.E. ADULT SUNDAY SCHOOL CLASSES, BIBLE STUDY GROUPS, PRAYER GROUPS, ETC.)?

_____ SEVERAL TIMES A WEEK   _____ SEVERAL TIMES A YEAR

_____ ABOUT ONCE A WEEK   _____ SELDOM

_____ SEVERAL TIMES A MONTH   _____ NEVER

6. IF YOU ARE NOT INVOLVED IN RELIGIOUS COMMUNITY ACTIVITY, HOW OFTEN DO YOU PARTICIPATE IN NON-RELIGIOUS COMMUNITY ACTIVITY? (Skip this question if you are involved in religious community activity.)

_____ NEVER   _____ SEVERAL TIMES A MONTH

_____ SELDOM   _____ ABOUT ONCE A WEEK

_____ SEVERAL TIMES A YEAR   _____ SEVERAL TIMES A WEEK

THE NEXT SECTION OF THE QUESTIONNAIRE ASKS HOW MUCH YOU AGREE OR DISAGREE WITH EACH ITEM.
PLACE A CHECK NEXT TO THE PHRASE WHICH BEST DESCRIBES YOUR FEELING FOR EACH ITEM.

7. WHILE DEALING WITH DIFFICULT TIMES IN MY LIFE, I DON'T GET MUCH PERSONAL STRENGTH
   AND SUPPORT FROM GOD.

   ____STRONGLY   ____MODERATELY   ____SLIGHTLY   ____SLIGHTLY   ____MODERATELY   ____STRONGLY
       AGREE   AGREE   AGREE   DISAGREE   DISAGREE   DISAGREE

8. PRIVATE PRAYER IS IMPORTANT IN MY LIFE.

   ____STRONGLY   ____MODERATELY   ____SLIGHTLY   ____SLIGHTLY   ____MODERATELY   ____STRONGLY
       AGREE   AGREE   AGREE   DISAGREE   DISAGREE   DISAGREE

THE NEXT SECTION OF THE QUESTIONNAIRE ASKS HOW TRUE YOU BELIEVE EACH STATEMENT TO BE ABOUT
YOU. CHECK THE PHRASE WHICH BEST DESCRIBES YOUR FEELINGS ABOUT EACH ITEM.

9. MY FAITH INVOLVES ALL OF MY LIFE.

   ____DEFINITELY   ____TENDS TO   ____TENDS NOT   ____DEFINITELY NOT   ____UNSURE
       TRUE OF ME   BE TRUE   TO BE TRUE   TRUE OF ME

10. IN MY LIFE I EXPERIENCE THE PRESENCE OF THE DIVINE (THAT IS, OF GOD).

   ____DEFINITELY   ____TENDS TO   ____TENDS NOT   ____DEFINITELY NOT   ____UNSURE
       TRUE OF ME   BE TRUE   TO BE TRUE   TRUE OF ME

11. ALTHOUGH I AM A RELIGIOUS PERSON, I REFUSE TO LET RELIGIOUS CONSIDERATIONS INFLUENCE
    MY EVERYDAY AFFAIRS.

   ____DEFINITELY   ____TENDS TO   ____TENDS NOT   ____DEFINITELY NOT   ____UNSURE
       TRUE OF ME   BE TRUE   TO BE TRUE   TRUE OF ME

12. NOTHING IS AS IMPORTANT TO ME AS SERVING GOD AS BEST AS I KNOW HOW.

   ____DEFINITELY   ____TENDS TO   ____TENDS NOT   ____DEFINITELY NOT   ____UNSURE
       TRUE OF ME   BE TRUE   TO BE TRUE   TRUE OF ME

13. MY FAITH SOMETIMES RESTRICTS MY ACTIONS.

   ____DEFINITELY   ____TENDS TO   ____TENDS NOT   ____DEFINITELY NOT   ____UNSURE
       TRUE OF ME   BE TRUE   TO BE TRUE   TRUE OF ME

14. MY RELIGIOUS BELIEFS ARE WHAT REALLY LIE BEHIND MY WHOLE APPROACH TO LIFE.

   ____DEFINITELY   ____TENDS TO   ____TENDS NOT   ____DEFINITELY NOT   ____UNSURE
       TRUE OF ME   BE TRUE   TO BE TRUE   TRUE OF ME

15. I TRY HARD TO CARRY MY RELIGION OVER INTO ALL MY OTHER DEALINGS IN LIFE.

_____DEFINITELY   _____TENDS TO   _____TENDS NOT   _____DEFINITELY NOT   _____UNSURE
     TRUE OF ME   BE TRUE   TO BE TRUE   TRUE OF ME

16. MY RELIGIOUS FAITH IS THE MOST IMPORTANT INFLUENCE IN MY LIFE.

_____ COMPLETELY TRUE   _____ MOSTLY TRUE   _____ MOSTLY UNTRUE   _____ COMPLETELY UNTRUE

THE FINAL SECTION OF THE QUESTIONNAIRE ASKS HOW MUCH YOU AGREE OR DISAGREE WITH EACH ITEM.
PLACE A CHECK NEXT TO THE PHRASE WHICH BEST DESCRIBES YOUR FEELING ABOUT EACH ITEM.

17. ONE SHOULD SEEK GOD'S GUIDANCE WHEN MAKING EVERY IMPORTANT DECISION.

_____DEFINITELY   _____TEND TO   _____TEND TO   _____DEFINITELY   _____UNSURE
     AGREE   AGREE   DISAGREE   DISAGREE

18. ALTHOUGH I BELIEVE IN RELIGION, I FEEL THERE ARE MANY MORE IMPORTANT THINGS IN LIFE.

_____DEFINITELY   _____TEND TO   _____TEND TO   _____DEFINITELY   _____UNSURE
     AGREE   AGREE   DISAGREE   DISAGREE

19. IT DOESN'T MATTER SO MUCH WHAT I BELIEVE AS LONG AS I LEAD A MORAL LIFE.

_____DEFINITELY   _____TEND TO   _____TEND TO   _____DEFINITELY   _____UNSURE
     AGREE   AGREE   DISAGREE   DISAGREE

20. PLEASE CHECK YOUR RELIGIOUS PREFERENCE.

_____ PROTESTANT   _____ CATHOLIC   _____ JEWISH   _____ NONE

21. IF YOU WERE EXPERIENCING GREAT EMOTIONAL DISTRESS, WERE VERY SICK OR
    NEAR DEATH, WOULD YOU LIKE YOUR PERSONAL PHYSICIAN TO PRAY WITH YOU?

_____YES,   _____YES,   _____NO,   _____NO,
     VERY MUCH   SOMEWHAT   PROBABLY NOT   DEFINITELY
                                                                 NOT

THAT CONCLUDES THE QUESTIONNAIRE. THANK YOU VERY MUCH FOR YOUR COOPERATION.
ALL RESPONSES ARE ANONYMOUS.

APPENDIX II: ORGANIZATIONS TO CONTACT FOR FURTHER INFORMATION

PROTESTANT

Federal Council of Churches of Christ
Special programs for the aged
includes 34 Protestant and Eastern Orthodox denominations

National Interfaith Coalition on Aging (NICA)
Thomas Cook
Athens, GA

Shepherds Centers International (established by United Methodist Church)
Community programs to involve older persons in helping each other
more than 50 to 60 centers currently established nationwide
for more information, contact:
   Thomas E. Akins, Executive Director
   5218 Oak St.
   Kansas City, MO 64112
   (816) 523–1080

Religion, Spirituality, and Aging Committee (American Society on Aging)
Jim Seeber, Chairman

Health and Welfare Ministries Division
Board of Global Ministries
Charles Frazier
Evanston, IL

Protestant Health and Welfare Assembly (Nursing homes, in particular)

Specific Denominations

Presbyterian Office on Aging
Thomas B. Robb
Atlanta, GA

Center on Aging
(under direction of Presbyterian School of Christian Education)

Episcopal Society for Ministry on Aging
Lorraine Chiaventone
Stafford, NJ

Senior Adult Ministries
Baptist Sunday School Board
Horace Kerr
Nashville, TN

National Lutheran Council
(special programs for the aged)

CATHOLIC

Committee on Justice and Peace
Office of Domestic Affairs
(under direction of the United States Catholic Conference
special programs for the aged)

Commission on Aging
(under direction of the National Conference of Catholic Charities)

Catholic Health Association
St. Louis, MO

Catholic Golden Age Association
(similar to AARP)

JEWISH

Jewish Communal Service
Jewish Institute of Religion
Los Angeles, CA

Union of American Hebrew Congregations
New York, NY

American Jewish Committee

PROFESSIONAL ASSOCIATIONS

Society for the Scientific Study of Religion

Association for the Sociology of Religion

BIBLIOGRAPHY

Acklin, M. W., Brown, E. C., and Mauger, P. A. (1983). "The Role of Religious Values in Coping with Cancer." *Journal of Religion and Health, 22* (4), 322–33.

Alexander, I., and Adlerstein, A. (1959). "Death and Religion." *The Meaning of Death*, H. Feifel editor. New York: McGraw-Hill, 271–83.

Allport, G. W. (1950). *The Individual and His Religion*. New York: Macmillan.

Allport, G. W. (1954). *The Nature of Prejudice*. Cambridge, Mass.: Addison-Wesley.

Allport, G. W., and Ross, J. M. (1967). "Personal Religious Orientation and Prejudice." *Journal of Personality & Social Psychology, 5,* 432–43.

Americana Healthcare Corporation (1980–81). *Aging in America: Trials and Triumphs*. Westport, Conn.: US–Research and Forecasts Survey Sampling Corp.

Ancona, L. (1961). "The Clinical Interpretation of Religious Behavior." *Archives of Psychology and Neurology, 22,* 7–28.

Anderson, R. (1979). "The Role of the Church in the Community Based Care of the Chronically Mentally Disabled: Reclaiming an Historic Ministry." *Pastoral Psychology, 28* (1), 38–52.

Anderson, R., Robinson, C., and Ruben, H. (1978). "Mental Health Training and Consultation: A Model for Liason with Clergy." *Hospital Community Psychiatry, 29,* 800–802.

Antonovsky, A. (1979). *Health, Stress and Coping*. San Francisco: Jossey-Bass.

Argyle, M., and Beit-Hallami, B. (1975). *The Social Psychology of Religion*. Boston: Routledge and Kegan Paul.

Armstrong, B., Merwyk, A., and Coates, H. (1977). "Blood Pressure in Seventh Day Adventist Vegetarians." *American Journal of Epidemiology, 105,* 444–49.

Atchley, R. C. (1985). *Social Forces and Aging*, 4th ed. Belmont, Calif.: Wadsworth Publishing Co.

Bahr, H. M. and Martin, T. K. (1983). "And Thy Neighbor as Thyself: Self-esteem and Faith in People as Correlates of Religiosity and Family Solidarity Among Middletown High School Students." *Journal for the Scientific Study of Religion, 22*, 132–44.

Baker, G. H. B. (1982). "Life Events Before the Onset of Rheumatoid Arthritis." *Psychotherapy and Psychosomatics, 38*, 173–77.

Baldree, K. S., Murphy, S. P., and Powers, M. (1982). "Stress Identification and Coping Patterns in Patients on Hemodialysis." *Nursing Research, 31* (2), 107–12.

Barron, M. L. (1958). "The Role of Religion and Religious Institutions in Treating the Milieu of Older People." *Organized Religion and the Older Person*, DL Scudder edition. Gainesville: University of Florida Press, 12–13.

Barron, M. L. (1961). *The Aging American*. New York: Thomas Crowell Co., 178–81.

Barsky, A. J. (1981). "Hidden Reasons Some Patients Visit Doctors." *Annals of Internal Medicine, 94* (part I), 492–8.

Bearon, L. B. (1987). Unpublished report. Geriatric Research Education and Clinical Center. VA Medical Center, Durham, N.C.

Beck, A. (1976). *Cognitive Therapy and Emotional Disorders*. New York: International University Press.

Beck, A. T., et al. (1961). "An Inventory for Measuring Depression," *Archives of General Psychiatry, 4*, 561–571.

Becker, A. (1986). "Pastoral Theological Implications of the Aging Process." *Journal of Religion and Aging, 2*(3), 13–30.

Beckman, L. J., and Houser, B. B. (1982). "The Consequences of Childlessness on the Social-Psychological Well-Being of Older Women." *Journal of Gerontology, 37*(2), 243–50.

Belgum, D. (1984). "The Practice of Pastoral Care: Revisiting the Generalist." *Journal of Religion and Health, 23*(1), 8–18.

Benson, H., et al. (1977). "Historical and Clinical Considerations of the Relaxation Response." *American Scientist, 65*, 441–45.

Berardo, F. M. (1967). "Social Adaptation to Widowhood Among a Rural-Urban Aged Population." *Agricultural Experiment Station Bulletin, 689*. Washington State University.

Berardo, F. M. (1970). "Survivorship and Social Isolation: The Case of the Aged Widower." *Family Coordinator, 19*(1), 11–25.

Berbert, B. (1979). "Psychological Aspects of Crohn's Disease." *Journal of Behavior Medicine, 3*, 41–58.

Bergin, A. E. (1980). "Psychotherapy and Religious Values." *Journal of Consulting and Clinical Psychology, 48*, 95–105.

Berkman, L. F., et al. (1979). "Social Networks, Host Resistance and Mortality: A Nine-year Follow-up Study of Alameda County Residents." *American Journal of Epidemiology, 109*, 186–204.

Bibliography on Religion and Mental Health 1960–1964 (1967). Public Health Service Publication 159, Department of Health, Education and Welfare. U.S. Government Printing Office.

Birren, J. E. and Schaie, W. (1977). *Handbook of the Psychology of Aging*. Toronto: Van Nostrand Reinhold Co.

Blazer, D. G. (1982a). *Depression in Late Life*. St. Louis: C. V. Mosby Co.

Blazer, D. G. (1982b). "Social Support and Mortality in an Elderly Community Population." *American Journal of Epidemiology, 115,* 684–94.

Blazer, D. G. and Palmore, E. (1976). "Religion and Aging in a Longitudinal Panel." *The Gerontologist, 16*(1), 82–85.

Blum, R. H. (1980). *The Management of the Doctor-Patient Relationship*. New York: McGraw-Hill, 282.

Bohrnstedt, G. W., et al. (1968). "Religious Affiliation, Religiosity and MMPI Scores." *Journal for the Scientific Study of Religion, 7,* 255–58.

Bowman, C. M. (1982, December). *Spiritual/Religious Awareness: 12 Areas of Measurable Change*. Project Report for Gerontology 476, Field Experience and Seminar, Madonna College, Tevonia, Michigan.

Bradburn, N. (1969). *The Structure of Psychological Well-Being*. Chicago: Aldine.

Braden, C. S. (1954). "Study of Spiritual Healing in the Churches." *Pastoral Psychology, 5,* 9–15.

Bradley, R. L. (1967). "Acute Peptic Ulcer in the Elderly: Similarity to Stress Ulcer." *Journal of the American Geriatrics Society, 15,* 254–64.

Breed, W. (1967). "Suicide and Loss in Social Interaction." *Essay in Self-destruction,* (F. Schnerdman editor). New York: Science House.

Briggs, K. A. (1987). *Religion in America: The Gallup Report*, No. 259. Princeton, N. J.: The Gallup Poll.

Britton, J. H. (1949). "A Study of the Adjustment of Retired School Teachers." *The American Psychologist, 4,* 308.

Broen, W. E. (1955). "Personality Correlates of Certain Religious Attitudes." *Journal of Consulting Psychology, 19,* 64–68.

Brown, G. W., and Prudo, R. (1981). "Psychiatric Disorder in a Rural and an Urban Population: 1. Aetiology of Depression." *Psychological Medicine, 11,* 581–99.

Bultena, G. L. (1974). "Structural Effects on Morale of the Aged: A Comparison of Age-segregated and Age-integrated Communities." *Late Life: Communities and Environmental Policy,* J. F. Gubrium, editor. Springfield, Ill.: Charles C. Thomas.

Burgess, E. W., Cavan, R. S., and Havighurst, E. W. (1948). *Your Attitudes and Activities*. Chicago: Science Research Associates.

Busse, E. W., and Pfeiffer, E. (1969). *Behavior and Adaptation in Later Life*. Boston: Little Brown and Co.

Busse, E. W., Barnes, R. H., and Silverman, A. J. (1954). "Studies of the Processes of Aging: Factors that Influence the Psyche of Elderly Persons." *American Journal of Psychiatry, 110,* 897–903.

Butler, A. M. (1968). "Hippocratic Oath, 1968." *New England Journal of Medicine, 278,* 48–49.

Butler, R., and Lewis, M. (1973). *Aging and Mental Health: Positive Psychosocial Approaches*. St. Louis: C. V. Mosby Company.

Byrd, R. (1986). "Three Cardiologists Report Prayers for Their Patients Are Answered." *Medical Tribune, 27,* 3.

Cahalan, D., Cisin, I. H., and Crossley, H. M. (1969). *American Drinking Practices.*

A National Study of Drinking Behaviors and Attitudes. New Brunswick, N.J.: Rutgers Center of Alcohol Studies.

Cameron, P. (1975). "Mood as an Indicant of Happiness: Age, Sex, Social Class, and Situational Differences." *Journal of Gerontology, 30,* 216–24.

Cameron, P., et al. (1973). "The Life Satisfaction of Non-normal Persons." *Journal of Consulting and Clinical Psychology, 41,* 207–14.

Campbell, A., et al. (1976). "Some General Influences on Reports of Satisfaction." *The Quality of American Life,* 151–69. New York: Russell Sage Foundation.

Cantril, H. (1965). *The Pattern of Human Concerns.* New Brunswick, N.J.: Rutgers University Press.

Carr, L. G., and Hauser, W. J. (1976). "Anomie and Religiosity." *Journal for the Scientific Study of Religion, 15,* 69–74.

Cavan, R. S., et al. (1949). *Personal Adjustment in Old Age.* Chicago: Science Research Associates.

Cavenar, J. O., and Spaulding, J. G. (1977). "Depressive Disorders and Religious Conversions." *Journal of Nervous and Mental Disease, 165,* 209–12.

Clark, M., and Anderson, B. (1967). *Culture and Aging.* Springfield, Ill.: Charles C. Thomas.

Clemente, F., and Sauer, J. (1976). "Life Satisfaction in the United States." *Social Forces, 54,* 621–31.

Clingan, D. F. (1975). *Aging Persons in the Community of Faith: A Guidebook for Churches and Synagogues on Ministry to, For and With The Aging.* Indianapolis: Commission on Aging and the Aged.

Cluff, C. B., and Cluff, L. E. (1983). "Informal Support for Disabled Persons: A Role for Religious and Community Organizations." *Journal of Chronic Disease, 36,* 815–20.

Coakley, D. V., and McKenna, G. W. (1986). "Safety of Faith Healing." *Lancet, i,* 444.

Cobb, S. (1971). *The Frequency of Rheumatic Diseases.* Cambridge: Harvard University Press.

Cobb, S., and Rose, R. M. (1973). "Hypertension, Peptic Ulcer, and Diabetes in Air Traffic Controllers." *Journal of the Americal Medical Assn, 224,* 489–492.

Cohen, D. I., Teresi, J., and Holmes, D. (1985). "Social Networks, Stress and Physical Health: A Longitudinal Study of an Inner-city Elderly Population." *Journal of Gerontology, 40(4),* 478–86.

Cohen, F., and Lazarus, R. S. (1979). "Coping With Stress and Illness." *Health Psychology—A Handbook.* Stone, G. C., Cohen, F., and Odler, N. E., editors. San Francisco: Jossey-Bass.

Cohen, F., and Lazarus, R. S. (1983). "Coping and Adaptation in Health and Illness." *Handbook of Health, Healthcare and the Health Professions,* D. Mechanic, editor. New York: Free Press, 608–35.

Cole, T. (1984). "Aging, Meaning, and Well-Being: Musings of a Cultural Historian." *International Journal of Aging and Human Development, 19(4),* 329–36.

Collipp, P. J. (1969). "The Efficacy of Prayer: A Triple Blind Study." *Medical Times, 97(5),* 201–4.

Comstock, G. W., and Partridge, K. B. (1972). "Church Attendance and Health." *Journal of Chronic Diseases, 25,* 665–72.

Connors, Q. (1985). "Seminary to Parish Transition." *Human Development*, 6(2), 37–39.

Conway, K. (1985–86). "Coping with the Stress of Medical Problems Among Black and White Elderly." *International Journal of Aging and Human Development*, 21(1), 39–48.

Covalt, N. K. (1960). "The Meaning of Religion to Older People." *Geriatrics*, 15, 658–64.

Cozzens, D. (1983). "When Ministry Becomes Therapy." *Human Development*, 4(4), 36–39.

Cranston, R. (1955). *The Miracle of Lourdes*. New York: McGraw-Hill.

Croog, S. H., and Levine, S. (1972). "Religious Identity and Response to Serious Illness: A Report on Heart Patients." *Social Science and Medicine*, 6, 17–32.

Cummings, E. A. (1940). "The Kings Highway." In *The Hymnal*. The Pension Fund of the Episcopal Church.

Cutler, S. J. (1976). "Membership in Different Types of Voluntary Associations and Psychological Well-being." *The Gerontologist*, 16(4), 335–39.

Dean, D. G. (1961). "Alienation: Its Meaning and Measurement." *American Sociological Review*, 26, 753–758.

Delgado, M. (1982). "Ethnic and Cultural Variations in the Care of the Aged: Hispanic Elderly and Natural Support Systems—a Special Focus on Puerto Ricans." *Journal of Geriatric Psychiatry*, 15(2), 239–51.

Denier, E. (1984). "Subjective Well-being." *Psychological Bulletin*, 95(3), 542–75.

Diagnostic and Statistical Manual of Mental Disorders (1987). Third Edition, Revised. Washington, D.C.: American Psychiatric Association.

Dillon, K. M., Minchoff, B., and Baker, K. H. (1985). "Positive Emotional States and Enhancement of the Immune System." *International Journal of Psychiatry in Medicine*, 15, 13–17.

Downey, A. M. (1984). "Relationship of Religiosity to Death: Anxiety of Middle-aged Males." *Psychological Reports*, 54: 811–22

Durkheim, E. (1951). *Suicide*, J. A. Spaulding and G. Simpson, translators. New York: Free Press.

Durkheim, E. (1965). *The Elementary Forms of the Religious Life*. New York: Free Press.

Editorial (1979). "Complete Care of the Whole Man." *Journal of the Mississippi State Medical Association*, 11(4), 193.

Editorial (1985). "Exploring the Effectiveness of Healing." *Lancet*, ii, 1177–78.

Editorial (1987). "Depression, Stress, and Immunity." *Lancet*, i, 1467–68.

Edwards, J. N., and Klemmack, D. L. (1973). "Correlates of Life Satisfaction: A Reexamination." *Journal of Gerontology*, 28, 497–502.

Elk, N., and Nash, E. (1985). "Hypertension in the Aged—Psychosocial and Psychiatric Concomitants in a Coloured Community." *South African Medical Journal*, 67, 1046–49.

Ellis, A. (1980). "Psychotherapy and Atheistic Values: A Response to A. E. Bergin's 'Psychotherapy and Religious Values' ". *Journal of Consulting and Clinical Psychology*, 48, 642–45.

Engel G. (1980). "The Clinical Application of the Biopsychosocial Model." *American Journal of Psychiatry*, 137 (5), 535–55.

Enstrom, J. E. (1975). "Cancer Mortality Among Mormons." *Cancer*, 36, 825–41.

Epperly, J. (1983). "The Cell and the Celestial: Spiritual Needs of Cancer Patients." *Journal of the Medical Association of Georgia*, 72, 374–76.

Etziony, M. B. (1973). *The Physician's Creed*. Springfield, Ill.: Charles C. Thomas, 59–61.

Fahey, C. (1985). *Catholic Trends, 16*(9), Washington, D.C., 1312 Massachusetts Avenue, N.W. 4.

Favazza, A. R. (1982). "Modern Christian Healing of Mental Illness." *American Journal of Psychiatry, 139*(6), 728–39.

Feagin, J. R. (1964). "Prejudice and Religious Types: A Focused Study of Southern Fundamentalists." *Journal for the Scientific Study of Religion, 4*, 3–13.

Fecher, V. J. (1982). *Religion and Aging: An Annotated Bibliography*. San Antonio: Trinity University Press, 23–27.

Feifel, H. (1959). "Attitudes Toward Death in Some Normal and Mentally Ill Populations." *The Meaning of Death*, H. Feifel, editor. New York: McGraw-Hill, 114–30.

Feifel, H. (1974). "Religious Conviction and Fear of Death Among the Healthy and Terminally Ill." *Journal for the Scientific Study of Religion, 13*, 353–60.

Feifel, H., and Nagy, V. T. (1981). "Another Look at Fear of Death." *Journal of Consulting and Clinical Psychology, 49*, 278–86.

Fichter, J. (1954). "Social Relations in the Urban Parish." *In Southern Parish*, Volume II. Chicago: University of Chicago Press.

Fichter, J. (1969). "Sociological Measurement of Religiosity." *Review of Religious Research, 10*, 169–77.

Folkman, S., and Lazarus, R. S. (1980). "An Analysis of Coping in a Middle-Aged Community Sample." *Journal of Health and Social Behavior, 21*, 219–39.

Folkman, S., and Lazarus, R. S. (1985). "If It Changes It Must be Process: A Study of Emotion and Coping During Three Stages of a College Examination." *Journal of Personality and Social Psychology, 48*, 150–70.

Folstein, M., et al. (1975). 'Mini-Mental State': A Practical Method for Grading the Cognitive State of Patients for the Clinician." *Journal of Psychiatric Research, 12*, 189–95.

Foster, D. W. (1982). "Religion and Medicine: the Physician's Perspective. *Health/Medicine and the Faith Traditions*, M. Marty and K. Vaux, editors, 245–70.

Fountain, (1986). "How to Assimilate the Elderly into Your Parish: The Effects of Alienation on Church Attendance." *Journal of Religion and Aging, 2*(3), 45–55.

Frankl, V. (1959). *Man's Search for Meaning*. New York: Simon and Schuster.

Frankl, V. (1975). *The Unconscious God*. New York: Simon and Schuster.

Fromm, E. (1979). *Greatness and Limitations of Freud's Thought*. New York: Harper Row.

Fukuyama, Y. (1961). "The Major Dimensions of Church Membership." *Review of Religious Research, 2*, 154–61.

Funk, R. A. (1956). "Religious Attitudes and Manifest Anxiety in a College Population." *American Psychologist, 2*, 375–77.

Galanter, M. (1982). "Charismatic Religious Sects and Psychiatry: An Overview." *American Journal of Psychiatry, 139*(12), 1539–48.

Galanter, M., and Buckley, P. (1978). "Evangelical Religion and Meditation: Psychotherapeutic Effects." *Journal of Nervous Mental Disease, 166*, 685–91.

Gallemore, J. L., Wilson, W. P., and Rhoads, J. M. (1969). "The Religious Life of Patients with Affective Disorders." *Diseases of the Nervous System, 30,* 483–6.

Galton, F. (1883). *Inquiries into Human Faculty and Its Development.* London: Macmillan, pp. 277–94.

Gardner, J. W., and Lyon, J. L. (1982a). "Cancer in Utah Mormon Women by Church Activity Level." *American Journal of Epidemiology, 116,* 258.

Gardner, J. W., and Lyon, J. L. (1982b). "Cancer in Utah Mormon Men by Lay Priesthood Level." *American Journal of Epidemiology, 116,* 243–57.

Gass, K. A. (1987). "The Health of Conjugally Bereaved Older Widows: The Role of Appraisal, Coping, and Resources." *Research in Nursing & Health, 10,* 39–47.

Gavras, H., and Gavras, I. (1985). "Risk of Stroke in Hypertensive Elderly Patients." *Geriatric Medicine Today, 4* (11), 72–75.

George, L. K. (1980). "Resources, Coping Skills, and Social Status Factors." *Role Transitions in Later Life.* Monterey, Calif.: Brooks/Cole Publishers, 25–30.

George, L. K. (1986). "Life Satisfaction in Later Life." *Generations, 10* (3), 5–8.

Gianturco, D. T., and Busse, E. W. (1978). "Psychiatric Problems Encountered During a Long-term Study of Normal Aging Volunteers." *Studies in Geriatric Psychiatry,* A. D. Isaacs and F. Post, editors. New York: John Wiley and Sons, 1–17.

Glock, C. Y., and Stark, R. (1965). *Religion and Society in Tension.* Chicago: Rand McNally.

Glock, C. Y., and Stark, R. (1966). *Christian Beliefs and Anti-Semitism.* New York: Harper & Row.

Goldberg, E. L., Van Natta, P., and Comstock, G. W. (1985). "Depressive Symptoms, Social Networks and Social Support of Elderly Women." *American Journal of Epidemiology, 121* (3), 448–56.

Goldman, N. S. (1985). "The Placebo and the Therapeutic Uses of Faith." *Journal of Religion and Health, 24* (2), 103–16.

Gorsuch, R. L. (1984). "Measurement—The Boon and Bane of Investigating Religion." *American Psychologist, 39* (3), 228–36.

Goulder, T. J. (1986). "Scientific Evaluation of Complementary Medicine." *Lancet, i,* 158.

Graham, T. W., et al. (1978). "Frequency of Church Attendance and Blood Pressure Elevation." *Journal of Behavior Medicine, 1,* 37–43.

Graney, M. J. (1975). "Happiness and Social Participation in Aging." *Journal of Gerontology, 30,* 701–6.

Grant, I., et al. (1974). "Recent Life Events and Diabetes in Adults." *Psychosomatic Medicine, 36,* 121–26.

Gray, R. M., and Moberg, D. O. (1962). *The Church and the Older Person.* Grand Rapids, Mich.: William B. Erdsmans Publishing Co.

Greer, S. (1983). "Cancer and the Mind." *British Journal of Psychiatry, 143,* 535–43.

Griffith, E. (1983). "The Impact of Sociocultural Factors on a Church-based Healing Model." *American Journal of Orthopsychiatry, 53* (2), 291–302.

Griffith, E., English, T., and Mayfield, V. (1980). "Possession, Prayer, and Testimony: Therapeutic Aspects of the Wednesday Night Meeting in a Black Church." *Psychiatry, 43,* 120–28.

Griffith, E., and Mahy, G. E. (1984). "Psychological Benefits of Spiritual Baptist 'Mourning.' " *American Journal of Psychiatry, 141,* 769–773.

Griffith, E., and Mathewson, M. (1981). "Communitas and Charisma in a Black Church Service." *Journal of the National Medical Association, 73*, 1023–27.

Griffith, E., Young, J. L., and Smith, D. L. (1984). "An Analysis of the Therapeutic Elements in a Black Church Service." *Hospital and Community Psychiatry, 35* (5), 464–69.

Grollman, E. A. (1963). "Some Sights and Insights of History, Psychology and Psychoanalysis Concerning the Father-God and Mother-Goddess Concepts of Judaism and Christianity." *American Imago, 20* (2) (Summer), 187–209.

Gubrium, J. F. (1973). "Apprehensions of Coping Incompetence and Responses to Fear in Old Age." *International Journal of Aging and Human Development, 4* (2), 111–25.

Guy, R. F. (1982). "Religion, Physical Disabilities and Life Satisfaction in Older Age Cohorts." *International Journal of Aging and Human Development, 15* (3), 225–32.

Hadaway, E. K. (1978). "Life Satisfaction and Religion: A Reanalysis." *Social Forces, 57*, 636–43.

Hall, J. W., and Henderson L. L. (1966). "Asthma in the Aged." *Journal of the American Geriatric Society, 14*, 779–85.

Hammond, P. (1981). "Churches and Older People." *Aging and the Human Spirit*, LeFevre, C. and LeFevre, P., editors. Chicago: Exploration Press, 222–37.

Hannay, D. R. (1980). "Religion and Health." *Social Science Medicine, 14A*, 683–5.

Haring, B. (1985). *In Pursuit of Wholeness*. Liguori, M.: Liguori Publications.

Harris, L., and Associates (1975). *The Myth and Realities of Aging in America*. Washington, D.C.: National Council on Aging.

Havighurst, R. J., and Albrecht, R. (1953). *Older People*. New York: Longmans, Green and Co., 203–4.

Hawkins, N. G., Davies, R., and Holmes, T. H. (1957). "Evidence of Psychosocial Factors in the Development of Pulmonary Tuberculosis." *American Review of Tuberculosis and Pulmonary Diseases, 75*, 5–11.

Haynes, S. G., et al. (1980). "The Relationship of Psychosocial Factors to Coronary Heart Disease in the Farmington Study III. Eight-year Incidence of Coronary Heart Disease." *American Journal of Epidemiology, 111*, 37–58.

Heenan, E. (1972). "Sociology of Religion and the Aged: The Empirical Lacunae." *Journal for the Scientific Study of Religion, 2*, 171–76.

Heschel, A. J. (1981). "The Older Person and the Family in the Perspective of Jewish Tradition." *Aging and the Human Spirit*, C. LeFevre and P. LeFevre, editors. Chicago: Exploration Press, 35–43.

Heschel, A. J. (1964). "The Patient as a Person." *Conservative Judaism, 19*, 7.

Heyman, D. K. and Gianturco, D. T. (1973). "Long-term Adaptation by the Elderly to Bereavement." *Journal of Gerontology, 28*, 359–62.

Hinkle, L. E., and Wolff, H. G. (1958). "Ecologic Investigations of the Relationship Between Illness, Life Experience, and Social Environment." *Annals of Internal Medicine, 49*, 1373–88.

Hinkle, L. E., and Wolf, S. (1952). "A Summary of Experimental Evidence Relating Life Stress to Diabetes Mellitus." *Journal of Mount Sinai Hospital, 19*, 537–550.

Hinton, J. (1967). *Dying*. Baltimore: Penguin.

Hoffman, L. M. (1970). "Medicine and Religion: A Natural Alliance." *Pennsylvania Medicine*, 73 (3), 71–2.

Hoge, D. R. (1972). "A Validated Intrinsic Religious Motivation Scale." *Journal for the Scientific Study of Religion*, 11, 369–76.

Holmes, T. (1962). "Psychosocial and Psychophysiological Studies of Tuberculosis." *Physiological Correlates of Psychological Disorder*, R. Roessler and N. Greenfield, editors. Madison: University of Wisconsin Press, 239-56.

House, J. S. (1974). "Occupational Stress and Coronary Heart Disease: A Review and Theoretical Integration." *Journal of Health and Social Behavior*, 15, 13.

House, J. S., et al. (1982). "The Association of Social Relationships and Activities with Mortality: Prospective Evidence from the Tecumseh Community Health Study." *American Journal of Epidemiology*, 116, 123–40.

Howe, R. (1953). *Man's Need and God's Action*. Greenwich, Conn.: The Seabury Press.

Hunsberger, B. (1985). "Religion, Age, Life Satisfaction, and Perceived Sources of Religiousness: A Study of Older Persons." *Journal of Gerontology*, 40 (5), 615–20.

Hunt, R. A., and King, M. B. (1971). "The Intrinsic-Extrinsic Concept." *Journal for the Scientific Study of Religion*, 10, 339–56.

Idler, E. L. (1987). "Religious Involvement and Health of the Elderly: Some Hypotheses and an Initial Test." *Social Forces*, 66, 226–38.

Jackson, T. (1984). *The Works of John Wesley*, 3rd ed. Vol. II. Peabody, Mass.: Hendrickson Publishers.

Jacobs, M. A., et al. (1970). "Life Stress and Respiratory Illness." *Psychosomatic Medicine*, 32, 223–28.

Jacobs, S., and Ostfeld, A. (1977). "An Epidemiological Review of the Mortality of Bereavement." *Psychosomatic Medicine*, 39 (5), 344–57.

James, W. (1902). *The Varieties of Religious Experience: A Study in Human Nature*. New York: Longmans, Green and Co.

Jarvis, G. K., and Northcott, H. C. (1987). "Religion and Differences in Morbidity and Mortality." *Social Science in Medicine*, 25, 813–24.

Jeffers, F. C., and Nichols, C. R. (1961). "The Relationship of Activities and Attitudes to Physical Well-being in Older People." *Journal of Gerontology*, 16, 67–70.

Jeffers, F. C., Nichols, C. R., and Eisdorfer, C. (1961). "Attitudes of Older Persons Toward Death: A Preliminary Study." *Journal of Gerontology*, 16, 53–6.

Jeffers, F. C., and Verwoerdt, A. (1966). "Factors Associated with the Frequency of Death Thoughts in Elderly Community Volunteers." *Proc. VII International Congress of Gerontology*, 149–52.

Johnson, D. M., Williams, J. S., and Bromley, D. G. (1986). "Religion, Health and Healing: Findings from a Southern City." *Sociological Analysis*, 47 (1), 66–73.

Johnson, S. B. (1979). "Psychosocial Factors in Juvenile Diabetes: A Review." *Journal of Behavior Medicine*, 3, 95–116.

Joyce, C. R. B., Welldon, R. M. C. (1965). "The Objective Efficacy of Prayer: A Double Blind Trial." *Journal of Chronic Diseases*, 18, 367–77.

Jung, C. (1933). *Modern Man in Search of Soul*. New York: Harcourt Brace Jovan-
    ovich.
Kane, R. A., and Kane R. L. (1981). *Assessing the Elderly: A Practical Guide to
    Measurement*. Lexington, Mass.: D. C. Heath and Company.
Kaplan, B. H. (1976). "A Note on Religious Beliefs and Coronary Heart Disease."
    Journal of S. Carolina Medical Assn. (suppl.), 72, 60–64.
Kaplan, B. H., Cassel, J. C., and Gore, S. (1977). "Social Support and Health."
    Medical Care, 15, 47–58.
Katz, R. L. (1975). *Toward A Theology of Aging*, Hiltner, S., editor. New York:
    Human Sciences Press. 135–150.
Kelsey, M. (1973). *Healing and Christianity: In Ancient Thought and Modern Times*.
    New York: Harper and Row, 141.
Keyser, A. (1986). "Legal Guardianship for the Elderly: A Volunteer Model."
    Journal of Religion and Aging, 2 (4), 41–54.
Khavari, K. A., and Harmon, T. M. (1982). "The Relationship Between the De-
    gree of Professed Religious Belief and Use of Drugs." *International Journal
    of Addictions*, 17 (5), 847–57.
Kiecolt-Glaser, J. K. and Glaser, R. (1985). "Psychosocial Enhancement of Im-
    munocompetence in a Geriatric Population." *Psychological Health*, 4, 25–
    41.
King, M. B., and Hunt, R. A. (1975). "Measuring the Religious Variable: Na-
    tional Replication." *Journal for the Scientific Study of Religion*, 14, 13–22.
Kisch, E. S. (1985). "Stressful Events and the Onset of Diabetes Mellitus." *Israel
    Journal of Medical Science*, 21, 356–58.
Kivett, V. R. (1979). "Religious Motivation in Middle Age: Correlates and Im-
    plications." *Journal of Gerontology*, 34, 106–15.
Kleinman, A., Eisenberg, L., and Good, B. (1978). "Clinical Lessons from An-
    thropologic and Cross-cultural Research." *Annals of Internal Medicine*, 88,
    251–8.
Knapp, K. (1981). "Respect for Age in Christianity: The Base of Our Concern
    in Scripture and Tradition." *Aging and the Human Spirit*, C. LeFevre and
    P. LeFevre editors. Chicago: Exploration Press, 21–33.
Knight, J. (1982). "The Minister as Healer, the Healer as Minister." *Journal of
    Religion and Health*, 21 (2), 100–14.
Koenig, H. G. (1986). "Shepherds' Centers: Elderly People Helping Them-
    selves." *Journal of the American Geriatrics Society*, 34, 73.
Koenig, H. G. (1988). "Religion and Death Anxiety in Later Life." *The Hospice
    Journal*, 4 (1), 3–24.
Koenig, H. G. (1987a). "The Relationship Between Age and Religious Activities:
    A Cross-Sectional Study." Southern Illinois University School of Medi-
    cine, Springfield, Ill. Unpublished data.
Koenig, H. G. (1987b). "Religious Characteristics of Senior Center Participants
    in a Three State Study." Southern Illinois University School of Medicine,
    Springfield, Ill. Unpublished data.
Koenig, H. G. (1987c). "Shepherds' Centers: Role of the Physician." *Geriatric
    Consultant*, May/June.
Koenig, H. G., and Blake, R. L. (1985). "Religious Behaviors, Coping, and Self-
    Perceived Health in Elderly." Unpublished manuscript presented at the
    32d Annual Meeting of the American Society on Aging, San Francisco.
Koenig, H. G., Moberg, D. O., and Kvale, J. N. (1988a). "Religious Activities

and Attitudes of Older Adults in a Geriatric Assessment Clinic." *Journal of the American Geriatric Society, 36*, 362–74.

Koenig, H. G., Kvale, J. N., and Ferrel, C. (1988b). "Religion and Well-being in Later Life." *The Gerontologist, 28*, 11–24.

Koenig, H. G., George, L. K., and Siegler, I. C. (1988c). "The Use of Religion and Other Emotion-regulating Coping Strategies Among Older Adults." *The Gerontologist, 28*, 303–10.

Koenig, H. G., Meador, K. G., Cohen, H. J., and Blazer, D. G. (1988d). "Depression in Elderly Hospitalized Patients with Medical Illness." *Archives of Internal Medicine*. In press.

Koenig, H. G., Bearon, L. B., and Dayringer, R. (1988e). "Physician Perspectives on the Role of Religion in the Physician-Older Patient Relationship." *Journal of Family Practice*. In press.

Koenig, H. G., Siegler, I. C., and George L. K. (1988f)."Religious and Non-religious Coping: Impact on Adaptation in Later Life." *Journal of Religion and Aging, 5* (4).

Koenig, H. G., Meador, K. G., Cohen, H. J., and Blazer, D. G. (1988g). "Self-rated Depression Scales and Screening for Major Depression in the Older Hospitalized Patient with Medical Illness." *Journal of the American Geriatrics Society, 36*, 699–706.

Kramer, M., et al. (1985). "Patterns of Mental Disorders Among the Elderly Residents of Eastern Baltimore." *Journal of the American Geriatrics Society, 33* (4), 236–45.

Krantz, L., et al. (1968). "Religious Beliefs and Suicidal Patients." *Psychological Report, 22*, 936–40.

Kuebler-Ross, E. (1969). *On Death and Dying*. New York: Macmillan.

Kuhlman, K. (1962). *I Believe in Miracles*. Englewood Cliffs, N.J.: Prentice-Hall.

Kuhn, M. (1981). "The Church's Continuing Role with the Aging." C. Lefevre and P. Lefevre, editors. *Aging and the Human Spirit*. Chicago: Exploration Press, 238–65.

Kulka, R., et al. (1979). "Social Class and the Use of Professional Help for Personal Problems." *Journal of Health and Social Behavior, 20*, 2–17.

Kurlychek, R. T. (1976). "Level of the Belief in Afterlife and Four Categories of Fear and Death in a Sample of 60+ Year Olds." *Psychological Reports, 38*, 228–30.

Kvale, J. N., Koenig, H. G., Ferrel, C., and Moore, H. R. (1988). "Life Satisfaction of the Aging Woman Religious." *Journal of Religion and Aging, 5* (4).

Lamere, F. (1953). "What Happens to Alcoholics." *American Journal of Psychiatry, 109*, 673.

Landis, B., et al. (1985). "Effect of Stress Reduction on Daily Glucose Range in Previously Stabilized Insulin-Dependent Diabetic Patients." *Diabetes Care, 8*, 624–26.

Laporte, J. B. (1981). "The Elderly in the Life and Thought of the Early Church." *Ministry with the Aging*, G. Clements, editor. New York: Harper and Row, 33–35.

Lardis, J. T. (1942). "Hobbies and Happiness in Old Age." *Recreation, 35*, 642.

Larson, D. B., et al. (1988). "The Frequency of Church Attendance, Importance of Religion, and Blood Pressure Status." *Journal of Religion and Health*. Manuscript in submission.

Larson, D. B., and Wilson, W. P. (1980). "Religious Life of Alcoholics." *Southern Medical Journal*, 73, 723–7.

Larson, R. (1978). "Thirty Years of Research on Subjective Well-being of Older Americans." *Journal of Gerontology*, 33 (1), 109–25.

Lawton, G. (1943). "Happiness in Old Age." *Mental Hygiene*, 27, 231–37.

Lawton, M. P. (1975). "The Philadelphia Geriatric Morale Scale: A Revision." *Journal of Gerontology*, 30, 85–89.

Lazarus, R. S. (1966). *Psychological Stress and the Coping Process*. New York: McGraw-Hill.

Lazarus, R. S. (1974). "The Psychology of Coping: Issues of Research and Assessment." *Coping and Adaptation*, G. V. Coelho, D. A. Hamburg, and J. E. Adams, editors. New York: Basic Books.

Lazarus, R. S., and Golden, G. Y. (1979). "The Function of Denial in Stress, Coping, and Aging." *Aging: Biology and Behavior*, McGaugh, editor. Orlando, Fla.: Academic Press, 283–307.

Lenski, G. (1961). *The Religious Factor*. Garden City, N.Y.: Doubleday.

Lenski, G. (1963). *The Religious Factor: A Sociological Study of Religion's Impact on Politics, Economics and Family Life*. Garden City, N.Y.: Doubleday.

Letzig, B. (1986). "The Church as Advocate in Aging." *Journal of Religion and Aging*, 2 (4), 1–11.

LeVeque, J. (1987). "Pastoral Caring: A Call to Growth." *Sisters Today*, 59 (1), 34–38.

Levin, L. S., and Idler, E. L. (1981). *The Hidden Health Care System: Mediating Structures and Medicine*. Cambridge, Mass.: Harper and Row.

Levin, J. S., and Markides, K. S. (1985). "Religion and Health in Mexican Americans." *Journal of Religion and Health*, 24 (1), 60–9.

Levin, J. S., and Markides, K. S. (1986). "Religious Attendance and Subjective Health." *Journal for the Scientific Study of Religion*, 25 (1): 31–40.

Levin, J. S., and Schiller, P. L. (1986). "Religion and the Multidimensional Health Locus of Control Scales."*Psychological Reports*, 59, 26.

Levin, J. and Schiller, P. L. (1987)."Is there a Religious Factor in Health?" *Journal of Religion and Health*, 26 (1), 9–36.

Levin, J. S., and Vanderpool, H. Y. (1987). "Is Frequent Religious Attendance Really Conductive to Better Health?: Toward an Epidemiology of Religion." *Social Science Medicine*, 24, 589–600.

Lin, N., et al. (1979). "Social Support, Stressful Life Events, and Illness. A Model and Empirical Test." *Journal of Health and Social Behavior*, 20, 108–19.

Lindenthal, J. J., et al. (1970). "Mental Status and Religious Behavior." *Journal for the Scientific Study of Religion*, 9, 143–49.

Lloyd, R. G. (1955). "Social and Personal Adjustment of Retired Persons." *Sociology and Social Research*, 39, 312–16.

Lohmann, N. L. P. (1977). "Comparison of Life Satisfaction, Morale, and Adjustment Scales on an Elderly Population" (Doctoral Dissertation, Brandeis University). *Dissertation Abstracts International*, 38, 418B. University Microfilms No. 77–15,272.

Longino, C., and Kitson, G. (1976). "Parish Clergy and the Aged: Examining Stereotypes." *Journal of Gerontology*, 31 (3), 340–45.

MacDonald, C. B., and Luckett, J. B. (1983). "Religious Affiliation and Psychiatric Diagnoses." *Journal for the Scientific Study of Religion,* 22 (1), 15–37.

McFadden, S. H. (1986). "Clergy Counseling of Elders: Topics of Concern Raised in Individual Contacts by Clergy with Older Persons." Paper presented at the Annual Meeting of the American Society on Aging, San Francisco, Calif., March 25, 1986.

McNeil, J. T. (1951). *The History of the Cure of Souls.* New York: Harper and Row.

MacNutt, F. (1974). *Healing.* Notre Dame: Ave Maria Press.

MacNutt, F. (1977). *The Power to Heal.* Notre Dame: Ave Maria Press.

Maddox, G. L. and Douglas, E. B. (1973). "Self-assessment of Health." *Journal of Health and Social Behavior,* 14, 87–93.

Mahoney, R. (1987). *Catholic Trends,* 18 (6). Washington, D.C., 1312 Massachusetts Avenue, N.W., 3.

Manfredi, C., Pickett, M. (1987). "Perceived Stressful Situations and Coping Strategies Utilized by the Elderly." *Journal of Community Health Nursing,* 4 (2), 99–110.

Maranell, G. M. (1974). "Religiosity and Personal Adjustment." *Responses to Religion,* G. M. Maranell, editor. Wichita: University Press of Kansas, 211–20.

Markides, K. S. (1983). "Aging, Religiosity, and Adjustment: A Longitudinal Analysis." *Journal of Gerontology,* 28, 621–5.

Markides, K. S., Levin, J. S., and Ray, L. A. (1987). "Religion, Aging, and Life Satisfaction: An Eight-Year Three-Wave Longitudinal Study." *The Gerontologist,* 27, 660–65.

Marsh, G. R., and Thompson, L. W. (1977). "Psychophysiology of Aging." *Handbook of the Psychology of Aging,* J. E. Birren and K. W. Schaie, editors. New York: Van Nostrand Reinhold.

Marshal, V. W. (1980). *Last Chapters: A Sociology of Aging and Dying.* Monterey, Calif.: Brooks/Cole Publishers.

Marty, M. E. (1980). "Social Service: Godly and Godless." *Social Services Review,* 54, 464–81.

Mathieu, J. (1972). "Dying and Death Role Expectations," doctoral dissertation. Los Angeles: University of Southern California.

Maves, P. B. (1960). "Aging, Religion and the Church." *Handbook of Social Gerontology,* C. Tibbitts, editor. Chicago: University of Chicago Press, 698–748.

Maves, P. B. (1986). *Faith for the Older Years.* Minneapolis: Augsburg Publishing House.

Maves, P. B., and Cedarleaf, J. L. (1949). *Older People and the Church.* Nashville, Tenn.: A Bingdon-Cokesbury Press.

Mayberry, J. F. (1982). "Epidemiological Studies of Gastrointestinal Cancer in Christian Sects." *J. Clin Gastroenterology* 4:115–21.

Mayo, S. C. (1951). "Social Participation Among the Older Population in Rural Areas of Wake County, N.C." *Social Forces,* 30, 53–59.

Mechanic, D. (1974). "Social Structure and Personal Adaptation: Some Neglected Dimensions." *Coping and Adaptation,* G. Coelho, D. Hamburg, and J. Adams, editors. New York: Basic Books, 33.

Meng, H., and Freud, E. L. (1963). *Psychoanalysis and Faith: The Letters of Oskar Pfister*. London: The Hogarth Press.

Merrill, G. G. (1981, December). "Health, Healing and Religion." *Maryland State Medical Journal, 30*, 45–47.

Merrill, G. G. (1982, December). "Religious Values in Treatment." *Maryland State Medical Journal, 31*, 33.

Miller, W. R., and Martin, J. E. (1988). *Behavior Therapy and Religion*. Newbury Park, Calif.: Sage Publications.

Mindel, C. H., and Vaughan, C. E. (1978). "A Multidimensional Approach to Religiosity and Disengagement." *Journal of Gerontology, 33* (1), 103–8.

Missinne, L. (1983). "Parish Ministry to the Elderly." *Human Development, 4* (3), 25–29.

Moberg, D. O. (1953a). "Church Membership and Personal Adjustment in Old Age." *Journal of Gerontology, 8*, 207–11.

Moberg, D. O. (1953b). "Leadership in the Church and Personal Adjustment in Old Age." *Sociology and Social Research, 37*, 312–16.

Moberg, D. O. (1953c). "The Christian Religion and Personal Adjustment in Old Age." *American Sociological Review, 18*, 87–90.

Moberg, D. O. (1956). "Religious Activities and Personal Adjustment in Old Age." *Journal of Social Psychology, 43*, 261–68.

Moberg, D. O. (1958). "Christian Beliefs and Personal Adjustment in Old Age." *Journal of American Science Affiliates, 10*, 8–12.

Moberg, D. O. (1965). "Religion in Old Age." *Geriatrics, 20*, 977–82.

Moberg, D. O. (1970). "Religion in the Later Years." *The Daily Needs and Interests of Older Persons*, A. M. Hoffman, editor. Springfield, Ill.: Charles C. Thomas.

Moberg, D. O. (1974). "Spiritual Well-being in Late Life." *Later Life: Communities and Environmental Policy*, J. F. Gubrium, editor, Springfield, Ill.: Charles C. Thomas, 256–76.

Moberg, D. O. (1975). "Needs Felt by the Clergy for Ministries to the Aging." *The Gerontologist, 15*, 170–75.

Moody, R. (1975). *Life After Life*. Covington, Ga.: Mockingbird Books.

Moos, R. H., Tsu, V. D. (1977). "The Crisis of Physical Illness: An Overview." *Coping with Physical Illness*. R. H. Moos and V. D. Tsu, editors. New York: Plenum Press, 14.

Morris, J. N., Wolf, R. S., and Klerman, L. V. (1975). "Common Themes Among Morale and Depression Scales." *Journal of Gerontology, 30*, 209–15.

Morris, P. A. (1982). "The Effect of Pilgrimage on Anxiety, Depression, and Religious Attitude." *Psychological Medicine, 12*, 291–94.

Naguib, S. M., Beiser, P. B., and Comstock, G. W. (1968). "Response to a Program of Screening for Cervical Cancer." *Public Health Reports, 83* (12), 990–98.

Nelson, A. A., Wilson W. P. (1984). "The Ethics of Sharing Religious Faith in Psychotheraphy." *Journal of Psychology and Theology, 12*, 15–23.

Nelson, F. L. (1977). "Religiosity and Self-destructive Crises in the Institutionalized Elderly." *Suicide and Life-threatening Behavior, 7* (2), 67–73.

Ness, R., and Wintrob, R. (1980). "The Emotional Impact of Fundamentalist

Religious Participation: An Empirical Study of Intragroup Variation."
American Journal of Orthopsychiatry, 50, 302–15.

Neugarten, B., Havighurst, R., and Tobin, S. (1961). "The Measurement of Life
Satisfaction." *Journal of Gerontology*, 16, 134–43.

The New American Bible. (1970). New York: P. J. Kenedy & Sons.

Nielsen, A. C. (1985). *Report on Devotional Programs: February, 1985*. New York:
A. C. Nielsen.

Nolan, W. A. (1974). *Healing: A Doctor in Search of a Miracle*. New York: Random
House.

Nouwen, H., and Gaffney, W. (1974). *Aging, The Fulfillment of Life*. New York:
Image Books, Doubleday and Co., Inc.

Oakes, C. G. (1974). "Conclusion: Aging in Perspective." *Foundations of Practical
Gerontology*, R. Boyd and C. Oakes edition. Columbia: University of South
Carolina, 227–28.

O'Brien, M. E. (1982). "Religious Faith and Adjustment to Long-term Hemodialysis." *Journal of Religion and Health*, 21 (1), 68–80.

Orbach, H. L. (1961). "Aging and Religion: A Study of Church Attendance in
the Detroit Metropolitan Area." *Geriatrics*, 16, 530–40.

O'Reilly, C. T. (1957). "Religious Practice and Personal Adjustments of Older
People." *Sociology and Social Research*, 43, 119–21.

O'Rourke, W. D. (1977). "The Relationship Between Religiousness, Purpose in
Life, and Fear of Death." *Dissertation Abstracts International*, 37 (11–A),
7046–47.

Ortega, S. T., Crutchfield, R. D., and Rushing, W. A. (1983). "Race Differences
in Elderly Personal Well-Being: Friendship, Family, and Church." *Research
on Aging*, 4, 101–18.

Osgood, N. J. (1985). "Identifying and Counseling the Suicidal Geriatric Patient." *Geriatric Medicine Today*, 4 (3), 83–92.

Osgood, N. J. (1982). "Suicide in the Elderly." *Postgraduate Medicine*, 72 (2), 123–
30.

Osler, W. (1910). "The Faith That Heals." *British Medical Journal* (June 18), 1470–
72.

Palmore, E. (1969). "Sociological Aspects of Aging." *Behavior and Adaptation in
Late Life*, E. Busse and E. Pfeiffer, editors. Boston: Little and Brown.

Palmore, E. (1980). "The Social Factors in Aging." *Handbook of Geriatric Psychiatry*,
E. Busse and D. Blazer, editors. New York: Van Nostrand Reinhold, 222–
48.

Paloutzian, R. F., and Ellison, C. W. (1982). "Loneliness, Spiritual Well-being,
and Quality of Life." *Loneliness: A Sourcebook of Current Theory, Research
and Therapy*, A. Peplau and D. Porlman, editors. New York: Wiley Inter
Science, 224–37.

Parfrey, P. S. (1976). "The Effect of Religious Factors on Intoxicant Use." *Scand.
Journal of Social Medicine*, 3, 135–40.

Pargament, K. I., et al. (1988). "Religion and the Problem-solving Process: Three
Styles of Coping." *Journal for the Scientific Study of Religion*, 27 (1), 90–104.

Pargament, K. I., and Hahn, J. (1986). "God and the Just World: Causal and
Coping Attributions to God in Health Situations." *Journal for the Scientific
Study of Religion*, 25 (2), 193–207.

Pargament, K. I. (1988). "God Help Me: Toward a Theoretical Framework of Coping for the Psychology of Religion." In *Research in the Social Scientific Study of Religion*, Bowling Green State University, Department of Psychology.

Parker, G. B., and Brown, L. B. (1982). "Coping Behaviors that Mediate Between Life Events and Depression." *Archives of General Psychiatry, 39*, 1386–91.

Pattison, E. M. (1965). "Social and Psychological Aspects of Religion in Psychotherapy." *Journal of Nervous and Mental Diseases, 141*, 586–97.

Pattison, E. M., Labino, N. A., and Doerr, H A. (1973). "Faith Healing: A Study of Personality and Function." *Journal of Nervous and Mental Diseases, 157*, 367–409.

Pattison, E. M., and Pattison, M. L. (1980). "Ex-gays: Religiously Mediated Change in Homosexuals." *American Journal of Psychiatry, 137*, 1553–62.

Payne, B. P., et al. (1972). "Social Background and Role Determinants of Individual Participation in Organized Voluntary Action." *Voluntary Action Research*. Boston: D. C. Health.

Payne, B. P. (1975). "Religious Life of the Elderly: Myth or Reality?" *Spiritual Well-being of the Elderly*, K. A. Thorson and T. C. Cook, Jr., editors. Springfield, Ill.: Charles C. Thomas Publisher.

Payne, B. P., and Brewer, E. (1982). "Denominational Community Roles in the Aging Enterprise." A paper presented at the Southern Sociological Society, Memphis, Tenn. April 15–17, 1982.

Payne, B. P. (1984). "Protestants." *Handbook on the Aged in the United States*, E. B. Palmore, editor. Westport, Conn.: Greenwood Press, 191–98.

Payne, B. P. (1988a). "Religious Patterns and Participation of Older Adults: A Sociological Perspective." *Journal of Educational Gerontology*.

Payne, B. P. (1988b). Unpublished update of inclusion of religion in gerontological textbooks cited in 1975 publication: *Religious Life of the Elderly: Myth or Reality? Spiritual Well-Being of the Elderly*, J. A. Thorson, T. C. Cook editors. Springfield, Ill.: Charles C. Thomas Publisher.

Payne, B. P., and Bull, N. C. (1979). "Report to the Andrus Foundation on the Longitudinal Study of the Older Volunteer." Paper for the Andrus Foundation, Atlanta, Ga.

Payne, E. C. (1975). "Depression and Suicide." *Modern Perspectives in the Psychiatry of Old Age*, J. Horvells, editor. New York: Brunner-Mazel.

Payne-Pittard, B. P. (1966). "The Meaning and Measurement of Commitment to the Church." Georgia State College Research Paper Number 13.

Pelligrino, E. (1978). "The Fact of Illness and the Act of Profession: Some Notes on the Source of Professional Obligation." *Implications of History and Ethics to Medicine Veterinary and Human*, L. B. McCullogh and J. P. Norris, editors. College Station: Texas A & M University, 78–89.

Pelligrino, E. (1979a). "To be a Physician." *Humanism and the Physician*. Knoxville: University of Tennessee Press, 222–30.

Pelligrino, E. (1979b). "Toward a Reconstruction of Medical Morality: The Primacy of the Act of Profession and the Fact of Illness." *Journal of Medicine and Philosophy, 4*, 32–56.

Perlman, L. V., Ferguson, S., and Bergum, K. (1971). "Precipitation of Congestive Heart Failure: Social and Emotional Factors." *Annals of Internal Medicine, 75*, 1–13.

Peterson, D. and Bolton, C. (1980). *Gerontology Instruction in Higher Education.* New York: Springer.

Peterson, J. A., and Briley, M. (1977). *Widows and Widowhood: A Creative Approach to Being Alone.* New York: Association Press.

Pflanz, M. (1971). "Epidemiological and Sociocultural Factors in the Etiology of Duodenal Ulcer." *Advances in Psychosomatic Medicine,* 6, 121–51.

Piedmont, E. B. (1968). "Referrals and Reciprocity: Psychiatrists, General Practitioners and Clergymen." *Journal of Health and Social Behavior,* 9, 29–41.

Pihlblad, C. T., and Adams, D. L. (1972). "Widowhood, Social Participation and Life Satisfaction." *International Journal of Aging and Human Development,* 3, 323–30.

Pilli, A. (1984). *Our Journey In Faith, Together: A Pastoral Letter to Adults and Their Loved Ones.* Cleveland: The Catholic Universe Bulletin.

Pressey, S. L., and Semcoe, E. (1950). "Case Study Comparisons of Successful and Problem Old People." *Journal of Gerontology,* 5, 168–75.

Princeton Religion Research Center (1976). *Religion in America.* Princeton, N.J.: The Gallup Poll.

Princeton Religion Research Center (1982). *1982 Religion in America.* Princeton, N.J.: The Gallup Poll.

Princeton Religion Research Center (1985). *1985 Religion in America.* Princeton, N.J.: The Gallup Poll.

Princeton Religion Research Center (1986). *Faith Development and Your Ministry.* Princeton, N.J.: The Gallup Poll.

Profiles of the *Guideposts* Reader (1981, June-July). Survey conducted by Trost Associates, Inc.

Rabkin, J., and Streuning, E. (1976). "Life Events, Stress and Illness." *Science,* 194, 1013–20.

Rawlings, M. S. (1978). *Beyond Death's Door.* Nashville: Thomas Nelson.

Rawlings, M. S. (1980). *Before Death Comes.* Nashville: Thomas Nelson.

Ray, R. O. (1979). "Life Satisfaction and Activity Involvement: Implications for Leisure Service." *Journal of Leisure Research,* 11, 112–19.

Redlener, I., and Scott, C. (1979). "Incompatibilities of Professional and Religious Ideology: Problems of Medical Management and Outcome in a Case of Pediatric Meningitis." *Social Science Medicine,* 13 (B), 89–93.

Reid, W. S., et al. (1978). "A Study of the Religious Attitudes of the Elderly." *Age and Aging,* 7, 40–45.

Reynolds, D. K., and Nelson, F. L. (1981). "Personality, Life-Situation, and Life Expectancy." *Suicide & Life-Threatening Behavior,* 11 (2), 99–110.

Reynolds M. M. (1982). "Religious Institutions and the Prevention of Mental Illness." *Journal of Religion and Health,* 21 (3), 245–53.

Riley, M., and Foner, A. (1968). *Aging and Society.* New York: Russel Sage Foundation.

Robb, T. B. (1985). *The Ministry of Older Presbyterians.* Atlanta: Presbyterian Office on Aging.

Robertson, M.H.B. (1985). "The Influence of Religious Beliefs on Health Choices of Afro-Americans." *Topics in Clinical Nursing,* 7 (3), 57–63.

Robinson, J. P., and Shaver, P. R. (1973). *Measures of Social Psychological Attitudes.* Ann Arbor: University of Michigan, Survey Research Center.

Rokeach, M. (1960). *The Open and Closed Mind.* New York: Basic Books.

Rosen, C. C. (1982). "Ethnic Differences Among Impoverished Rural Elderly in

Use of Religion as a Coping Mechanism." *Journal of Rural Community Psychology, 3,* 27–34.

Rosen, I. M. (1974). "Some Contributions of Religion to Mental and Physical Health." *Journal of Religion and Health, 13* (4), 289–94.

Rosenman, R. H., et al. (1975). "Coronary Heart Disease in the Western Collaborative Group Study: Final Followup Experience of 8½ Years." *Journal of the American Medical Association, 233,* 872–7.

Rosenman, R. H., and Friedman, M. (1974). "A Predictive Study of Coronary Heart Disease: The Western Collaborative Group Study." *Journal of the American Medical Association, 189,* 15–22.

Ross, D. C., and Thomas, C. B. (1965). "Precursors of Hypertension and Coronary Disease Among Healthy Medical Students: Discriminant Function Analysis, III. Using Ethnic Origin as the Criterion, with Observations on Parental Hypertension and Coronary Disease on Religion." *Bulletin of the Johns Hopkins Hospital, 117,* 37–57.

Schinder, T. (1984). "Back to the Bible." Personal Communication. Lincoln, Neb.: The Good News Broadcasting Association.

Schmidt, J. F. (1951). "Patterns of Poor Adjustment in Old Age." *American Journal of Sociology, 57,* 33–42.

Schoenfeld, C. G. (1962). "God the Father—and Mother: Study and Extension of Freud's Conception of God as an Exalted Father." *American Imago, 19* (3) (Fall), 213–34.

Scotch, N. A. (1963). "Sociocultural Factors in the Epidemiology of Zulu Hypertension." *American Journal of Public Health, 53,* 1205–13.

Scott, F. G. (1955). "Factors in the Personal Adjustment of Institutionalized Aged." *American Sociologist Review, 20,* 538–40.

Selye, H. (1956). *The Stress of Life.* New York: McGraw-Hill.

Sevensky, R. L. (1982). "The Religious Physician." *Journal of Religion and Health, 21* (3), 254–63.

Shanas, E. (1962). "The Personal Adjustment of Recipients of Old Age Assistance." *The Church and the Older Person,* R. M. Gray and D. O. Moberg, editors. Grand Rapids, Mich.: Erdmans.

Shapiro, A. K., et al. (1976). "Prognostic Correlates of Psychotherapy in Psychiatric Outpatients." *American Journal of Psychiatry, 133,* 802–813.

Shekelle, R., et al. (1981). "Psychological Depression and 17-year Risk of Death from Cancer." *Psychosomatic Medicine, 43,* 117–125.

Simons, R. L., and West, G. E. (1985). "Life Changes, Coping Resources, and Health among the Elderly." *International Journal on Aging and Human Development, 20* (3), 173–187.

Singh, B. K., and Williams, J. S. (1982). "Satisfaction with Health and Physical Condition Among the Elderly." *Journal of Psychiatric Treatment and Evaluation, 4,* 403–408.

Smiley, M. (1985). "Attitudes of Women Religious in Retirement." Unpublished Data. Incarnate Word College, San Antonio, Tex.

Smiley, M. (1987a). "Women Religious and Aging: A Reflection." *Sisters Today.* Manuscript in submission.

Smiley, M. (1987b). "The Elders Speak: A Survey." Unpublished. Incarnate Word College, San Antonio, Tex.

Smith, D. K., Nehemkis, A. M., and Charter, R. A. (1983–84). "Fear of Death, Death Attitudes and Religious Conviction in the Terminally Ill." *International Journal of Psychiatry in Medicine, 13* (3), 221–232.

Smith, D. M. (1986). "Safety of Faith Healing." *Lancet, i,* 621.

Sorokin, P. A. 1954. *The Ways and Power of Love.* Boston: Beacon Press.

Spielberger, C. D., Gorsuch, R. L., and Lushene, R. E. (1970). Calif.: Consulting Psychologists Press, Inc.

Spilka, B., Mullin, M. (1977). "Personal Religion and Psychological Schemata: A Research Approach to a Theological Psychology of Religion." *Character Potential, 18*(2), 57–66.

Spinks, G. S. (1963). *Psychology and Religion: An Introduction to Contemporary Views.* London: Methuen and Co.

Spreitzer, D., and Snyder, E. (1974). "Correlates of Life Satisfaction Among the Aged." *Journal of Gerontology, 29,* 454–58.

Stack, S. (1983). "The Effect of Religious Commitment on Suicide: A Cross-national Analysis." *Journal of Health and Social Behavior, 24,* 362–74.

Starbuck, E. D. (1899). *The Psychology of Religion.* New York: Charles Scribner's Sons.

Stark, R. (1968). "Age and Faith: A Changing Outlook at an Old Process." *Sociological Analysis, 29,* 1–10.

Stark, R. (1971). "Psychopathology and Religious Commitment." *Review of Religious Research, 12,* 165–76.

Stark, R., and Glock, C. (1970). *American Piety: The Nature of Religious Commitment.* Berkeley: University of California Press.

Steele, C., Lucas, M. J., and Tune, L. E. (1982). "An Approach to the Management of Dementia Syndromes." *Psychiatry Clinic: Johns Hopkins Hospital, 151*(6), 362–68.

Steinitz, L. Y. (1980). "Religiosity, Well-being, and Weltanschaung among the Elderly." *Journal for the Scientific Study of Religion, 19,* 60–67.

St. George, A. S., McNamara, P. H. (1984). "Religion, Race and Psychological Well-Being." Journal for the Scientific Study of Religion, 23, 351–63.

Strachey, J. (1959). *Sigmund Freud. Collected Papers,* vol. 2. N.Y.: Basic Books.

Strachey, J. (1962). *The Standard Edition of the Complete Psychological Works of Sigmund Freud.* London: The Hogarth Press.

Strickland, B. R., Shaffer, S. (1971). *Journal for the Scientific Study of Religion, 10,* 366–69.

Sturdevant, R. A. (1976). "Epidemiology of Peptic Ulcer." *American Journal of Epidemiology, 104,* 9–14.

Swanson, W. C., and Harter, C. L. (1971). "How Do Elderly Blacks Cope in New Orleans?" *International Journal on Aging and Human Development, 2,* 210–16.

Swenson, W. M. (1961). "Attitudes Toward Death in Aged Population." *Journal of Gerontology, 16,* 49–52.

Taylor, C. (1984). *Growing On: Ideas about Aging.* New York: Van Nostrand Reinhold.

Taylor, R. J. (1986). "Religious Participation Among Elderly Blacks." *The Gerontologist, 26,* 630–5.

Tellis-Nayak, V. (1982). "The Transcendant Standard: The Religious Ethos of the Rural Elderly." *Gerontologist*, 22 (4), 359–363.

Tessler, R., and Mechanic, D. (1978). "Psychological Distress and Perceived Health Status." *Journal of Health and Social Behavior*, 19, 254–62.

Timio, M. (1985). "Study of Nuns Supports Stress Factor in Blood Pressure Increase with Age." *Family Practice News*, 15(9), 87.

Tobin, S. S., Ellor, J. W., and Anderson-Ray, S. M. (1986). *Enabling the Elderly: Religious Institutions Within the Community Service System*. Albany: State University of New York Press.

Toseland, R. and Rasch, J. (1979–80). "Correlates of Life Satisfaction: An AID Analysis." *International Journal of Aging and Human Development*, 10, 203–11.

Trost and Associates (1984). Profile of the *Guideposts* Reader. *Daily Guideposts*. Carmel, N.Y.

Tyroler, H., Heyden, S., and Hanes, C. (1975). "Evans Country Studies of Blacks and Whites." *Epidemiology and Control of Hypertension*. P. Oglesby, editor. New York: Stratton Intercontinental Medical Book Association, pp. 177–204.

United States Census, 1980. U.S. Bureau of the Census. Washington, D.C.

Vachon, M., et al. (1982). "Predictors and Correlates of Adaptation to Conjugal Bereavement." *American Journal of Psychiatry*, 139(8), 998–1002.

Vanderpool, H. Y. (1977). "Is Religion Therapeutically Significant?" *Journal of Religion and Health*, 16, 255–59.

Vanderpool, H. Y. (1980). "Religion and Medicine: A Theoretical Overview." *Journal of Religion and Health*, 19(1), 7–17.

Vaux, K. (1976). "Religion and Health." *Preventative Medicine*, 5, 522–36.

Walsh, A. (1980). "The Prophylactic Effect of Religion on Blood Pressure Levels among a Sample of Immigrants." *Social Science Medicine*, 148, 59–63.

Ward, R. A. (1984). *The Aging Experience*, 2nd ed. New York: Harper & Row Publishers.

Wardwell, W. I., et al. (1963). "Stress and Coronary Heart Disease in Three Field Studies. *Journal of Chronic Diseases*, 17, 73–84.

Webber, I. L. (1954). "The Organized Social Life of the Retired: Two Florida Communities." *American Journal of Sociology*, 59, 340–46.

Weber, Max (1946). *Essays in Sociology*. H. H. Gerth and C. W. Mills, translators. New York: Oxford University Press.

Weber, Max (1963). *The Sociology of Religion* (originally published 1922). Boston: Beacon Press.

Webster, A. M. (1981). *Webster's New Collegiate Dictionary*. Springfield, Mass.: The G & C Meriam Company.

Webster, N. (1983). *American Dictionary of the English Language*. San Francisco: Foundation for American Christian Education.

Weikart, R. (1986). "Cooperation Between Clergy and Family Practice Physicians: A New Area of Ministry." *Journal of Pastoral Care*, 40(2), 151–57.

Williams, M. (1974). *Community in a Black Pentecostal Church*. Pittsburgh: University of Pittsburgh Press.

Williams, R. L., and Cole, S. (1968). "Religiosity, Generalized Anxiety, and

Apprehension Concerning Death." *Journal of Social Psychology, 78,* 111–17.

Wilson, B. (1968). "The Fellowship of Alcoholics Anonymous." *Alcoholism,* E. Cantanzaro, editor. Springfield, Ill: Charles C. Thomas.

Wilson, J. (1978). "The Measurement of Religiosity." *Religion in American Society.* Englewood Cliffs, N.J.: Prentice-Hall, Inc., p. 440.

Wilson, R., and Maddox, G. (1974). "Relating Life Change to Psychological Distress: Further Research." *Southern Sociological Society.* Atlanta.

Wilson, W., and Miller, H. L. (1968). "Fear, Anxiety and Religiousness." *Journal for the Scientific Study of Religion, 7,* 111–15.

Wilson, W. P. (1972). "Mental Health Benefits of Religious Salvation." *Journal of Diseases of the Nervous System, 36*(6), 382–86.

Wilson, W. P., Hohman, L. B., and Gallemore, J. L. (1969). Unpublished observations. Department of Psychiatry, VA and Duke University Medical Centers, Durham, N.C.

Wilson, W. P., Larson, D. B., and Meier, P.D. (1983). "Religious Life of Schizophrenics." *Southern Medical Journal, 76,* 1096–1100.

Wingard, D. L. (1982). "The Sex Differential in Mortality Rates: Demographic and Behavioral Factors." *American Journal of Epidemiology, 115,* 205–16.

Wingrove, C., and Alston, J. (1971). "Age, Aging and Church Attendance." *The Gerontologist, 11*(1), 356–58.

Wittkowski, J., and Baumgartner, I. (1977). "Religiosity and Attitude Toward Death and Dying in Elderly Persons." *Zeitschrift für Gerontologie, 10*(1), 61–68.

Wolff, K. (1959a). "Group Psychotherapy with Geriatric Patients in a State Hospital Setting: Results of a Three Year Study." *Group Psychotherapy, 12,* 218–22.

Wolff, K. (1959b). *The Biological, Sociological, and Psychological Aspects of Aging.* Springfield, Ill.: Charles C. Thomas, p. 75.

Wolff, K. (1970). "The Problem of Death and Dying in the Geriatric Patient." *Journal of the American Geriatrics Society, 18,* 954–61.

Yahn, G. (1979). "The Impact of Holistic Medicine, Medical Groups, and Health Concepts." *Journal of the American Medical Association, 242,* 2202–5.

Yater, W. M., et al. (1948). "Coronary Artery Disease in Men 18–39 Years of Age." *American Heart Journal, 36,* 334–72, 481–526, 688–722.

Yates, J. W., et al. (1981). "Religion in Patients with Advanced Cancer." *Medical and Pediatric Oncology, 9,* 121–128.

Youmans, E. G. (1963). *Aging Patterns in a Rural and Urban Area of Kentucky,* Bulletin 681, 45. Lexington: University of Kentucky Agricultural Experiment Station.

Young, G., and Dolwing, W. (1987). "Dimensions of Religiosity in Old Age: Accounting for Variation in Types of Participation." *Journal of Gerontology, 42,* 376–380.

Zimberg, S. (1977). "Sociopsychiatric Perspectives on Jewish Alcohol Abuse: Implications for the Prevention of Alcoholism." *American Journal for Drug and Alcohol Abuse, 4,* 571–79.

Zuckerman, D. M., et al. (1984). "Psychosocial Predictors of Mortality Among the Elderly Poor." *American Journal of Epidemiology, 119,* 410–23.

Zung, W. (1965). "A Self-rated Depression Scale." *Archives of General Psychiatry*,
    12, 63–68.
Zung, W. W. K. (1972). "How Normal is Depression?" *Psychosomatics*, *13*, 174–
    78.

OTHER PUBLICATIONS AND REFERENCES

BOOKS AND CHAPTERS
(RELIGION AND HEALTH—THE ELDERLY)

Aging and the Human Spirit: A Reader in Religion and Gerontology. C. LeFevre and P. LeFevre, eds. Chicago (Chicago Theological Seminary): Exploration Press, 1985 (37 articles).

"Aging, Religion, and the Church." P. B. Maves. In *Handbook of Social Gerontology*. C. Tibbitts, ed. Chicago: University of Chicago Press, 1960.

"Church Participation and Adjustment in Old Age." D. O. Moberg and M. J. Taves. In *Older People and Their Social World*. A. M. Rose and W. A. Peterson, eds. Philadelphia: Davis, 1965.

The Daily Needs and Interests of Older People. A. M. Hoffman, ed. Springfield, Ill.: Charles C. Thomas Publications, 1970.

New Directions in Religion and Aging. D. Olover, ed. New York: Haworth Press, 1986.

"Religion in America Today." W. C. Roof, special ed. *The Annals* (American Academy of Political and Social Science), Vol. 480, July, 1985.

Role of the Church in Aging. M. Hendrickson, ed. New York: Haworth Press, 1986.

"Spiritual Well-Being in Late Life." D. O. Moberg. In *Late Life: Communities and Environmental Policy*. J. F. Gubrium, ed. Springfield, Ill.: Charles C. Thomas Publications, 1974.

Spiritual Well-Being of the Elderly. J. A. Thorson and T. C. Cook, eds. Springfield, Ill.: Charles C. Thomas Publications, 1980.

Other Reference Books

Encyclopedia of Aging. G. L. Maddox, ed. New York: Springer Publishing Co., 1987. "Religion," pp. 559–61; "Religious organizations," pp. 561–63).

Handbook on the Aged in the United States. E. B. Palmore, ed. Westport, Conn.: Greenwood Press, 1984. Note Chapters 9–11 "Catholics," Ch. 9, by C. J. Fahey and M. A. Lewis; "Jews," Ch. 10, by E. Kahana and B. Kahana; "Protestants," Ch. 11, by B. P. Payne).

Religion and Aging: An Annotated Bibliography. V. J. Fecher. San Antonio, Tex.: Trinity University Press, 1982.

BOOKS AND CHAPTERS (RELIGION AND HEALTH— ALL AGES)

Health: A Whole Person Approach to Primary Health Care. D. A. Tubesing. New York: Human Sciences Press, 1979.

Health/Medicine and the Faith Traditions. M. E. Marty and K. L. Vaux, eds. Philadelphia: Fortress Press, 1982.

Life After a Heart Attack. Croog and Levine. New York: Human Sciences, 1982.

The Psychology of Religious Belief. L. B. Brown, ed. Orlando, Fl.: Academic Press, 1987.

Religion and Pain: The Spiritual Dimension of Health Care. J. H. Fichter, ed. New York: Crossroads, 1981.

Religious Doctrine and Medical Practice. R. T. Barton, ed. Springfield, Ill.: Charles C. Thomas Publications, 1958.

Spiritual Well-Being: Sociological Perspectives. D. O. Moberg, ed. Washington, D.C.: University Press of America, 1979.

Classics

Becoming. Gordon Allport. New Haven: Yale University Press, 1955.

The Future of an Illusion. Sigmund Freud. New York: Doubleday, 1957.

The Individual and His Religion. Gordon Allport. New York: The Macmillan Co., 1972.

Jesus and Logotherapy: The Ministry of Jesus as Interpreted through the Psychotherapy of Viktor Frankl. R. C. Leslie. Nashville: Abingdon Press, 1965.

Man's Search for a Meaningful Faith. R. C. Leslie, Nashville: Graded Press, 1967.

Man's Search for Meaning. Viktor Frankl. New York: Simon and Schuster, 1959.

Modern Man in Search of Soul. Carl Jung. New York: Harcourt, Brace and World, Inc., 1933.

Moses and Monotheism. Sigmund Freud. New York: Vintage Books, 1939.

Psychoanalysis and Faith: The Letters of Sigmund Freud and Oskar Pfister. H. Meng and E. L. Freud, eds. New York: Basic Books, 1963.

Psychology and Religion. Carl Jung. New Haven: Yale University Press, 1938.

Psychotherapy and a Christian View of Man. D. E. Roberts. New York: Charles Scribner's Sons, 1950.

Religions, Values, and Peak-Experiences. A. H. Maslow. Columbus: Ohio State University Press, 1964.

The Self in Pilgrimage. E. A. Loomis. New York: Harper and Row, 1960.

Totem and Taboo. Sigmund Freud. New York: Vintage Books, 1918.

The Unconscious God. Viktor Frankl. New York: Simon and Schuster, 1975.

The Varieties of Religious Experience: A Study in Human Nature. William James. New York: Longmans, Green and Co., 1902.

The Vital Balance. Karl Menninger et al. New York: The Viking Press, 1963.

Other Reference Books

American Mainline Religion: Its Changing Shape and Future. W. C. Roof and W. McKinney. New Brunswick and London: Rutgers University Press, 1987.

Behavioral Therapy and Religion. W. R. Miller and J. E. Martin. Newbury Park, Calif.: Sage Publications, 1988.

Emerging Trends. Princeton Religion Research Center. Princeton, N.J.: Gallup Poll (reports of Gallup surveys published monthly).

The Encyclopedia of Religion. Mircea Eliade, ed. New York: Macmillan, 1986.

Religion in America. Princeton Religion Research Center. Princeton, N.J.: Gallup Poll (compendium of Gallup surveys on religious practices and attitudes of Americans; published every 2–3 years).

Yearbook of American and Canadian Churches. [editor and publisher unknown] (demographics of protestant church members).

JOURNALS, SPECIAL ARTICLES (RELIGION AND HEALTH—THE ELDERLY)

Journal of Aging and Judaism. K. M. Olitzky, ed. New York: Human Sciences Press.

Journal of Religion and Aging. W. M. Clements, ed. New York: Haworth Press.

"The Spiritual Dimension of Elder Care." E. McSherry. *Generations* (journal of the American Society on Aging), Fall, 1983.

JOURNALS (RELIGION AND HEALTH—ALL AGES)

Books and Religion (monthly Duke University Divinity School journal).

Journal for the Scientific Study of Religion. D. Capps, ed. Society for the Scientific Study of Religion. Catholic University of America. Washington, D.C.

Journal of Judaism and Psychology. R. P. Bulka, ed. New York: Human Sciences Press.

Journal of Religion and Health. H. C. Meserve, ed. New York: Human Sciences Press.

Pastoral Psychology. L. O. Mills, ed. New York: Human Sciences Press.

Review of Religious Research. E. C. Lehman, Jr., ed. Religious Research Association. Storrs, Connecticut.

Sociological Analysis. B. Hargrove, ed. Association for the Sociology of Religion. Catholic University of America. Washington, D.C.

NURSING AND RELIGION BIBLIOGRAPHY

Compiled by Richard Fehring, DNSc., R.N., Assistant Professor of Nursing, Marquette University and modified by Ruth M. Stollenwerk, DNSc., R.N.,

Associate Professor of Nursing, Marquette University; without specific reference to the elderly.

L. W. Brallier. "The Nurse as Holistic Health Practitioner." *Nursing Clinics of North America*, 13 (4), 643–55, 1978.

A. M. Buys. "Discussion Series Sensitizes Nurses to Patients Spiritual Needs." *Hospital Progress*, 62, 44–45, 1981.

S. Fish and J. A. Shelly. *Spiritual Care: The Nurse's Role*. Downers Grove, Ill.: Inter Varsity Press, 1983.

V. Carson. "Prayer—an Effective Therapeutic and Teaching Tool." *Journal of Psychiatric Nursing*, 7, 34–37, 1979.

R. Cass. "Sin and Guilt: A Secular-Psychological and Biblical Comparison." *Nurses Lamp*, 33, 2–4, 1982.

M. Colliton. "The Spiritual Dimension of Nursing." In *Clinical Nursing: Pathophysiological and Psychosocial Approaches*, L. Beland and J. Posse, eds. New York: Macmillan, 1981.

S. C. Dickenson. "The Search for Spiritual Meaning." *American Journal of Nursing*, 75, 1789–94, 1975.

D. Ellis. "Whatever Happened to the Spiritual Dimension?" *Canadian Nurse*, 76 (8), 42–43, 1980.

R. Fehring and A. McLane. "Value Belief." In *Clinical Nursing*. J. Thompson et al., eds. St. Louis: C. V. Mosby Co., 1843–57, 1986.

S. L. Granstrom. "Spiritual Nursing Care for Oncology Patients." *Topics in Clinical Nursing*, 7 (1), 39–45, 1985.

M. R. Hassett. "Nursing is a Ministry." *Kansas Nursing*, 58 (3), 8–9, 1983.

F. M. Highfield and C. Cason. "Spiritual Needs of Patients: Are They Recognized." *Cancer Nursing*, 6, June, 1983.

J. Hungelmann et al. "Spiritual Well-Being in Older Adults: Harmonious Interconnectedness." *Journal of Religion and Health*, 24 (2), 147–53, 1985.

M. Kiening. "Spiritual Needs of the Psychiatric Patient." In *Mental Health Concepts and Nursing Practice*. L. Dunlap, ed. New York: Wiley, 1978.

G. R. Kittelson. "Tips on Health and Healing from the Bible." *Australian Nurses Journal*, 9, 57–58, 1979.

M. A. Lucas. "Praying with the Terminally Ill." *Hospital Progress*, 59, 66–70, 1978.

J. F. Miller. "Assessment of Loneliness and Spiritual Well-Being in Chronically Ill and Healthy Adults." *Journal of Professional Nursing*, 1 (2), 79–85.

M. E. O'Brien. "The Need for Spiritual Integrity." In *Human Needs 2 and the Nursing Process*. H. Yura, M. B. Walsh, eds. Norwalk, Conn.: Appleton-Century-Crofts, 1982.

M. L. Peck. "The Therapeutic Effect of Faith." *Nursing Forum*, 20 (2), 153–66, 1981.

V. Penrose et al. "Spiritual Needs in Sickness." *Nursing Mirror*, 10, 38–39, 1982.

R. Piepgras. "The Other Dimension: Spiritual Help." *American Journal of Nursing*, 68, 2610, 1960.

J. B. Pumphrey. "Recognizing Your Patient's Spiritual Needs." *Nursing 77*, 7 (12), 64–70, 1977.

E. Rankin. "Sick, Injured Get Spiritual Care." *Occupational Health Nursing*, 28 (1), 32–33, 1980.

D. Saylor. "The Spiritual Self." *Journal of Practical Nursing, 27* (8), 16–17, 30, 1977.

I. J. Scott. "The Spiritual Element in Healing." *Australian Nurse's Journal, 4* (11), 27, 1976.

M. Shannon. "Spiritual Needs and Nursing Responsibility." *Imprint, 27,* 23, 1980.

J. A. Shelby. "God as a Need Meeter—Toward a Psychology of Believing." *Nursing Lamp, 33,* 1–2, 1981.

J. A. Shelly. "Spiritual Care . . . Planting Seeds of Hope." *Critical Care Update, 9* (12), 7–13, 15–17, 1982.

R. L. Shelton. "The Patient's Need of Faith at Death." *Topics in Clinical Nursing, 3,* 55–59, 1981.

B. Simpsen. "Spiritual Dimension." *New Zealand Nursing Journal, 69* (1), 12–14, 1976.

J. Stallwood et al. "Spiritual Dimensions of Nursing Practice." In *Clinical Nursing* Beland et al., eds. New York: Macmillan, 1975.

R. I. Stoll. "Guidelines for Spiritual Assessment." *American Journal of Nursing, 9,* 1574–77, 1979.

J. Travelbee. *Interpersonal Aspects of Nursing.* Philadelphia: F. A. Davis, 1966.

Sr. M. C. Vaillet. "Hope: The Restoration of Being." *American Journal of Nursing, 70,* 270, 1970.

D. B. Young. "Spiritual Dimensions of Nursing Practice." *Nursing Lamp, 29* (5), 3–4, 1978.

INDEX

About the Authors

HAROLD GEORGE KOENIG, M. D., is a Geriatric Medicine Research and Clinical Fellow at the Duke University Center for Aging and Human Development and the GRECC VA Medical Center. He has published extensively in the field of geriatrics.

MONA SMILEY is Assistant Professor of Adult Education, Incarnate Word College.

JO ANN PLOCH GONZALES has a Master's degree in Education from Incarnate Word College.